Richard Wagner

❖ FRITZ LANG ❖ AND

THE NIBELUNGEN

RICHARD WAGNER

❖ FRITZ LANG ❖ AND

THE NIBELUNGEN

The Dramaturgy of Disavowal

DAVID J. LEVIN

PRINCETON UNIVERSITY PRESS · PRINCETON, NEW JERSEY

Copyright © 1998 by Princeton University Press
Published by Princeton University Press, 41 William Street,
Princeton, New Jersey 08540
In the United Kingdom: Princeton University Press,
Chichester, West Sussex

Library of Congress Cataloging-in-Publication Data

Levin, David J., 1960–
Richard Wagner, Fritz Lang, and the Nibelungen : the dramaturgy
of disavowal / David J. Levin
p.   cm. — (Princeton series in opera)
Includes bibliographical references (p.   ) and index.
ISBN 0-691-02621-1 (alk. paper)
1. Wagner, Richard, 1813–1883. Ring des Nibelungen.
2. Lang, Fritz, 1890–1976—Cirticism and interpretation.
3. Music and society—Germany.   4. Motion pictures—
Social aspects—German.   5. Germany—Civilization—
19th century.   6. Germany—Civilization—20th century.
I. Title.   II. Series
ML410.W22L48   1997
782.1'092—dc21   97-27022

This book has been composed in Trump Medieval

Photo on title-page spread: Siegfried speared. From Fritz Lang's film
Die Nibelungen (1924). Photo courtesy of the Film Stills Archive,
The Museum of Modern Art, New York.

Princeton University Press books are printed on acid-free paper
and meet the guidelines for permanence and durability of the
Committee on Production Guidelines for Book Longevity
of the Council on Library Resources

http://pup.princeton.edu

Printed in the United States of America

1   2   3   4   5   6   7   8   9   10

Contents

List of Illustrations

Preface

THIS PROJECT originated in a question posed during a meeting of dramaturgs at the Frankfurt Opera. Dramaturgy is a wonderfully German institution—essentially a *conceptual* director, a dramaturg is responsible for developing a reading of a work and then, during rehearsals, lobbying the director on its behalf, attempting to insure that the production remains true to that reading. The dramaturg's task is invariably contentious and often thankless, but it affords literary and cultural theorists a rare opportunity to put their ideas to some real-life use. It is comical but true: the theater, for some literary scholars, is about as close to real life as we get when it comes to professional engagement. And in my case, at least, it has been an enormously interesting engagement—as demanding as the classroom and of an entirely different order. For one thing, the dramaturg is not accorded any immediate respect in the rehearsal process. With the rug of institutional authority pulled out from under me, I had to struggle to be heard and my ideas had to persuade on merit. (In this sense, it is useful to come to German dramaturgy from the United States, where professors are not accorded all that much respect anyway—in any case, not nearly as much respect as their German colleagues.) On the other hand, there is, in certain German theaters—and, of course, not just there—a thoroughgoing commitment to the project of critically rereading the classics. It is hard to express how exciting this can be. In such theaters, dramaturgs and dramaturgs-cum-literary theorists are presented with a culture of rereading and a vibrant, public forum for it. Rather than simply staging the work for the umpteenth time in its familiar form, such theaters have committed themselves to producing serious rereadings of canonical works.

For a decade from 1978 to 1988, the Frankfurt Opera under Michael Gielen was such a place.[1] Gielen made a point of hiring some of the most interesting and innovative production teams—stage directors as well as set and costume designers—and insisted that they work together with, yes, dramaturgs. And with the help of a relatively young ensemble and extraordinarily generous rehearsal times, the Frankfurt Opera made a name for itself by presenting a series of controversial stagings of ostensibly familiar works by Mozart, Verdi, and Wagner, among others. Gielen crowned his years in Frankfurt with a production of Wagner's *Ring* by the controversial East German director Ruth Berghaus. Fresh out of college, I had the great fortune to work as one of Berghaus's assistants on her centennial production of Wagner's *Parsifal* in Frankfurt in 1982; years later, and in the midst of graduate studies, I went back to Frankfurt to work with her again on her production of the *Ring*. Which brings us to the meeting of dramaturgs, chaired by Klaus Zehelein, the chief dramaturg of the Frankfurt Opera at the time (he has since moved on and is currently director of the Stuttgart Opera). Zehelein asked a group of us working on the production where we would locate the linden-leaf spot marking Siegfried's vulnerability in the *Ring*. In many of the source materials, including the medieval epic *Das Nibelungenlied*, Siegfried attains physical invulnerability by bathing in the blood of a dragon. There is, of course, an important exception: a linden leaf falls upon his back, thus leaving him vulnerable at that one spot, the so-called linden-leaf spot. In the *Ring*, however, there is no such spot on Siegfried's back. Zehelein did not ask the predictable philological query—why isn't there such a spot?—rather he wanted to know where it was despite its absence. We didn't have a good answer for him. It was just one in an avalanche of such queries, but one that stuck with me. It is a question that I attempt to address here. In doing so, I consider the dissemination of the Nibelungen material, its reworking for the operatic stage (in Wagner's tetralogy) and the silent screen (in Fritz Lang's film). For in both of these works, the spot that marks the vulnerability of the hero is intimately bound up with problems of representation.

A number of institutions, colleagues, and friends have helped along the way. A great deal of thanks is due two writing groups: the first, at Berkeley (Michel Chaouli, Lisa Freinkel, Elizabeth Maddock-Dillon, and Natalie Melas) where this work found its original incarnation as a dissertation; then, more recently, at Columbia (Adam Bresnick, Michael Levine, Nelson Moe, Daniel Purdy, and James Schamus). Both groups read portions of the manuscript and subjected them to criticism that was alternately searing and amusing, but always helpful. In addition, a number of friends and colleagues read and responded to portions of the manuscript with exceptional generosity, including Carolyn Abbate, Adam Bresnick, Michel Chaouli, Marie Deer, Andreas Huyssen, Martin Jay, Michael Jennings, Anton Kaes, Winfried Kudszus, George Makari, Rosalind Morris, Thomas J. Saunders, Hinrich C. Seeba, Michael P. Steinberg, Helen Tartar, Katie Trumpener, Dorothea von Mücke, and Marc A. Weiner. My thanks to each of them. I also want to thank my colleagues and the staff at the Department of Germanic Languages at Columbia, who have provided an unusually vibrant and supportive intellectual community; my students at Columbia, especially Joe Compton, Ehren Fordyce, and Tamsen Wolff, who have helped to focus my thinking on this topic and responded very generously to my ideas; my research assistant Abigail Zitin, who brought to the relatively mundane task of library research the same imagination, energy, and intelligence that has characterized her academic work; Ed Dimendberg at the University of California Press, who provided his usual expert professional advice; Robert Brown of Princeton University Press, who ushered the manuscript through production with generosity and speed; my brother Tom and my parents, Evi and Walter, who augmented the comforts of various homes with intense intellectual engagement; and Walter Lippincott at Princeton University Press, whose enthusiasm for the project was as important to its realization as his patience in awaiting its completion.

A number of institutions provided financial and research assistance, for which I am very grateful, including the Junior Faculty Development Program at Columbia University, the Columbia University Council for Research in the Humanities, and the Berlin Program for Advanced German and European Studies, jointly administered by the Freie Universität Berlin and the Social Science Research Council. Archivists at the Stiftung Deutsche Kinemathek in Berlin graciously provided a wealth of materials, including—can it be?—Thea von Harbou's script for Fritz Lang's film, long assumed to have been lost forever. The stills archive at the Museum of Modern Art provided a storehouse of images, for which I am most grateful. Finally, my thanks to Claudia Edwards, whose editorial zeal when it came to the manuscript was augmented by an impressive arsenal of encouragement, affection, and good cheer.

Richard Wagner

❖ Fritz Lang ❖ and

The Nibelungen

FIGURE 1. The Nibelungen encounter Hollywood: King Gunther and his chaplain share the stage with Oliver Stone's *Natural Born Killers*. Photo by Ingolf Seidel, courtesy of the Volksbühne Berlin.

Chapter One

Representation's Bad Object

THE NIBELUNGEN, AGGRESSION, AND AESTHETICS

𝕴N MAY OF 1995, Frank Castorf, the controversial artistic director of the Volksbühne (People's Theater) in East Berlin, presented a radical reworking of Friedrich Hebbel's grandiloquent mid-nineteenth-century drama *Die Nibelungen*. Castorf's production bore the marks of its aspiration to radicalism on its sleeve, or at least in its title: "*Die Nibelungen*: Born Bad." The newly amalgamated title did not just span languages, it spanned cultures, epochs, and genres, for Castorf drew his subtitle from Oliver Stone's *Natural Born Killers*. The juxtaposition of Hebbel and Stone was not limited to the title; rather it kept popping up during the course of the production, which spanned a grueling 6½ hours in two evenings. Several video monitors were visible on stage and at selected moments fragments from Stone's film appeared on-screen while the soundtrack rumbled through the theater.

In one sense, Castorf's gambit was transparent: he assumed the directorship of the Volksbühne with the explicit charge of attracting a more youthful audience. In playing Hebbel off against Stone, he juxtaposed the ostensibly stodgy and remote concerns of the mid-nineteenth-century drama with Stone's hip and accessible, even outrageous, work. (Stone's film had aroused a good deal of hand-wringing when it arrived in Germany. Initial screenings were accompanied by debates about cinematic nihilism and the responsibilities of cinema in a democratic culture.) The bridge that Castorf built to ease his target audience into the work also afforded him an escape from—or at least an opportunity to resituate—the work's historical and national specificity. Once Castorf had his

young audience in tow, he took them and the work for a ride in formulaically unfamiliar territory. That is, he packed up the work and the kids
and whizzed by the Third Reich in order to land Hebbel and company in
the wild, wild west.

Beyond the marketing strategy, there is also a dramaturgical polemic
implicit in Castorf's production. It is not that we see the *Nibelungen*
differently as a result of an individual directoral interpretation, which
was the case, for example, with Thomas Langhoff's production of *Kriemhild's Revenge* (the second part of Hebbel's two-part drama) at the Deutsches Theater just across town.[1] There, Langhoff offered a reading of the
text in a traditional sense, although his reading was certainly not traditional. His rendering reinflected the work by critically reinflecting its
text: thus, in Langhoff's reading, Hagen emerges as an utterly charis-
matic military leader while Siegfried is unusually passive. On the other
hand, Castorf staged the text as unreadable, riven by its discursive and
ideological entwinements. Like Hans-Jürgen Syberberg, Castorf did not
seek to present the text as such, but rather its cultural, historical, and
political saturation. But unlike Syberberg, who famously renders that
saturation with heaps of ambivalent *ur*-German bric-a-brac, Castorf
looked abroad to reinflect the work's voice with the jargon of Generation
X. Here, but not just here, the *Nibelungen* spoke of and to Germany's
tortured historical identity.

My readers will certainly not be surprised by the assertion that the
Nibelungen material is ideologically rife or historically overdetermined.
Indeed, a number of scholars have undertaken detailed surveys of the
ideological content and historical appropriation of this material; I will
not do so here.[2] Of course, the ideology of the work is found not only in
its content and reception. Indeed, in recent years a sizable body of criticism has relocated the ideologies of national representation in aesthetic
form.[3] Thus we might ask, if the various Nibelungen works have so
much to tell us about the relationship of the Germans to their history,
are we looking in the right places for their testimony? The question is
unduly coy, for it hides a polemic that needs to be stated plainly. Over
the course of the past thirty-five years, we have learned a good deal about
the astonishing historical and ideological trajectory of this material. But
critics have traced that trajectory largely in terms of content and reception; I propose instead that we examine it on the level of aesthetics. Each
of the works I will consider poses its principal concerns—including questions of community, identification, and power—as properly aesthetic.

This is not to say that the political is only or merely aesthetic, but rather that it is important to examine the ways in which these works render their politics in an aesthetic register.

I seek to account for the politics of aesthetics in two famous—and famously perplexing—renderings of the Nibelungen material: Richard Wagner's operatic tetralogy *Der Ring des Nibelungen* and part one of Fritz Lang's two-part film *Die Nibelungen*. Wagner's tetralogy and Lang's film have played crucial roles not just in the history of Nibelungen adaptations, but in the overall history of their respective genres and, more important, in the elaboration of what we might term an aesthetics of national identity. In *Musica Ficta*, Philippe Lacoue-Labarthe argues that "Wagner's aesthetic politics has nothing of a political aestheticism or of an 'aesthete' politics . . . rather it aims at what Benjamin and Brecht, speaking of Nazism, called an *aestheticization of politics*."[4] The same holds for Lang's film. These works have consciously, even programmatically, addressed the question, What is German? They have, at the same time, provided a vision of what is *not* German. Both works pose and respond to these questions in the aesthetic realm as *properly aesthetic problems*. For example, Siegfried is inflected in both of these works as explicitly Germanic, heroic, fearless. His death, then, is the death of a prototypically Germanic hero. These are noteworthy—and familiar—points. But in Wagner's *Ring*, Siegfried is killed in the course of reciting an impromptu tale, an autobiography of sorts; in Lang's *Die Nibelungen*, he is killed while—indeed, *for*—bearing a visual mark over whose production he has no control. I will argue that these moments—recourse to autobiography or loss of control over the visual realm—tell us a great deal about the politics of these works. But they do so only indirectly. That is, these works repeatedly formulate their ethical judgments in aesthetic terms. What these works endorse as good (an ethical judgment) will be presented as good art (an aesthetic judgment); and conversely, what is ethically bad is marked as aesthetically bad. Thus, a good character in these works is marked by aesthetic qualities that the work endorses, while a bad character is marked by aesthetic qualities that the work loathes. Why would this be? And how does it come to pass? These are questions addressed in this study.

❖

In the Introduction to his 1816 edition of the *Nibelungenlied*, Friedrich Heinrich von der Hagen offers the following assessment of the work:

> The saga of the Nibelungen, of Siegfried and Criemhild—one of the greatest and most meaningful anywhere, and especially for us—is a German *ur*- and tribal-saga; unto itself it is rooted, reposes, and keeps watch. It rises above history and is itself one of its oldest monuments. . . . Although so much of what really happened in those olden days remains hidden to us, the saga offers us the oldest and truest inner history. It reigns and creates according to its own inner laws, just as the so-called "wondrous" within it goes its way alongside the ordinary.[5]

Von der Hagen's claims, and their hyperbolic presentation, are typical for scholarly accounts of the *Nibelungenlied* in the early nineteenth century. The first argument, that the epic represents "a German *ur*- and tribal-saga," is quite familiar, if also highly charged in criticism of the *Nibelungenlied*. Since the early 1970s, a growing number of critics have subjected that claim to rigorous historical and ideological interrogation, examining how the work came to be appropriated by the volatile forces of German nationalism.[6] This appropriation culminated in the wildly chauvinistic reception of the *Nibelungenlied* in the literary criticism of the National Socialists, and many contemporary critics write with at least one eye to the work's dubious destiny between 1933 and 1945. Thus, we possess a detailed map of the uneven ideological terrain occupied by the *Nibelungenlied* since its reintroduction into German culture in the latter half of the eighteenth century.

Von der Hagen's second claim is more convoluted and less familiar. He argues that although much of the historical evidence of "what really happened in those olden days" is lost, the work offers "the oldest and truest inner history." The term *Geschichte* that von der Hagen employs is famously ambiguous—designating history as well as story—and both meanings are at play in the claim. The *Nibelungenlied* redresses the paucity of concrete *Geschichte* (in the sense of historical evidence) by providing an internal *Geschichte* (in the sense of a story).

There are a number of reasons why von der Hagen would inflect his claim in this way. The need for cultural legitimation had become particularly acute with the dissolution of the Holy Roman Empire—and with it the external, political traces of the German nation—in 1806.[7] Von der Hagen was seeking to join the battle for national legitimacy on the cultural front: without political history in his favor, he struck out in search of an alternative. Not surprisingly, he hedged history into story under cover of *Geschichte*, abandoning the depressing facticity of Germany's history in favor of a more reassuring, "inner" story. The *Nibelungenlied* provided just the sort of cultural cover he needed. Here, the story would pick up where history left off. Like many of his compatriots, von der Hagen turned to the *Nibelungenlied* to tell a tale that he longed to tell: the prehistory of the German nation. That tale, in turn, has been told and retold: in every epoch since the early nineteenth century, in every conceivable genre—in painting, poetry, ballet, sculpture, literature, drama, opera, and on screen.[8] And although we have a strong sense of the political appropriation of these works, we know comparatively little about the politics of representation within them.[9] This is odd, because the historical appropriation and functionalization of the work are prefigured on the level of representation: here, the inner *Geschichte* tells and retells the story of how very treacherous representation can be and how important it is to control its production.

Of course, representation will mean different things in different works, especially when those works span genres, source materials, and epochs. Nonetheless, each of these works displays a recurring concern with the politics of representation and, more precisely, the politics of reiteration. In Lang's film of the mid-twenties, the concern involves control over spectatorial absorption and physical appearance; in Wagner's *Ring*, it involves control over one's own tale. I read both works allegorically: in both, control over narrative dissemination is shown to be essential to power. As these works embody the perils of a narrative appropriated in the service of a greater—devious, unethical, nihilistic—cause, they also figure those perils within the work. That figuration takes the form of a *mise-en-abyme*, where problems of content—such as control of one's appearance—are also rendered as problems of form. This happens repeatedly and in various guises in these works—this study examines how.

The problem in these works is not unlike the problem in Castorf's production. In each, a good deal of anxiety accrues to the very project of narrative totalization; the project, that is, of producing a fully fledged, totalizing account of the nation. In the following pages, I will attempt to account for the genesis and terms of this project of narrative totalization. For now, I want to suggest that once a narrative is fully rendered in these works, vulnerability ensues. This is how we can explain Castorf's determination to break up Hebbel's work with snippets of Stone's film. When it comes to the Nibelungen material—and in this sense, the material arguably stands in for a problem that dogs an aspiration to a totalizing representation of "Germanness"—a full, totalizing rendering repeatedly produces vulnerability.

THE DRAMATURGY OF DISAVOWAL

Lang's film and Wagner's tetralogy are both reworkings of earlier material. But how is that reflected and figured in the works? How does the project of reformulating the material relate to the recurring scenes of reiteration that they present?

To begin with, reiteration in these works is bound up with scheming and aggression. In Wagner's *Ring*, reiteration constitutes a celebrated compositional technique (in the form of the *Leitmotif*) and an ambivalent dramaturgical tick (in the form of narratives that are formulated and reformulated during the course of the tetralogy). While heroic characters in Wagner's work often narrate without a conscious intent to manipulate or mislead, less appealing characters use narration as a weapon to deceive and ensnare. Thus, a malevolent character such as Mime, who narrates with great fervor and then repeats those narratives *ad nauseam*, is distinguished by that fact: his corruption is signaled by his recourse to narration, and, more important, his conscious manipulation of it. On the other hand, Siegfried, who is, of course, a heroic figure, is killed in the course of narrating his past. And not just narrating it, but reiterating his narration. That is, the tale that Siegfried tells of his past in act III, scene ii of Wagner's *Götterdämmerung* diverges in one extremely important feature from the tale of his past recounted in act I, scene ii of the same opera. Hagen, who sets up both scenes, makes good use of the discrepancy in Siegfried's story: he kills Siegfried for perjury. Of course, he does not kill Siegfried solely because the latter retells his life story. But there is a recurring scene of trickery played out in these works that seems to converge around a desire to revisit and refigure a tale. Why would this be? Why would the scene of retelling yield aggression? And whence the determination to control that scene?

In the Nibelungen film, reiteration and its functionalization take a different form. Here, the project of rendering the epic on film produces a set of concerns that have less to do with narration than with cinema. As I show in chapter three, the film is produced in response to anxieties concerning the role of German film and German film audiences in the face of Hollywood's broad success in Germany in the early twenties. These concerns do not just surround the production of the film; they play an important part within it. Thus, characters from the saga are re-inflected with qualities—such as naive spectatorship and loss of control over appearances—that can be understood in terms of contemporary anxieties about German film culture. Those qualities emerge in the film's reformulation of the source material for a prototypically national-ist cinematic culture in the mid-twenties.

We can gain a preliminary sense of what distinguishes these two works from one another and what similarities they share by returning to the scene considered above, the scene of Siegfried's death. In the film, Siegfried dies not while retelling a tale but for appearing to have betrayed his master. My argument will apply a great deal of pressure to this notion of appearance, since Siegfried does not simply appear to have betrayed Gunther, rather Hagen makes it (and him) appear thus. In chapter three, I suggest that Siegfried becomes vulnerable when he cedes to others his own explicitly magical control over appearances. Thus, both the film and the tetralogy depict an aesthetic problem—be it visual or narrative dissemination—as a central dramaturgical concern. But this sounds more like a dramaturgy of reflexivity than a dramaturgy of disavowal, promised in my title. How are the two related? I will argue that they are related through villainy.

Both of these works offer a vision of villainy that has landed them in hot water. And for similar reasons: their villains have tended to look and sound like "Jews".[10] In Wagner's case, the problem is well known. Theo-dor Adorno was one of the first to formulate it, and his claim is as con-troversial as it is familiar: "All the rejects of Wagner's works are cari-catures of Jews," Adorno wrote in the late 1930s, "the gold-grubbing, invisible, anonymous, exploitative Alberich, the shoulder-shrugging, lo-quacious Mime, overflowing with self-praise and spite, the impotent, intellectual critic Hanslick-Beckmesser."[11] Adorno's position was and remains hotly contested: a slew of recent publications attests to the pas-sions it still arouses.[12] In Lang's case, the critique is similar, but less familiar; it comes from no less august a voice, although its formulation is more difficult to trace. In her biography of Lang, Lotte Eisner mentions that Siegfried Kracauer was incensed by the virulently anti-Semitic stereotyping of the figure of Alberich, king of the Nibelungen, in part one of Lang's film. Like Adorno's claim about Wagner, this is, of course, a controversial claim and, strangely enough, one that is impossible to locate in Kracauer's published writings; Eisner does not cite a source for it.[13] The philological status of Kracauer's claim is, of course, less important than its implications for a reading of the character and the film. Even if we agree that Alberich appears as a stereotypical "Jew" in the film, we still need to account for his function—which is also to say, the function of his appearance.

The "Jewish question" in these works leads us back to the debate about aesthetics and ideology that I raised earlier. To the extent that they take place at all, discussions of the place and circulation of Jews in these works—and of course, not just there—tend to privilege questions of content, intentionality, and biography over questions of form. That is, we tend to ask, Are these figures *supposed* to be Jews? Are their qualities coincidental or intentional? Are there real-life analogs for them? And if the works can be said to resort to anti-Semitic stereotyping, must they—and their creators—be seen as anti-Semitic? In this book, I seek to pursue the same problem with a different set of questions. First and foremost, I want to examine these figures in terms of their aesthetic functions. After all, Wagner's Mime and Lang's Alberich—the two characters I focus upon in this regard—are, of course, aesthetic constructs. As such, their appearance has interesting things to tell us, not just about how Jews are seen in cultural artifacts, but about how they operate within them. In Wagner's tetralogy and Lang's film, they operate in extremely suggestive ways, for they come to embody their villainy on an aesthetic level. In the following, I will argue that they are not just marked as terribly unappealing figures, but that their lack of appeal takes the form of a terrible aesthetic identity. Thus, Mime is repeatedly shown to be narrating (a terrible thing in Wagner's eyes and his works) while Alberich embodies a version of "Hollywood" cinema (a terrible thing in Lang's eyes and his work).

Both of these villains are notable not just for what they do and what they represent within these works, but for what befalls them. But what *do* they do? In both cases, the aesthetics they embody are closely, even integrally, related to the properties of the work in which they appear. Here, then, are the outlines of a dramaturgy of disavowal. Each of these characters comes to embody in his aesthetic traits precisely what the work would want to disavow. These are not works that simply contain none of the dreaded characteristics. Rather, both works go about embodying those characteristics in order to depict their expulsion. Thus, I will argue that these works figure their own aesthetic shortcomings, but fob them off onto a character within the work who is eventually unmasked and killed off as an aesthetic bad object.[14]

In Melanie Klein's coinage, the bad object is split off from and thus counterposed to the ideal object; but both share the corporeal form of the primary object—generally, the breast.[15] The infant splits the primary object into two parts, the ideal object and the bad object: the ideal object is associated with love and good feeling while the bad object is associated with deprivation and pain.[16] For Klein, the bad object is essentially projected, enabling a deflection of elemental assaults upon the ego. In my argument, the process is similar although the forum is different; I would like to use the term to designate an object that is the purported source of an assault upon the integrity of the artwork. To return to the terms I introduced above, the aesthetic bad object serves as an agent within the work who is nonetheless foreign to it. It is important to keep in mind the aesthetic components of this agency: Mime (in the *Ring*) and Alberich (in the film), are not just foreigners within the work, they embody aesthetic practices that the works would want to inflect—or, in Klein's vocabulary, to *de*flect—as foreign, threatening, bad.

In this capacity as a kind of foreign agent, the aesthetic bad object serves as a repository of all that persecutes the aesthetic integrity of the work.[17] That persecution will prove to be all the more important given the aspiration to totalization and completion that characterizes these works—an aspiration that we will consider shortly. The bad aesthetic object figures as an inhibitor in, and to, that aspiration, an impediment on the road to an aesthetic ideal. The works do not merely figure this aesthetic impediment, they figure it in order to disavow it.

In addition to examining the scene of disavowal as it occurs within these works, I will also seek to explain how it moves between them. This is not to say that the scene takes the same form in each work, or that it travels particularly well, lithely negotiating historical or generic boundaries. But because the object of focus here is a recurring scene, I will want to examine the forces that account for that recurrence. In order to do so, I will make use of narratological as well as psychoanalytic models—including Freud's analyses of the relation between representation, reiteration, and aggression, as well as Lacan's sense of the commerce between the imaginary and symbolic realms.[18] In addition to serving as a tool for analysis, psychoanalysis will come in for its own analysis as well. For in the course of explaining the clinical efficacy of reiteration in psychoanalytic practice, Freud sets a scene that is remarkably similar to a recurring scene in the works under consideration here.

FREUD, REITERATION, AND THE NIBELUNGEN

The retellings of the Nibelungen myth involve a resituation of vulnerability, its transformation to an abstract quality from a physical manifestation on the hero's body (such as a spot between the shoulder blades). I will argue that the linden-leaf spot on Siegfried's back—German mythology's equivalent of Achilles' heel—can be understood as a spot in his tale as well as on his back, and it is this spot in the tale that marks his vulnerability and leads to his undoing.

Both of these works will show that this formal flaw is the necessary by-product of a characterological flaw: Siegfried is simply too naive. That is, this prototypically fearless hero is also presented as a prototypically good, trusting soul. While he is a true hero in battle (he slays the dragon that none before has been able to vanquish), he is a dupe when it comes to the pitfalls of cultural communication, falling prey to elementary cultural manipulations that a moderately savvy hero should be able to avoid. Why would this be? In part, Siegfried has been consistently stylized since the early nineteenth century as an agent of a long-lost natural state, one where men were strong and wise in the ways of the forest, but necessarily less adept in the ways of civilization. Thus Siegfried has served as a player in a critique of culture, where his wonderful qualities attest to the appeal of the precivilized state of nature and his tragic ruin attests to the corruption at the heart of culture. That corruption, though, takes a clear form: someone out there is intent on misrepresenting Siegfried. And once Siegfried loses control over his self-representation, he is lost. We need to account for this fantasy of controlling the means of narrative dissemination. In order to do so, we need to venture into psychoanalytic territory.

Between the premiere of Wagner's work in 1876 and Lang's in 1924, another significant drama of reiteration is being rehearsed—the analytic scene. It is a scene that has at its core a struggle for and around representation. Thus, it shares a number of the concerns that are central to Wagner's tetralogy and Lang's film, from the determination to elicit a narrative that will reveal a weak spot, to the desirability of gaining control over the means and terms of narrative dissemination.

In their respective projects, Freud, Wagner, and Lang share an aspiration—even a determination—to tell all. According to Franco Moretti, it is an aspiration that is shared by all world texts: "to represent the social totality—while at the same time *addressing* it."[19] And while Moretti places the *Ring* in the august company of Goethe's *Faust* and Joyce's *Ulysses*, we can easily extend his point to Lang's film as well as Freud's study. In Wagner's case, that aspiration is consistent with a megalomaniacal streak that runs through his works as early as the mid-1840s, a streak that is colored not just by a recurring claim to mythic grandeur, but, more important, by an intense and programmatic determination to produce an artwork that will encompass everything there is to represent. The totalizing dramaturgy of the *Gesamtkunstwerk* aspires to a totalizing representation, one that will allow the tale to be rendered from start to finish, in all of its complexity.

In Freud's case, the aspiration to tell all is central to the project of psychoanalysis and is one of its utopian qualities. Psychoanalysis would bring psychic processes to light by speaking them and having them spoken—that is, by identifying them and allowing them to identify themselves through the analytic process. Unlike Wagner, whose aspiration to a totalizing representation is famously willful and absolute, Freud repeatedly notes the utopian—and in his more discouraged moments, the Sisyphean—nature of his project.[20] Despite his powerful understanding of the remoteness and tenacious resilience of psychic processes (such as defensive distortion and instinctual drives), Freud remains intent upon gaining access to the most inaccessible recesses of human subjectivity. The means of access is narrative.

For Lang and his longtime collaborator Thea von Harbou, who wrote the screenplay to the Nibelungen film, the aspiration is less explicitly totalizing than amalgamative. Thus, Harbou claims that the film represents an ideal amalgamation of Nibelungen works, culled from the best moments in all of the Nibelungen works of all times, and incorporating the most famous modes of transmitting the saga—from epic recitation to domestic drama to operatic melodrama.[21] But here the work will be retold in what Lang and Harbou characterize as a prototypically German style: that is, the film will gather together the best of the disparate moments in the various source materials and render them in a new, national cinematic style. As in Wagner's work and Freud's project, the revision occurs most distinctly in the course of a new *form* of vision, one that will represent differently as it represents all.

For each of these works, the aspiration to a totalizing representation is beset with ambivalence. Freud accounts for this ambivalence much more explicitly than Wagner or Lang. Nonetheless, I will argue that Freud's determination to produce a comprehensive account of psychical processes leads him to employ a metaphorics of aggression. Wagner and Lang do not so much reflect upon this aggression as they stage it, rendering the downfall of their hero at the hands of representation itself. We need to sort out why this might be.

It is, of course, a truism that in its music and dramaturgy, the *Ring* implicitly claims to tell us the whole story, from the very beginning to the very end. What Theodor Adorno termed Wagner's "phantasmagoria" is, at least in part, this penchant for totalization.[22] And it is not just a penchant for *narrative* totalization, since the very notion of the *Gesamtkunstwerk* involves a consolidation of the means of expression— musical, dramatic, textual, visual. But narrative totalization does play a major role in the *Ring*: it is hard not to notice that characters repeatedly tell and retell their stories *in toto*. Thus, the tetralogy provides us with an overarching tale, told from beginning to end, and a proliferation of recapitulations, mini-tales of individual characters reminding us of what they have done and where they have been.

Carolyn Abbate has shown that narration made and kept Wagner anxious as he worked on the libretti for the cycle, which were published years before he composed the music for the *Ring*.[23] Throughout his work on the cycle, Wagner was dogged by doubts concerning the relative prominence of action or presentation vs. recitation or representation.[24] Although he consciously opted for the former, his work evidences the tenacity, indeed, the predominance of the latter. This conflict between presentation and representation finds its way into the *Ring*, such that Wagner's crisis—which is a crisis about the need and desire to dispense with narration—becomes *Siegfried*'s crisis. In chapter two, I examine the extent to which Siegfried could be said to stand in—and fall—for the problems which beset *Siegfried*; problems, as I have suggested here, that are born of an excessive reliance upon narration.

For Freud, the ability to relate the whole story is dependent upon the ability to elicit a narrative from the analysand. On a number of occasions Freud outlines his method of narrative eduction, a method that has aroused a great deal of critical interest.[25] In the following, I will focus on the process of eduction outlined in the *Interpretation of Dreams*. As I suggested above, Freud's project in the *Interpretation of Dreams* is no less ambitious than Wagner's or Lang's—he too would tell the whole story, in this case, of psychic processes that seem designed to resist just such a totalizing account. But while the project may be as ambitious, its terms are less overtly problematic, largely because he explicitly recognizes its limitations. That recognition does not prevent Freud from describing the project in particularly suggestive terms. Here is how he puts and responds to the question of the limits of his project:

> The question whether it is possible to interpret *every* dream must be answered in the negative. One must not forget that in interpreting a dream one is opposed by the psychical forces which were responsible for its distortion. It thus becomes a question of relative strength whether one's intellectual interest, capacity for self-discipline, psychological knowledge and practice in interpreting dreams make it possible to master one's internal resistances.[26]

Note that Freud has set a sharply oppositional scene: thus, to interpret a dream is to engage in a battle for mastery. As Freud puts it, it is a question of relative strength, pitting revision against distortion, pitting the determination to account for internal resistances against the account provided by those resistances. As long as Freud engages in auto-analysis, the scene remains a private one: it is Freud vs. Freud, his own desire to know versus his internal resistances to that knowledge. But it is not always private: in the analytic scene, it is the patient vs. the patient, or even Freud vs. the patient, where Freud embodies the determination to know and the patient necessarily embodies some amount of resistance to that determination.

Freud's wording is suggestive in that it alerts us to the nexus of representation, eduction, and aggression that is at play in his work and in the Nibelungen works we will consider. We can note in his formulation some preliminary traces of the aggression that attends the process of eliciting and interpreting a narrative. Freud's determination to outwit the patient's resistance to that process generates a certain subterranean bravado in his writing: thus he would scout out the distortion, ambush it. At times, Freud admits, the patient's initial account will be confusing or otherwise difficult to engage. In those instances, Freud is faced with the challenge of gaining access to an apparently inaccessible point behind the account:

> In analyzing the dreams of my patients I sometimes put this assertion to the following test, which has never failed me. If a patient's account of a dream initially strikes me as hard to understand, I ask him to repeat it. In doing so he rarely uses the same words. But the parts of the dream that he describes in different terms are by that fact revealed to me as the weak spots in the dream's disguise: they serve me as the embroidered mark on Siegfried's cloak serves Hagen. That's where the interpretation of dreams can begin.[27]

It is easy to overlook Freud's reference here, which is, after all, one among many such literate references in his book. But the allusion is worth lingering over, since it affords us insight not only into Freud's project, but more important, into the variegated dynamics of the Nibelungen works we will examine.

In *Towards Reading Freud*, Mark Edmundson has argued convincingly for an allegorical reading of Freud's reading in *The Interpretation of Dreams*. According to Edmundson, "the Oedipus complex, whatever else it may be, manifests itself in the text of *The Interpretation of Dreams* as an allegory of Freudian reading and writing, a myth about the genesis of Freud's text in which the powers of the new science declare themselves against prior cultural forms, and particularly against literary forms."[28] In the following, my argument about Freud's relation to *The Nibelungenlied* could be said to apply Edmundson's insight to a different, but similarly foundational text. Let us begin by sorting out the terms of Freud's allusion. The Hagen that he refers to appears in the *Nibelungenlied* and again in Lang's *Siegfried*; he is not the same Hagen as appears in Wagner's *Ring*. This distinction is important because each Hagen bears a different, and crucial, relation to reiteration. In the film as in the medieval epic, Hagen famously has to determine whether Siegfried is vulnerable to physical attack: thus he tricks Kriemhild into telling him that her husband *is* vulnerable—albeit only on one tiny spot on his back; and to mark the spot, he has her sew a cross upon his garment. That cross "serves" Hagen by marking the only spot where he can (and does) mortally wound the hero. Later in this chapter, we will consider the scene from the epic in greater detail.

Freud evidently refers to this episode in the *Nibelungenlied* because it successfully captures an important concept in his dream theory, that of the unwitting mark (for Freud, a mark of revision; for Hagen, a mark of vulnerability). At the same time it gives a characteristically pithy literary referent to his metaphor of the garment [*Gewand*], an image that Freud has been applying to the analysand's account of the dream to render its quality as the outermost layer. But the image does more than that, and, I suspect, more than Freud would have it do. For it also captures an instance of identification (with Hagen) and a dynamic of deception essential to the analytic and interpretive process: the analysand/Siegfried accordingly bears an unwitting mark of vulnerability elicited by the analyst/Hagen. We will attend to the specifics of this mark and its production later in this chapter. At this point we can simply ask what is a character like Hagen doing in a text like Freud's *Interpretation of Dreams*?

Hagen, after all, is one of the most ambivalent characters in German literary history.[29] And yet, in important ways, Freud arguably shared, or at least envisioned himself sharing many of the fictional figure's ambivalent qualities. Thus, for example, Freud could be seen as—and arguably saw himself—displaying Hagen's famous qualities, including his status as an outsider and his unwavering, selfless fidelity to the greater cause: in Hagen's case, the master is Gunther (in the *Nibelungenlied* and in the Nibelungen film); in Freud's, it is the very project of psychoanalysis. Of course, Hagen goes so far as to kill Siegfried in order to protect and uphold the king's reputation. Freud's service to the cause fits into this scenario, if less neatly, since the psychoanalytic project as defined in Freud's book can be read as an attempt to replace a popular and naive conception of childhood and, more generally, human subjectivity, with a much more complex vision. That vision famously includes matters that were previously unthinkable and unmentionable in polite society, such as aggressive impulses and sexual drives. We can, I think, read Siegfried as a figuration of precisely the sort of idealized vision of childlike naiveté that Freud, like Hagen, sought to dispense with.[30] Freud's appeal—like Hagen's—arguably resides in his unself-conscious lack of appeal: unlike everyone else at court, he has contempt for surface appeal, dedicating himself instead to a comprehensive, no-holds-barred interrogation of what is going on beneath the surface. That contempt arguably extends to those who don't share it—those, like Siegfried, whose naiveté allows them to lose control over representation. There is, then, a certain grandiloquence lurking within Freud's allusion ("Hagen, *c'est*

moi"), and yet it is an apt grandiloquence and, I suppose, a sad one, insofar as it shows Freud identifying with such an unsavory and ambivalent
(anti-)hero.

While it is important to examine the terms of Freud's relationship
with Hagen, I want to emphasize that the analogy between them is structural. That is, they employ certain similar methods in radically different
projects. And while I intend to explore the methodological grounds they
share, it is important to keep in mind the immense ideological and conceptual gulfs between them. To begin with, Freud and Hagen share an
explicit plot to ambush a powerful, even apparently invincible opponent, be it Siegfried or the neurosis, and both plots operate by eliciting a
revision from an unwitting interlocutor. Freud's reference to Hagen and
Siegfried elucidates more than his own argument and its unwitting
terms. For while it offers Freud an opportunity to crystallize some of his
concepts of the dream and dream interpretation, it will also prove helpful to our examination of the various versions of the Nibelungen tale.
How so? By linking Hagen's deception to his own professional and analytic need to deceive, Freud forges a link between Hagen's plot machinations and his own practice of strategic deception. It is not just that Freud
is acting like Hagen in soliciting the mark of revision, but Hagen—in
basing his deception upon narrative eduction—acts a good bit like Freud.

The blind spot rendered visible in the narrative is the spot where
Freud and Hagen meet, since both are fascinated by and—in different
ways—engaged in its production and exploitation. In the following section, I shall concentrate upon this spot so as to move beyond the relatively simple question of what happens to the tale when reiterated at
different times, by different figures, in different genres, to the more perplexing question of what happens to the telling in its retelling.

FUNCTIONALIZING NARRATION IN THE
NIBELUNGENLIED

It is hard to know where to start—or for that matter, where to
stop—in the search for retellings of the Nibelungen saga.[31] It is not simply that each of the works needs to be situated in a long line of previous
tellings, but that these tellings in turn feature diegetic scenes of retelling.
Where do we locate the original telling? Within the work? In literary

history? In its popular reception? Rather than account for all tellings, or the earliest one, I propose to offer a brief consideration of the most famous of early tellings, the work that has come to bear the greatest historical and ideological burden of the Nibelungen works: the *Nibelungenlied*. As anyone familiar with the early institutional history of German studies knows, and as Friedrich von der Hagen's claim, cited earlier in this chapter, makes clear, the *Nibelungenlied* has repeatedly served as a privileged object—if not a fetish—in the fervent search for an origin in German cultural identity. (Indeed, recent scholarship indicates that the work's status as fetish has in turn been fetishized, such that German nationalism's good object has in turn become a bad object for progressive cultural criticism since the 1970s.) Before we consider the operations of retelling in later Nibelungen works—even one, like Wagner's, that does not derive from the same source materials—I propose to review the operations of retelling in the work that occupies the position of the original telling. Let me be clear: I do not mean to claim that the *Nibelungenlied* *is* the original telling; rather, it has, over the course of the past two centuries, repeatedly been assigned that function.[32]

From the very outset, the purported site of origin seems to anticipate and complicate any claim to originality. Let us recall the famous opening lines of the work:

> Uns ist in alten mæren   wunders vil geseit
> von helden lobebæren,   von grôzer arebeit,
> von fröuden, hôchgezîten,   von weinen und von klagen,
> von küener recken strîten   muget ir nu wunder hoeren sagen.
>
> [We have been told in ancient tales many marvels of famous heroes, of mighty toil, joys, and high festivities, of weeping and wailing, and the fighting of bold warriors—of such things you can now hear wonders unending!][33]

From the start, then, the narrative voice sets a scene of retelling and situates itself within it: the work's originary gesture, the first words of the first strophe recount a scene of previous telling. The current version of that tale alluded to in the concluding line of the strophe is accordingly presented as the product of that transmission, a reiteration of the tales recounted long ago.

This scenario of an old tale revisited and told anew is not just important to the structure of the work, but will assume importance for its characters. Thus, for example, when Siegfried first arrives at the Burgundian court in Worms, Hagen is called upon by King Gunther's collected and somewhat agitated inner circle to provide an impromptu sort of intelligence briefing. After some preliminary disclaimers, Hagen identifies Siegfried and launches into a detailed account of his background.[34] He ends his briefing at Siegfried's encounter with the dragon, his bath in its blood, and his reputed invulnerability:

> Noch weiz ich an im mêre   daz mir ist bekant.
> einen lintrachen   den sluoc des heldes hant.
> er badet' sich in dem bluote;   sîn hût wart húrnîn.
> des snîdet in kein wâfen.   daz ist dicke worden scîn.

> [But I know more concerning him. This hero single-handedly slew a dragon and bathed in its blood, from which his skin grew invulnerable. As a result, no weapon will cut through it, as has been shown time and time again.][35]

This account is accurate as far as it goes, which is not very far, since Hagen has left out the linden-leaf episode. Hagen's story bears a flaw, or if you will, its own weak spot, a spot that will be redressed through retelling. That weak spot is, of course, the claim that Siegfried has none, that he is invulnerable. By leaving out the linden-leaf episode in this initial version of Siegfried's tale, Hagen sets the stage for the revision that he himself will elicit. That revision will yield the tale of Siegfried's vulnerability in place of and, more importantly, as a *revision* of the tale of his invulnerability told—or, more precisely, retold—here. Read in terms of the division of narrational responsibilities outlined in the *Interpretation of Dreams*, the unfolding of this revision involves a shift in Hagen's role, from the narrator who produces the tale, to the analyst who solicits its revision. And once produced, the narrative difference will prompt action. But what are we to make of Hagen's dual roles as narrator and analyst?

In the *Nibelungenlied*, Hagen relates a good part of the tale of Siegfried's past.[36] Thus, Hagen is temporarily but significantly aligned with the narrative voice of the epic, assuming its function and even reproducing some of its terms.[37] Insofar as Hagen assumes the role of the narrator, Siegfried becomes his narrated. This has some important consequences for the nature of power associated with the two heroes. Here, as in the rest of the works we will be considering, Siegfried becomes an object of narration; his power is shown to be unusually ephemeral, strangely dependent upon the medium of its representation. In the *Nibelungenlied*, as in Wagner's *Ring*, the medium of that representational paradise—gained and lost—is narration; in Lang's film, it is vision. Here, then, is a recurring ideological kernel in the overdetermination of the Siegfried figure: in a sense that will only gain allegorical force with time, Siegfried is shown to be very much the product of his representation. Thus, in the epic, he maintains his invulnerability as long as he is reputed to be invulnerable, and as soon as he is said to be vulnerable, he is killed. Either way—that is, as a super-hero and as a chump—in an oddly literal sense, he is spoken for. We can see his initial invulnerability as the effect of telling and his subsequent vulnerability as the effect of a subsequent reiteration and, more broadly, of representation. In this sense, his strength and weakness in the epic are produced by the narratives that surround him: the former, as we have seen, produced by Hagen's "introduction," the latter educed from Kriemhild by Hagen's invitation to a revision.

If Siegfried is an object of enunciation, we might describe Hagen as its master. Thus, for example, in introducing Siegfried to the Burgundian court, he exercises power over the young hero's introduction into its narrative economy. Hagen returns—and returns us—to Siegfried's narrative in the fifteenth adventure, when he elicits the tale of the linden-leaf spot. At this point, he has formulated a plot to kill Siegfried, who is, however, invulnerable to attack, or so the story—*Hagen's* story in adventure three—goes. As I suggested above, Hagen needs to have Siegfried's origins retold in order to encounter the weak spot in the narrative of his origins, a narrative that Hagen had originally formulated. In order to have the tale redone, Hagen abandons the role of narrator and assumes the dual role of elicitor and guardian of the narrative. His description of the plot against Siegfried is telling, for it is explicitly a plot to procure a story or tale, a *Mære*: "so ervar ich uns diu mære, ab des küenen recken wîp" [thus I will procure the tale for us from the brave man's wife].[38]

Translators have tended to explain this passage either by footnote or by amplification which, although it makes the text clearer, is not faithful to its terms.[39] To translate *Mære* as "secret" (Hatto) or *Geheimnis* (Brackert) is to elide the grounding of that secret in narration. In coming to possess Siegfried's story, Hagen comes into possession of his vulnerability. The blank spot in the narrative, an unwitting gap produced in the course of its telling, only becomes visible as such through repetition. The "x" that will mark the spot of Siegfried's physical vulnerability also marks the spot of narrative revision, the point where the narrative gap was opened up in reiteration. Initially, of course, Hagen directs Kriemhild to sew the mark of that revision on Siegfried's garment. In the end, that spot—elicited in the tale—will also be marked there.

But in order for the physical vulnerability to be revealed, the tale has to be revealed, and Kriemhild will serve as the compliant teller. Kriemhild's willingness to speak Siegfried's vulnerability is prepared by a series of instances where both she and Brünhild are explicitly shown to be incapable of the most elementary suppression of a desire to speak. This recurring lapse—inflected in the work as female, all-too-female—causes the quarrel between the two queens, which in turn leads to Hagen's plot, Kriemhild's revelation, Siegfried's assassination, and all-out war.

The quarrel between the queens is presented as a battle of unchecked tongues, with Kriemhild repeatedly bemoaning Brünhild's inability (or unwillingness) to keep quiet.[40] Brünhild, for her part, characterizes Kriemhild as "daz wortræze wîp" or "the sharp-tongued woman."[41] In the aftermath of their quarrel, Siegfried is called upon to make an example of his wife, one that shows who's in discursive charge: "Man sol sô vrouwen ziehen," Siegfried announces to Gunther and the court,

> daz si üppeclîche sprüche   lâzen under wegen.
> verbiut ez dînem wîbe,   der mînen tuon ich sam.
> ir grôzen ungefüege   ich mich wærlîchen scham.
>
> [Women should be trained to avoid irresponsible chatter . . .
> forbid your wife to indulge in it, and I shall do the same with
> mine. I am truly ashamed at her unseemly behavior.][42]

But the training in suppression comes too late, since Kriemhild is already too practiced in impromptu revelations. Thus, despite the beating she receives from Siegfried as punishment for her earlier lapse into unchecked speech, Kriemhild is still easy prey for Hagen's prying.[43] In expressing dismay at Kriemhild's revelation—"si sagt' im kundiu mære, diu bezzer wærén verlân" [she divulged tales that were known to her, that would have better been left un-divulged][44]—the narrative voice simply joins a (male) chorus formed in the previous adventure to disparage female narration. Kriemhild, it seems, is just a chatterbox.

Initially, Kriemhild's account to Hagen of her husband's past reiterates the account Hagen offered in adventure three.[45] However, the repetition is followed by elaboration—Kriemhild continues where Hagen left off:

> Iedoch bin ich in sorgen,   swenn' er in strîte stât
> und vil der gêrschüzze   von helde handen gât,
> daz ich dâ verliese   den mînen lieben man.
> hey waz ich grôzer leide   dicke úmbe Sîfriden hân!
>
> Ich meld' iz ûf genâde,   vil lieber vriunt, dir,
> daz du dîne triuwe   behaltest ane mir.
> dâ man dâ mac verhouwen   den mînen lieben man,
> daz lâz' ich dich hoeren;   deist ûf genâdé getân.
>
> [Nevertheless, whenever he is in battle amidst all the javelins
> that warriors hurl, I fear I may lose my dear husband. Alas, how
> often I suffer cruelly in my fear for Siegfried! Now I shall reveal
> to you in confidence, dearest kinsman, so that you may keep
> faith with me, and I shall let you hear, trusting utterly in you,
> where my dear husband can be harmed.][46]

Having elicited the narrative and acted as its privileged recipient, Hagen directs Kriemhild to mark the spot of vulnerability onto Siegfried's garment.[47] Here then is a condensed performance of Freud's practice of educing a dream narrative: have the tale retold and mark the spot of revision, rendering visible the otherwise invisible spot of vulnerability.

I have suggested that the mark sewn upon Siegfried's garment condenses the spot of narrative revision with the spot of physical vulnerability. In this reading, the aggression is directed at Siegfried's vulnerability. But in two senses, the act of eliciting that mark can also be read as an act of aggression against Kriemhild. On the one hand, her willingness to speak her mind here and in her argument with Brünhild arguably turns the work against her. As Jerold Frakes, among others, points out, free speech is not an option available to women in the work.[48] By manipulating her to speak freely yet again, Hagen in a sense entraps her and will dole out the punishment that—according to the logic of the work—is her due. Here, we are presented with the genesis of an aesthetic bad object. Kriemhild, so lovely at the outset of the work, becomes intolerable by virtue of—or at least, her nascent intolerability is figured by—her free,

unfettered speech. That speech is not simply to be read in terms of narrative content; it also bears implications on the level of form. For the work
that situates itself as an oral performance—and that arguably was performed orally—represents, within the *fabula*, the perils of an unchecked
oral performance. Kriemhild loses Siegfried and Siegfried loses his life by
losing control over his narrative reproduction. In another sense, we
could say that in having her sew the mark, Hagen exacts the punishment
for the narrative authority she wielded (in telling the tale of Siegfried's
vulnerability) and marks the transfer of that authority which he has effected (in now knowing the tale, Hagen can reassume the position of the
master of discourse). Having known more than the master narrator—
which is to say, having had greater mastery over the narrative material—
Kriemhild is made to sew the target for Hagen's plot.

But something odd happens on the way to the assassination: the mark,
so elaborately produced, is forgotten. That is, on the day of the hunt,
Siegfried wears hunting clothes in place of the garb he wore into battle
with the fictitious foreign assailants on the previous day. Kriemhild
sewed the mark on the latter, but Siegfried dons the former. No one in
the work—not even the narrator—seems to notice. One and all proceed
as if the mark is still there. In this way, the mark can be more readily
seen, in its absence, as marking overdetermination, designating the
point of vulnerability as a point apart from the physical spot on Siegfried's back. Let us review briefly the specific details of how the spot is
made to vanish.

Hagen's plot to kill Siegfried involves sending out a group of messen-
gers who will arrive at court and fraudulently declare war on the Burgundians. Here, Hagen reassumes the role of master plotter: he invents
a tall tale and then directs its presentation, first narrating its prospective
unfolding.[49] The plot is not particularly inventive—it is a rather straightforward example of dastardly deception. More interesting is its imbrica-
tion with narration, for the plot involves a proliferation of false tales:
first, the staged declaration of war, which will in turn allow Hagen to
procure the tale of Siegfried's vulnerability. If we apply some pressure to
the brief exchange between Hagen and the king, the stakes of narration
become clearer: "wie möhte daz ergân?" the king asks, to which Hagen
replies, "ich wilz iuch hoeren lân" ["how is this supposed to happen?" "I
will let you hear it"].[50] As the plot takes form, it takes the form of a
narrative, one involving a politically significant division of narrative responsibilities, with Hagen as the master narrator, and the king as his

auditor. Thus the overt goal and its formal qualities both involve narration. On the level of concrete political objectives, the goal is to kill Siegfried by duping him.[51] But by routing that objective through narration, Hagen also situates himself as the driving force behind its realization. In this plot, Hagen will do the talking and will dictate to the king his cues and lines.

If we were to try to characterize the differences between Siegfried and Hagen as they are crystallized in the epic, we might say that Siegfried makes history—recall, for example, his remarkable victories on the battlefield and over the dragon—while Hagen makes stories. As in Lang and Wagner, the *Nibelungenlied* will demonstrate that Hagen's powers of and over representation will win out over Siegfried's physical powers. Hagen's plot depends for its success upon Siegfried's singular—and, as I suggested above, his characteristic—lack of skepticism as a listener: in this sense, Hagen could be said to reproduce and exploit the distinction between his own role as the master of enunciation and Siegfried's role as its object. What distinguishes them is a different relation to representation: while Hagen is inventive and duplicitous, Siegfried is merely reactive and gullible. Siegfried's death is the product of this distinction: Hagen dupes Siegfried and Kriemhild into believing that war is imminent, and then dupes Siegfried into believing it has been called off. Thus we can describe a twofold plot: in addition to his plot to kill Siegfried (and in order to realize that plot), Hagen assumes what appears to be total control over the plot.

In plotting to procure the tale of Siegfried's vulnerability from Kriemhild, Hagen plots ahead of himself and even ahead of the plot, for the spot of Siegfried's vulnerability exists in Hagen's mind before it is produced (as planned) in his exchange with her. The later conversation lends physical specificity to this earlier mental image. But soon the spot on Siegfried's body returns to its position in Hagen's imagination, a transition that is not explained in the epic.

The morning after Hagen's fateful conversation with Kriemhild, Siegfried dons the secretly marked garment and rides off, leading the Burgundian troops into battle. Hagen rides alongside Siegfried, who bears the mark of his (and Kriemhild's) naive narrating habits on his back. When Hagen sees the mark, he sends out a new pair of men to tell "a new tale": that "Liudeger had sent them to King Gunther to say that Burgundy would be left at peace."[52] Upon their return to court, Siegfried rides straight to the king, who sticks to the script Hagen had prepared for him, announcing a hunt for the following day.[53] The murder takes place during a banquet that follows the hunt, a full day after the war excursion. By the time Hagen is finally set to kill Siegfried, the latter has changed out of the garment upon which Kriemhild sewed the mark of his vulnerability and into his "glorious" hunting outfit. And it is this hunting outfit that Siegfried explicitly dons as a handicap in an impromptu race against Hagen.

The race is the final in Hagen's series of amazingly convoluted, dastardly machinations—ranging from the fictitious declaration of war to the staged race for the spring—intended to position Siegfried properly for the kill. As part of this last plot, Hagen arranges the catering for the banquet and intentionally omits the drinks. When Siegfried complains of thirst, Hagen proposes that they drink from a nearby spring. Siegfried agrees, and agrees to race to the spring as well, bearing all of his hunting regalia.[54] When Siegfried wins the race and drinks from the stream, Hagen hurls his spear "through the cross."[55] Hagen explicitly sees the spot marked on the outfit, although the text has indicated that it was marked elsewhere. But no one—neither Hagen nor the text—notices that the mark is missing: in fact, Hagen still sees it.[56]

In leaving behind his marked garment, Siegfried is still a marked man. But instead of being marked by a spot on his garment, he is marked by his relation to representation. And given Hagen's explicit and sustained control over the narrative, he could be said to take aim at the mark that he educed in Siegfried's tale as much as he takes aim at the absent mark upon Siegfried's body. In killing Siegfried, Hagen marks himself as the master of the plot—not just the plot to kill Siegfried, but the plot of the tale itself.

SIEGFRIED'S DEATH BY NARRATION

In the *Ring*, Siegfried dies a hero, and is certainly commemorated as one, but his death is not especially heroic. When he is killed in act III of *Götterdämmerung*, Siegfried is not battling a bear or a dragon; indeed, the opera *Siegfried* has shown us that he and nature are particularly congenial—the bear is his spontaneous companion, and the woodbird engages Siegfried in some lengthy and significant conversations.[57] Nature, it appears, will not be Siegfried's undoing; this natural hero will die a most *un*natural death. And so, given the binary terms of Wagner's dramaturgical logic, if it is not nature that is going to destroy Siegfried, then it is almost certainly going to be culture. But culture in what sense? For Siegfried is not assassinated while engaged in political agitation, or at the gambling table, or in a shoot-out. Instead, he is killed while telling, or more precisely, *retelling* his story, an abbreviated version of his auto-biography.

I propose to examine the strategic deployment and manipulation of narrative in the *Ring* on two levels, within the work and outside it. This raises two questions: first, on an extra-diegetic level, how does Wagner control the production of narrative information; then, within the diegesis, how do his characters do so? In the tetralogy, power is not just de-rived from access to the ring itself. Instead, power in the *Ring* and over the ring means the power to produce—and control the production of—narrative information. In order to show this, I will consider Siegfried's relationship to his own story and his death in the process of recounting it. By framing Siegfried's death in these terms (or by viewing his death as thus framed), I will then move on in the next chapter to a wider consider-ation of the operations of auto-narration in the *Ring* and its function in Wagner's conception of the artwork (and art form) of the future.

The extent of the connection between Siegfried's death and narration becomes clear when we compare the scene of his murder in the *Nibe-lungenlied* with the same scene in *Götterdämmerung*. In both, Siegfried, Hagen, Gunther, and their crew have gone out for a day of hunting. And in both works, Hagen needs to position Siegfried just right, so he can stab him where he is vulnerable. In the medieval epic, that positioning has to be more precise than in the Ring, since the spot marking Siegfried's vul-nerability is only as big as a leaf—even if, as I have suggested, the mark of that leaf has disappeared. In the *Nibelungenlied*, as we have seen, Hagen contrives a lack of wine, induces Siegfried to race with him to the spring, waits for Siegfried to kneel, and then stabs him. In *Götterdäm-merung* there is no intended shortage of beverages: indeed, there is plenty to drink, and Hagen serves as the conniving bartender. Rather than racing Siegfried to a spring, Hagen guides him along the course of his life story and drugs him so that he will take a sudden and unexpected turn. Having served Siegfried a drink in act I, scene ii of *Götterdämme-rung* that caused him to forget Brünnhilde and his consummated love for her, Hagen now serves him another, which enables him to remember. In recounting past events differently, Siegfried appears to be telling a differ-ent story, singing a different tune. As Siegfried approaches the right spot in the narrative, Hagen creates a swerve in the tale—and the shift from the familiar, accepted terms of the tale as recounted in act I, to the unexpected, ostensibly shocking terms produced here in act III authorizes Hagen's attack. Hagen says so himself: when his men ask him what he has done, Hagen replies simply and directly—"Meineid rächt ich" or—"I've avenged perjury." The aggression is authorized by the act of perjury; at the same time, that perjury is produced by the interlocutor who avenges it.

In the *Ring*, there is no linden-leaf spot on Siegfried's back, nor does he gain (limited) invulnerability by bathing in the dragon's blood. Instead, Brünnhilde has rendered his body largely invulnerable, choosing to protect everything except his back, since, she reasons, he would never turn his back upon an enemy.[58] Thus, the incidental mark of Siegfried's vulnerability in the *Nibelungenlied* has been rendered quite differently in the *Ring*. In the medieval epic, the linden-leaf spot results from an act of nature—the wind blew and, in the process, blew the hero's chances of being invulnerable; in the *Ring*, Siegfried's vulnerability is produced by Brünnhilde. The scene of that production is not shown on stage; instead, Brünnhilde recounts it upon Hagen's prompting. This is one of the first indications that Siegfried's vulnerability will be closely connected to narration, as it was in the epic. As the scene of his assassination unfolds, that connection becomes tauter until eventually, Siegfried's narration precipitates his death.

Hagen's attentiveness to the swerve in Siegfried's narrative strikes a familiar chord, for Hagen essentially duplicates some important features of the analytic scene, getting Siegfried to repeat the tale, and using the marks of narrative difference for his own purposes. But it is important to note that those purposes are threaded through—and presented as a response to—Siegfried's life story. The betrayal here involves a deception enacted by the listener. In that sense, Hagen's mode of plotting in the *Ring* seems remarkably similar to Freud's in the *Interpretation of Dreams*: in both we encounter a surreptitious plot to gain access to vulnerability through narration. The aggression attending Hagen and Freud's interventions is all the more effective because it is surreptitious, where the appearance of disinterested inquiry is in fact part of the plot. Indeed, to the extent that the plot is bound up with the act of narration, it takes the form of a plot against and around a plot. Both Freud and Hagen share an ulterior motive: initially, to find the weak spot; ultimately, and here they diverge, Hagen wants to kill, Freud wants to heal.

What, we might ask, does it take for Freud to set his project in motion? It takes a narrative that changes when repeated, and it takes someone who is willing to tell the tale. And those are Hagen's needs too. In fact, the image of force is quite forcefully rendered in the text: for Hagen, the weak spot invites the sword; for Freud, it invites interpretation.

Whence this plot? Whence the conviction that narration is a mark of vulnerability? These questions bring us back to the notion of a work where narration is out of place. By examining the place of narration in Wagnerian music-drama, we will seek to determine the extent to which Siegfried is made to suffer for Wagner's dramaturgical dilemma.

Chapter Two

Where Narration Was,

There *Darstellung* Shall Be

WAGNER AND THE SCENE OF NARRATION

Is It Plastic Yet?

*I*N THE BEGINNING, there was narration.

But soon enough, Richard Wagner realized that his latest music drama (already christened *Siegfrieds Tod* [*Siegfried's Death*]) relied far too heavily upon what he termed *Erzählung* or narration.[1] Thus, in early May of 1851, on the very day he concluded the first prose sketch of the work, he sent a letter to his friend Theodor Uhlig announcing his decision to write what we might label a "prequel," a prefatory work that would pave the way for his commissioned rendering of Siegfried's demise.[2] Without such a prefatory work, Wagner was convinced that *Siegfried's Death* was doomed: "When I took a closer look at *Siegfried's Death* with a serious view to having it performed in Weimar next year, the whole thing inevitably struck me as utterly impossible. Where would I find the performers and audience for it?"[3]

Wagner's search for the right audience and performers occupied him from the very beginning of his thoughts on the *Ring* and continued to occupy him for the rest of his life.[4] The search for the proper audience culminated in May of 1872 in Bayreuth, when Wagner broke ground for his own theater, much as he had imagined it twenty years earlier: somewhere off the beaten track, patronized by his friends, and dedicated entirely to his works.[5] The second search, for the proper performers, did not lend itself to such a ready resolution. For Wagner, the difficulty in locating the right performers, the right *Darsteller*, was not merely one of body types or voices; beyond that, it was a problem of performance, embodiment, and representation—in short, a problem of *Darstellung*.

Throughout his writings from the late 1840s and early 1850s, during the composer's exile in Zurich, Wagner expresses an increasingly urgent determination to redirect his theatrical practice by reconceiving *Darstellung*, moving away from narration to a more immediate, dramatic mode of enactment. Thus, for example, in *The Artwork of the Future*, published in 1849, Wagner sketches a typically idiosyncratic history of artistic expression in ancient Greece, arguing that the shift from epic poetry to tragedy can be explained in terms of a concomitant shift from description (*Beschreibung*) to presentation (*Darstellung*). Wagner's account of that shift involves a modified Trojan Horse scene, where Thespis secrets a new mode of aesthetic expression into Athens—one committed to *Darstellung*—thus duping the clueless intellectuals who are struggling to preserve a dead form of art associated with mere description:

> the professors and literary scholars were up in the prince's castle laboring at the construction of a *literary Homer*—pampering their own unproductivity by marveling at their own wisdom, thanks to which they could only understand what had long since been lost and passed away. Meanwhile, *Thespis* had already rolled his cart into Athens, set it up beside the palace walls, prepared the *stage* and, stepping from the chorus of the *Volk*, set foot on the stage; and *ceased to describe* the deeds of heroes, as in the epic, but *enacted them as the hero himself* [*stellte sie selbst als dieser Held dar*].[6]

If, in Wagner's account, the birth of tragedy was attributable to the spirit of *Darstellung*, its death resulted from the same misfortunes that befell epic poetry: the spirit of the *Volk* was splintered, thus eviscerating the art form, which made it fair game for the meddling of intellectuals.[7] (Indeed, in *Die Meistersinger von Nürnberg*, Wagner arguably enacts what he narrates here, staging many of the features of this recurring anti-intellectual fantasy about the decline of a noble art on account of the prominence of pedants who suppress true artistic innovation.[8]) Upon tragedy's decline, Wagner claims, poetry no longer presented events, but merely described them: "The lonely art of poetry—*poeticized* no more; she no longer enacted, but only described ... [*sie stellte nicht mehr dar, sie beschrieb nur*]."[9]

The evolution of the *Ring* is imbued with many of the same terms. Thus, in the same letter to Uhlig of May 10, 1851, Wagner writes:

> *Young Siegfried* has the enormous advantage of conveying the important myth to an audience by means of actions on stage [*im Spiel*], just as children are taught fairy-tales. It will all imprint itself vividly by means of sharply defined sensory perceptions, it will all be understood,—so that by the time the more serious *Siegfried's Death* comes along, the audience will know everything that had to be taken for granted or simply hinted at there—and . . . the more so in that . . . *Young Siegfried* will give the *performers* a practical opportunity to train and prepare themselves for solving the greater task presented by *Siegfried's Death.*[10]

In opting to expand his Siegfried project from one opera (*Siegfried's Death*) to two (*Young Siegfried* and *Siegfried's Death*), Wagner seems less immediately concerned with substantive dramatic content than with an adequate mode of presentation and reception. In effect, the earlier work will offer a training ground where the audience and the players can prepare themselves for the presentation to come, learning what they need to know in anticipation of the far greater challenge posed by *Siegfried's Death*. But beyond this, the move from one opera to two also allows Wagner to move from one mode of *Darstellung* to another. This is what Wagner has in mind when he describes the fantastic advantage to be gained when the public is offered the myth in dramatized form, "im Spiel."

According to the logic of Wagner's thinking as set out in various letters and pamphlets from the Zurich period, the alternatives were clearcut: *Darstellung*, in the sense of dramatic enactment, engaged the senses and thus, by virtue of its "plasticity," produced immediate comprehension; narration, on the other hand, took a different and artistically less viable route, addressing itself to the understanding, which produced rumination and inhibited immediate sensory comprehension. For Wagner, the move from one opera to two enabled a move from narration to another, supposedly purer mode, committed to the plasticity of dramatization (a kind of Wagnerian *Darstellung an sich*).

The distinction becomes important for the conception and realization of the *Ring* as early as 1848. In his autobiography *Mein Leben*, Wagner recalls reading an early version of *Siegfried's Death* to Eduard Devrient,[11] who argued that the proposed confrontation between Siegfried and Brünnhilde (when the latter is brought to the Gibichungen court) needed to be preceded by a scene that showed their great love for one another, since a mere description of that love would not suffice.

> I had actually begun the poem of *Siegfried's Death* precisely with those scenes that form the first act of *Götterdämmerung*, and had resorted to a lyric-epic dialogue in order to explain to the listener everything bearing upon the previous relationship of Siegfried to Brünnhilde. This explanation would occur solely through a dialogue between the heroine, left alone on her rock after his departure, and a band of Valkyries passing by. Devrient's hint, to my delight, at once gave me the idea for the scenes which I have worked out as the prologue to this drama.[12]

Although this passage contains all of the makings of a realization that *Darstellung* is preferable to narration, the realization has not yet fully gelled. By 1851, however, Wagner's position has attained programmatic force. The terms of his campaign against narration and its implications for the *Ring* are outlined in a series of letters from November of 1851, including a famous letter to Liszt, dated November 21, 1851.[13] The circumstances leading to this letter are quite similar to those that led Wagner to write Uhlig six months earlier; only this time Wagner announces that the projected pair of operas (*Young Siegfried* and *Siegfried's Death*) has ballooned into a tetralogy. Following is a rather lengthy excerpt from Wagner's missive, where he explains that *Young Siegfried*, the previously announced "prequel," is but a fragment of a larger whole, itself in need of an introductory work:

> Even this *Young Siegfried* is only a fragment and, as an individual whole, it can only make its rightful and indubitable impression when it assumes its necessary place within the completed whole, a place which—in accordance with the plan I have now conceived—I am now assigning to it, together with *Siegfried's Death*. In both these dramas a wealth of necessary allusions was left simply in narrative form [*Erzählung*] or else had to be worked out for himself by the listener: everything that gives the intrigue and the characters of these two dramas their infinitely moving and far-reaching significance would have had to be omitted from the stage action [*Darstellung*] and communicated on a merely conceptual level.[14]

Wagner's rhetoric and his overall objective have a familiar ring to them—this expansion from two operas to four, like the previous expansion from one to two, is designed to dispense with narration and substitute *Darstellung* in its place.[15] If we put a Wagnerian spin on a Freudian locution, we might say that "where narration was, there *Darstellung* shall be."[16] Thus he replaces the retrospective mode of narration with a (temporally) recursive itinerary of works, each one bearing the good tidings of *Darstellung*—or at least, that is what he sets out to do. So, for example, instead of having someone *tell* us how Alberich encountered the Rhine-maidens, Wagner plans to *show* us that encounter.[17] But in order to do so, he has to go farther and farther back in the tale, impelled each time by the imperatives of *Darstellung*. Having made the (latest) case for a further expansion of the project, Wagner describes it in some detail:

> This plan will now comprise three dramas: 1st, *The Valkyre*. 2nd, *Young Siegfried*. 3rd, *Siegfried's Death*. In order to present everything complete, these three dramas must additionally be preceded by a great prelude: *The Theft of the Rhinegold*. It takes as its subject the complete depiction [*vollständige Darstellung*] of all that occurs in *Young Siegfried* in narrative form [*erzählungsweise*], as it relates to the theft of the gold, the origins of the Nibelung hoard, the abduction of this hoard by Wodan, and Alberich's curse. Thanks to the clarity of presentation which will thus have been made possible, I shall now—by discarding, at the same time, all the narration-like passages which are now so extensive or else by compressing them into a number of much more concise moments—acquire sufficient space to exploit to the full the wealth of emotive associations contained in the work, whereas previously, with my earlier, half-epic mode of presentation, I was obliged to prune everything laboriously and thus to weaken its impact.[18]

In expanding the project, Wagner envisions dispensing with the generic impurity of half-epic *Darstellung* that weakened the work and led to the difficulties of "beschneiden" (translated here as "laborious pruning"), posing as it does the vague threat of an aesthetic circumcision. More than a fantasy of generic or aesthetic purity, Wagner's fantasy here involves a determination to arrive at the place that precedes the story, a *Vor-stelle* of *Darstellung*, a point prior to the tale that he intends to show. Indeed, Wagner does not merely want to arrive at that place, he wants to capture it in all of its fullness, because it itself would capture the fullness that he seeks. The problem is that this fullness is not full in and of itself, but is conceived as dependent, a supplement to the other, narration-ridden work. Thus, Wagner does not describe *The Theft of the Rhinegold* as a "complete depiction" unto itself; instead it offers "the complete depiction of all that occurs in *Young Siegfried* in narrative form, as it relates to the theft of the gold, the origins of the Nibelung hoard, the abduction of this hoard by Wodan, and Alberich's curse." The fullness of *Darstellung* in *Das Rheingold* would complete the incompleteness of narration in *Young Siegfried*, just as *Young Siegfried* would complete *Siegfried's Death*.

The completion Wagner would attain through *Darstellung* is solicited by the inherent incompleteness of narration. But the cycle of replacement (whereby *Darstellung* is introduced as a replacement for narration) puts Wagner in a bind, for while he aspires to a complete *Darstellung* per se, his works are mere completions of one another. Wagner is trapped by his own peculiar itinerary of *Darstellung*: his need to *show* is dependent upon his need *not to* tell. By producing works that replace telling with showing, he is blocked, in the *Ring*, from producing works that would simply show without reference to a prior scene of telling. Rather than "a great prelude," as Wagner puts it, *Das Rheingold* rehearses the cycle of inscription and erasure that characterizes the rest of the *Ring*. As such, it poses the very problems and is characterized by the very incompleteness that it is designed to redress. For if *Das Rheingold* will solve the problem of incompleteness posed by *Young Siegfried*, what will solve the problem of incompleteness posed by *Das Rheingold*? Later in this chapter I will return to this problem, arguing that story-telling is left partially but significantly unredeemed: while providing the necessary dramaturgical redemption for *Young Siegfried*, *Das Rheingold* comes off without a redemption of its own.

We could read this recurring recourse to *Darstellung* without narration as a response to the preponderance of narration in Wagner's texts. In this way, the genesis of the tetralogy would be akin to the operations of the famous "fort/da" game described by Freud in *The Interpretation of Dreams*: here narration is expelled in order to return as *Darstellung*. In that return, Wagner would hope to regain a semblance of control over representation, redirecting its affective range by shifting the work's address from the intellect to the senses. To what extent can we say that Wagner's bind is not merely the result of his dependence upon narration, but is, instead, the result of his dependence upon his independence from narration? Insofar as each work is produced in order to render superfluous the narration in its precursor (which is also to say, its successor), Wagner seems to need narration in order to produce works which would free him of that dependence. So how does narration fit into this economy of production? It seems to gain at least some of its vitality by virtue of its incompatibility with *Darstellung*, as *Darstellung*'s necessarily unnecessary counterpart, desirable for its undesirability. This, as we shall see, is a familiar structure in Wagner.

THE PROBLEM OF NARRATION IN THE *RING*

Prior to the writings of the Zurich period, narration does not appear to have been of particular concern to Wagner. The early stage works feature some important and famous scenes of narration, such as the Rome narrative in act III of *Tannhäuser*, but narration does not constitute a particularly volatile presence—or absence—in the works preceding the *Ring*.[19] In the late 1840s and early 1850s, Wagner began to work out a vision of the *Gesamtkunstwerk* that would distinguish itself from his earlier work and, more importantly, define his work in contradistinction to the prevailing aesthetics of operatic composition, production, and reception.[20] Wagner's most important programmatic statement of these ideas came in book form, in *Opera and Drama*, a rambling yet exceedingly ambitious work originally published in three volumes in 1852.[21] Here Wagner outlines a counteraesthetics of opera, including a point-by-point denunciation of many of the major works and movements in operatic history. In addition to this wide-ranging account of all that is wrong in operatic aesthetics, the work features a bombastic and largely self-congratulatory announcement of the proper path that opera needs to take. Wagner is loath to send opera down that path encumbered by the weight of its aesthetic baggage.

According to Wagner, traditional number opera was in large measure so inane because of its formulaic dramaturgical and compositional construction, a sort of tag-team arrangement whereby dialogue, aria, and spectacle alternately worked over the audience, leaving it in a dazed stupor—to the extent that they were paying any attention in the first place. In Wagner's eyes (and ears), nothing made sense in these works: in some, the music and words bore no meaningful relation to one another; in others, words or music were merely formulaic or ornamental and bore no discernible meaning of their own. Here is how he describes the state of opera in a famous passage from "Art and Revolution," a pamphlet published in 1849:

> Opera has become a chaos of sensuous elements flitting by one another without rhyme or reason, from which one may choose at will what best suits one's fancy—here the alluring leap of a ballerina, there the *bravura* passage of a singer; here the dazzling effect of a triumph by the set designer, there the astounding efforts of an orchestral eruption. Do we not read every day that this or that new opera is a masterpiece because it contains many fine arias and duets, and the instrumentation is extremely brilliant, etc. etc.? The aim which alone can justify the employment of such disparate means,—the great dramatic aim,—people no longer give that so much as a thought.[22]

Wagner was, of course, suffused with a messianic determination to dispense with this purportedly senseless amalgam of effects in order to restore dramatic and musical focus to opera—to its composition, performance, and reception. That focus necessitates a shift in form and content: rather than inane spectacle, he envisions works with an unusual musico-dramatic integrity, works that will model as they impart a coherent conception. And yet who would tolerate such works, let alone celebrate them? After all, the works in the operatic repertory of Wagner's day were not going to solve the problem—indeed, they *were* the problem. And insofar as those very works were popular, the operatic audience was unlikely to flock to works that were less amusing and more demanding. It is a problem that Wagner recognized:

> Let us suppose for an instant, that somehow or other we acquired the capacity to effect the performers and a performance—from the standpoint of artistic intelligence—to such a degree that the highest dramatic-aim would be fully realized in this performance. Then for the first time we would have to come to terms with the fact that we lacked the real enabler of the artwork, namely, a public that needs the artwork, and from this need, becomes an all-powerful co-producer of the artwork. The public of our theatres has no *need* for the artwork; it wants to *distract* itself in the theatre, not *collect* itself; and he who is

addicted to distraction has a need for artificial *details* [künstliche *Einzelheiten*] but not for artistic unity [künstlerische *Einheit*].[23]

So what happens to Wagner's messianic spirit in the face of these circumstances? Not surprisingly, he sets about converting the heathen. And, as James Treadwell has pointed out, narration plays an important role in this process.[24] That is, narration is a preferred vehicle in Wagner's campaign—waged largely in the prose works of 1848 to 1852—to gain support for his self-proclaimed program of aesthetic revolution.

In a subtle and provocative article entitled "The *Ring* and the Conditions of Interpretation," Treadwell notes that the prose works from the Zurich period repeatedly return to scenes of disjunction—between the present and the past and between the present and the future. When it comes to the retrospective narrations—Wagner's tales of the good old days of ancient Greece, for example—the teleology is clear: back then, things were great; then they fell apart; in the future they will get better again.[25] But the route to this idealized future is more difficult for Wagner to negotiate than one might imagine. The *Ring*, in Wagner's writings, will find a home in that future utopian era, and in order for the work to be properly performed and understood, that era needs to be inaugurated. According to Treadwell:

> In [the Zurich] writings, a discontinuity arose between the texts and the events they referred to, because the world they described always remained elusive and remote. This perpetually deferred utopia was identified with the significant (that is, rightly interpretable) performance of the *Ring*. In the absence of visible and certain revelation, the texts substituted narrative, with its yearning appeal for an enabling hermeneutic reciprocity. The poem's narratives play exactly the same role.[26]

That is to say, the works do not offer a clear vision of that utopia or a clear map of how to get there, and yet they depend upon that utopia's existence. Narrative fills the space of this ambivalent reticence and is itself ambivalent. But in order to understand how this is so, we need to examine the place of narration in the *Ring*.

As the project expanded from one work to four, one would expect the role of narration to decrease: having gained more space in which to unfold the actions that preceded *Siegfried's Death*, there was presumably less of a need to explain those events in narrative form, since there was no need to tell people what they had already seen. But as the project grew, so too did the instances of narration. Thus results what Carolyn Abbate has described as the "great paradox in the *Ring*'s history, and what many consider to be the great flaw in its text: that the narratives, despite Wagner's glee over their elimination, were kept."[27] How can we account for this paradox? Abbate offers a structural-biographical explanation: "Knowing the *Ring* text's history, we may indeed be inclined toward an explanation of the *Ring*'s narratives in terms of Wagner's creative evolution. The narratives in the finished tetralogy are his way of insinuating his authorial self into the *Ring* text."[28] But to what end? Abbate's explanation does not satisfy:

> By retaining both modes [narrative accounts and dramatic enactment], Wagner reminds us that our experience of the sequence—enactment, followed by narrative retelling—is the inversion of his own creative process—making enactment from a précis. By inventing narratives that deal in unseen actions, he urges us as listeners to complete gaps and form our own supplementary stretches of libretto. At these nodes, we replay the same Wagnerian process of "making plastic" that drew forth dialogue and stage action from epic summaries, to make the *Ring* from *Siegfrieds Tod*.[29]

It strikes me as singularly implausible that Wagner would be intent upon reminding us that our experience as listeners inverts his creative process. Why would this reminder be necessary, let alone desirable? Even more implausible is the quasi-Bakhtinian vision of Wagner as the willing creator of open, dialogic artworks, works where the audience is "urged" to suture gaps individually, and thus "supplement" his works through imaginative investment. It is hard to think of an artist more opposed to the Bakhtinian ethos, more single-minded in his determination to close off the meaning of his librettos and reserve to himself the right to adjudicate that meaning. Wagner's letters, the documentary evidence surrounding his creation of the *Ring*, and his extensive theoretical writings on operatic aesthetics reveal an artist obsessed with anticipating, sealing, and reinforcing every imaginable breach in his aesthetic constructs. The total work of art was hardly partial when it came to narrative strategy. If the presence of narration in the *Ring* were to remind us that our experience inverts his, then it would also show us that his announced project—to address his work to the senses and not to the intellect—had failed miserably.

But if Abbate's explanation is unsatisfying, how can we account for the paradox she identifies with such precision? Treadwell offers an alternative, comparing the preponderance of narration in the prose with its recurrence in the tetralogy. He notes that "Wagner's constant creation of retrospective narratives" in the prose works

> has often been confused with, and therefore criticised as, historiography, but the selectivity and speculativeness of his narratives of the past are not really relevant. The histories are supposed to be mythic: that is, their facticity is subordinate to their narrative function. They exist not to provide an accurate picture of the past, but to press the past into the service of the present act of telling.[30]

This is an astute and convincing point. Indeed, Treadwell's examination of the narrative function of various "acts of telling" in the Zurich writings is perceptive and original. The problem arises when he moves from the prose works to the *Ring* poem. Treadwell argues that narration, transported from the prose works into the tetralogy, functions in much the same way in both:

> The refrain of the theoretical works' discussion of theatrical audiences is the demand that they be "brought to consciousness." Each moment of narration in the *Ring*, from Wotan's huge monologue down to Brünnhilde's tiny story "Lang' war mein Schlaf; ich bin erwacht [Long was my sleep; awakened am I]," pulls the drama out of its mimetic flow and images the experience of listening. The reader is always being reminded of his or her own hermeneutic activity.[31]

This seems absolutely right—and yet it is also contrary to the theory of the tetralogy. The distinction between the reader of Wagner's prose and the auditor/viewer of his stage works needs to be sharply drawn, for the reader may be "reminded of his or her own hermeneutic activity" but the auditor/viewer should not be.[32] Indeed, according to Wagner, the proper audience for true (read: his) works of art should be emotionally absorbed rather than hermeneutically engaged. That is what distinguishes art lovers from art critics and, indeed, the artwork of the future from the artworks of the past.[33] And that, in short, is the problem of narration for Wagner: it produces reflection by addressing itself to the mind, while he aims for a stronger—we might say, more abject—identification on the part of his audience, insofar as he addresses the work to "the senses."[34]

According to Treadwell, scenes of narrative in the *Ring* "stage a hermeneutic relation, a *process* of speaking/listening. In non-narrative passages, the text mimes action, making events happen and describing them happening. In narration, however, the text mimes itself, representing itself as a sheer act of speech, a voice demanding to be heard."[35] Treadwell's image of the text "miming itself" in narration may enable us to clarify the problem of narration in the *Ring*. It is not just a theoretical problem but one that finds dramatic expression within the work. After all, Mime is arguably presented as a character who mimes himself in the tetralogy and is loathsome for this very reason. (The irony is clear, since the only mimetic moment in Mime's character is his name, which enacts his status as one whose commitment to representation essentially bars him from enactment.[36]) The problem involves address and modality: in Wagner's idiosyncratic conception of narration versus enactment, enactment is desirable because it bypasses thought; narration is undesirable because it directs itself to thought. Put in colloquial terms, Mime is all talk and no action. Indeed, in the following pages I hope to show that this is his overt predicament: unable to act, all he can do is talk, and the talk that he talks is the dissembling language of culture.[37] Eventually that will be his undoing: in invoking the "Erziehungslied" (or "rearing song" that recounts his travails in raising Siegfried), Mime distorts reality; in repeating it, he merely mimics his own distortion. Siegfried will kill the dwarf for the deception underlying the practice.

But Siegfried too will be killed in the act of narration. What are we to make of this? In my view, neither Treadwell nor Abbate fully accounts for the ways in which narration, incorporated within the work, is fundamentally problematic once it's left there. In the following, I will argue that the preponderance of narration is a problem in and for the *Ring*, one that becomes the stuff of representation. Like an increasing number of critics, including Treadwell and Jean-Jacques Nattiez, I am convinced that we can best understand the operations of narration in the *Ring* by examining the accounts of its place and function in Wagner's writings from the period. In thus revisiting familiar territory, I will arrive at a different destination. For while Treadwell and Abbate both end up with a scene of mutual exchange and artistic power relinquished (where Wagner and the individual auditor share and fill out the work's interstices[38]), I envision a much less jovial scene, where narration hounds the work and ultimately causes its hero's demise.

DARSTELLUNG'S PREFACE: MUSIC, LANGUAGE,
AND ORIGINS IN DAS RHEINGOLD

Consistent with its label as a *Vorabend*, *Das Rheingold* occupies a rhetorical and dramaturgical position as the pre-tale. In his autobiography, Wagner described it as such and the best of critics have dutifully understood it accordingly.[39] Thus, for example, Thomas Mann retells the tale of the genesis of the *Ring*:

> [Wagner] felt an overwhelming need to present these earlier events in sensuous form. And so he began to write the work backwards: he composed *Der junge Siegfried*, then *Die Walküre*, then *Das Rheingold*, and would not rest until he had put everything on to the stage in fully present form—the whole story in four evenings, starting with the primeval cell, the ultimate beginning, the first E flat of the double bassoon that opens the *Rheingold* Prelude, with which he solemnly, almost inaudibly began to tell the story.[40]

But does this work really satisfy Wagner's need to make the pre-tale available to the senses? If the work does not constitute the prehistory to end (or begin) all prehistories, what does it do? It seems to serve as a partial prehistory for *Siegfried*, or rather, to *enact* certain moments described there. Indeed, the work "completes" the *Ring* by staging a later moment, not an aboriginal one.

So in what sense does *Das Rheingold* represent the ultimate beginning? What is prefatory about this prefatory work? Perhaps its beginning? Dramatically, *Das Rheingold* begins as much *in medias res* as the other three operas in the *Ring*. But linguistically, *Das Rheingold* starts off quite differently. Both *Die Walküre* and *Siegfried* begin with a solitary character in more or less desperate straits; *Götterdämmerung*, on the other hand, begins in the midst of a full-fledged conversation.[41] Unlike these scenes, the opening scene of *Das Rheingold* hovers unstably between declamation and conversation. This is in part because the infamous opening lines would appear to be more musical than linguistic: the meaning is hardly clear when Woglinde opens the tetralogy with the exclamation "Weia! Waga! Woge, du Welle, walle zur Wiege! wagala weia! wallala weiala weia!"[42] Her song renders in (proto-) words the allegory of origination suggested by the famous 136-bar musical prelude, retracing in language the route that the musical prelude travels from the very beginnings of sound.[43]

In *Mein Leben*, Wagner describes how the musical prelude to *Das Rheingold* came to him in a feverish state of somnambulism in La Spezia, Italy:

> I suddenly had the feeling of being immersed in rapidly flowing water. Its rushing soon presented itself to me in the musical sound of the chord of E-flat major, resounding in persistent broken chords. . . . I recognized at once that the orchestral prelude to *Das Rheingold*, that I had long carried about within me, but had been unable to find, had at last been revealed to me . . .[44]

Wagner's account makes for a fine autobiographical tale, but most critics have dismissed it as a retrospective invention.[45] While the origins of the prelude remain in question, critics have offered strong evidence that the music itself represents an account or rendering of origins.[46] Thus, for example, Ernest Newman writes that "the first sound we hear is a long-held E flat deep down in the double-basses, a primordial element, as it were, out of which the world of water represented by the Rhine will come into being by slow differentiation."[47] The depth of the tone (a low E flat), its instrumentation (played solely by the double basses), as well as its harmonic simplicity and static quality make its beginnings almost unnoticeable. That unnoticeable quality was undoubtedly reinforced by Wagner's audacious decision to submerge the orchestra beneath the Bayreuth stage and darken the auditorium before beginning the performance.[48] In thus rendering invisible the moment of the work's beginning (Wagner had also made the conductor invisible from the auditorium), Wagner added to its indeterminacy: here the commencement of the musical evocation of origins is rendered strangely undecidable. The E-flat harmony shifts abruptly in Bar 137 with the rise of the curtain and the onset of Woglinde's refrain. But while the harmony shifts (to A flat), we could say that Wagner's musical evocation of origins spills over into language so that the dramatic enactment begins at (or at least near) language's purported beginnings.[49]

But Woglinde's protolinguistic song breaks off as Wellgunde breaks in; thus it becomes clear that her song does not retrace very much or extend very far. Instead, her opening snippet marks a point near the beginnings of linguistic development; with her next line, she leapfrogs a vast expanse of that development to land in mid-conversation. Called upon "from above," Woglinde (and with her, Wagner) shifts from the proto-infantile mode to a comprehensible form of language:

> *Woglinde*:
> . . . Wagala weia!
> Wallala weiala weia!
>
> *Wellgundes Stimme* [von oben]:
> Woglinde, wachst du allein?
>
> *Woglinde*:
> Mit Wellgunde wär ich zu zwei.
>
> [*Woglinde*: . . . Wagalaweia, wallala weiala weia!
> *Wellgunde's voice* (from above): Woglinde, watching alone?
> *Woglinde*: With Wellgunde there would be two of us!][50]

The gulf traversed between Woglinde's first refrain and her exchange with Wellgunde deserves exploration. For when Woglinde lands in mid-conversation, she does not land in the language of the mid-nineteenth century. Instead, she arrives at a willfully archaic (and historically inde-terminate) point, a linguistic point sometime before language took off in the wrong direction, abandoning its roots in nature and the *Volk*. In *Opera and Drama*, Wagner fervently and repeatedly insists on the point: language was corrupted as it moved farther and farther away from its natural roots. But for Wagner, that point is not just polemical, it is also stage-worthy: thus, in the *Ring* he would return to a point when language *was* rooted, a time *back then* when language was still organically con-nected to its origins, a point, if you will, of pre-deracination. Woglinde's exchange with Wellgunde speaks to this point as it speaks from it.[51]

THE COMPOSER'S NEW CLOTHES: WAGNER'S
VERSION OF THE ORIGINS OF LANGUAGE

So far in this chapter we have encountered two scenes of re-turn: the first involved Wagner's recursive spiral in search of an initial and initiatory scene for his Nibelungen project, a place where the work could properly originate as *Darstellung*. The second scene was the fruit of the first, its realization in the music and words that opened *Das Rheingold*. Here, in the opening bars of the tetralogy, we encountered a musical evocation of origins. As the Prelude concluded, the return took linguistic form: Woglinde's entrance marked the return of a lost form of language. In order to understand this return, we need to go back to the account of linguistic origins and the rift between good and bad language in *Opera and Drama*.

The opening lines of *Das Rheingold* offer a concise introduction to an elaborate and idiosyncratic theory of language that Wagner presented in the Zurich writings. The most immediately striking linguistic feature of the scene is arguably the most important component of the theory: the predominance of alliteration, or to use Wagner's term, *Stabreim*. In *Opera and Drama*, *Stabreim* represents the innovation, or more precisely, the innovative archaism that would allow Wagner to return language to its roots.[52] But before Wagner can resuscitate the German language, he has to rescue *Stabreim*, which has long lain discarded and forgotten on the trash heap of German poetics.

According to Wagner, *Stabreim* once embodied a mythic sameness of language and nature. As that sameness was ruptured, *Stabreim* was replaced by end-rhyme, which in turn reflected the distance separating language and nature. By reintroducing *Stabreim*, Wagner would erase that distance and reestablish the connection. How did all of this come about? A brief review of Wagner's account of linguistic origins may help to explain the prominence of *Stabreim* in his aesthetics and its role in the opening lines of the *Ring*.

In the beginning, Wagner theorizes, there was sound-language (*Tonsprache*), a primal mode of utterance that Man originally shared with beasts.[53] Sound-language consisted of individual open sounds (*tönende Laute*), that lent spontaneous and singular expression to inner feeling. As that expression gained range, it became *melody*, which expressed a range of inner feeling (rather than the single impression expressed in sound-language). Melody was produced by stringing together the individual open sounds that form sound-language, and was soon accompanied by bodily gestures, which provided rhythm and added outer expression to the inner expression of the voice. Because pure sound-language and melody only gave expression to feeling, registering its (internal) impressions of external events, feeling in turn sought a way to signify objects in the world, or "external" objects. It found this signification in voiceless consonants (*stumme Laute*), which provided the feeling with an objective expression derived from an attribute of the object itself. This mute sound was added (as prefix or suffix) to either end of the open sounds that signified inner feeling, thus further differentiating expression. Here, then, in the new clothing of mute tones, Wagner locates the roots of language: "The vowels thus clothed, and distinguished by their clothing, form the *roots of language* through whose assembly and combination the whole sensuous edifice of our endlessly-branching word-language has been erected."[54]

Outfitted with this theoretical model, Wagner fits it into an extended domestic metaphor, and essentially plays house. Thus, word-language is presented as the child who left its father and mother in order to go off into the "wide world" on its own.[55] At first, language kept quite close to home, weaning itself only very gradually from its "mother's nourishing breast" (melody), and her "milk" (the open tone).[56] As it moved "ever so cautiously" away from home, it kept an eye on nature and developed a desire to impart its view. Since its vision organized things according to natural likenesses, setting only the kindred and analogous together, language created natural roots that accorded with this vision. According to Wagner, this creative moment where language creates its own roots is encapsulated in *Stabreim*, which represents "the very oldest attribute of all poetic language."[57] *Stabreim* brings together related linguistic roots, presenting a composite sound to the ear and a unified appearance to feeling.[58]

The problem is that word-language's attention soon faltered, and thus the nexus of feeling-nature-language fell apart. The child who left home with an eye trained upon nature had been able to grasp it with its feelings, creating new and natural roots for new objects. But soon enough, the child lost focus and began to look elsewhere for creative sustenance. This was a grievous error. For in turning away from nature, word-language lost an instinctive understanding of its roots and their relation to what Wagner terms "that nourishing mother-melody."[59] Suddenly, word-language was forced to create its own roots, usually by simply stringing together already extant ones, generating confusion and imprecision where previously there had been clarity and natural correspondence.

Wagner's account of linguistic history recalls some of the most vivid thematic preoccupations in his dramatic works. This shift from natural to artificial roots and from a natural heritage to a self-made one is familiar enough in Wagnerian dramaturgy.[60] In Wagner's works we repeatedly encounter male figures (including especially the Flying Dutchman, Siegfried, and Parsifal) who have somehow lost track of their roots and must reinvent them. And in Wagner's theory, language not only shares the same impulse toward reabsorption that impels each of these figures, it also follows the same route to attain it, a route that involves some form of return to those natural origins.

But before language can return home it has to go astray. In *Opera and Drama*, the wrong turn occurs, as I suggested above, when language turns away from nature. This parting of the ways is marked by the advent of end-rhyme over *Stabreim*. Where *Stabreim* had rendered the underlying connections among melodic intonations with ease, end-rhyme barely tagged along with melody, having lost any organic connection to it. As the distance separating word-language from natural designation increased, so too did its estrangement from the primal melody, until finally word-language simply lost even the faintest recollection of its origins. For Wagner, the move from *Stabreim* to *Endreim* was literally misleading, taking German expression farther and farther away from its roots and severing the signifier from the signified.[61] In returning to the scene of this deracination, Wagner seeks to repair these rifts and return German art to a proper, natural mode of expression.

The distinction between end-rhyme and *Stabreim* finds its corollary in *Opera and Drama* in a distinction that Wagner draws between the modern language of the intellect (so to speak, the offspring of the wayward offspring) and the antiquated language of feelings (the neglected offspring of the abandoned ancestors). Confronted with the increasing complexity of life in modern society, word-language addressed itself not to feeling but to reason. In gaining complexity, it made no effort to regain its organic connection to the signified. Thus mediation came to characterize the language of modernity.

While modern society propagates the highly mediated and mediating language of reason, the *Volk*, which remains closest to nature, cultivates the aboriginal field of the German language. It speaks what is left of the antiquarian language of the feelings—the language that *Wortsprache*, the wayward son, would have spoken had he not left the straight and narrow. The *Volk* speaks unconsciously, thus recalling the unsullied and naive impulse toward simple, unmediated, natural expression. In speaking thus and in remaining close to the land, the *Volk* ostensibly sustains the language and its roots as well:

> But beneath the frosty mantle of its civilization the *Volk* preserves, in
> the instinctiveness of its natural mode of language, the roots through
> which it remains connected to nature's ground; and everyone may

come by an instinctive understanding of those roots, if he turns from the hubbub of our official-State-business language-intercourse (*unseres staatsgeschäftlichen Sprachverkehres*) to seek a loving view of Nature, and thus makes these roots available to feeling, through an 'unconscious' use of their *kindred* qualities.[62]

For Wagner, the language of feeling is much closer to the roots of expression—both in principle and in fact, a proximity that is borne out by its suffusion with original linguistic roots. This distinguishes it from modern language, which is at once rootless and overgrown with roots, having lost track of its roots in the course of its headlong rush into reason, and having produced new and artificial ones to replace them. Without guidance from home, modern language is at a loss: overburdening its own imagination by having to invent new roots, and killing off the very language it had inherited by neglecting its natural roots.[63]

Wagner's response to the predicament of language is unequivocal: since true works of art cannot be created with modern language, he intends to return to language's roots, creating works that are as elevated as they are grounded.[64] In doing so, he will right the wrong by reconnecting language to nature, thus reinvigorating language's "withered flesh." Of course, Wagner cannot claim to reinvent this aboriginal language—to do so would compromise its status as aboriginal; instead, he merely rediscovers it. Or perhaps more appropriately, it discovers him. Thus, as he realizes that he cannot produce a *Siegfried* in modern language—even in the modern language of poetry—the aboriginal source for the myth presents him with an adequate form of expression. Without such an adequation, Wagner reasons, the project itself would be at risk:[65]

> I must have straightway let my *Siegfried* go, had I been restricted to such [conscious, modern] verse. Thus I had to conceive of another language-melody. And yet, in truth, there was no need for me to conceive, but merely to decide; for at the primal mythic spring [*ur-mythische Quelle*] where I had found the fair young Siegfried-man, I also came, automatically, upon the sensually complete mode of utterance [*Sprachausdruck*] wherein alone that man could express himself. This was the *alliterative verse*, accommodating itself in the most natural and lively rhythm to the actual accents of our language, yielding itself so readily to endless shades of the most variegated expression,—that *Stabreim* in which the people itself once wrote, when it was still both poet and creator of myths.[66]

There is a certain intertextual irony to Wagner's claim that he happened upon the only fitting language at the primal mythic spring. For as I suggested in the introductory chapter, the *Quelle* has a particularly dubious history within the *Nibelungenlied*, since it is where Siegfried is killed. Thus its overdetermination as a place of purity and refreshment is ironized when Hagen plays his dastardly plot off against it. In the *Ring*, Siegfried will not die at the physical site of the *Quelle*, but insofar as we take Wagner at his word (that he derives the language of the *Ring*—and even more specifically, Siegfried's language—from the *Ur-Quelle*), we could say that in an important sense Siegfried *does* die at the *Quelle*. For as I pointed out at the conclusion of the preceding chapter, Siegfried dies in the course of recounting his tale. This only adds to the irony of Wagner's claim that he has saved the project with this "sensually complete mode of utterance," for the mode of expression that saves *Siegfried* will in turn undo Siegfried. If Siegfried in the *Nibelungenlied* became vulnerable as he bathed himself in invulnerability, Siegfried in the *Ring* becomes vulnerable at a similar juncture, if in a different way: as Wagner envelops him within the aboriginal language of the source, it is his relegation to that very language that will prove his undoing. Made to speak the language of nature, and thus spared the corruption that supposedly afflicts those who speak the language of culture, Siegfried will die on account of his inability to fend for himself in the language he would have spoken had he not been thus protected. Here, then, we can locate the missing linden-leaf episode, in this scene where Wagner would save his hero and the entire Nibelungen project, rendering them invulnerable to the debilitating and corrupting effects of modern language—a language directed to the intellect, the language of description rather than *Darstellung*—by outfitting them with the language of the *Ur-Quelle*.

In stumbling upon this language at the *Ur-Quelle*, Wagner encounters a proliferation of aboriginality—the aboriginal language of the *Ring*, derived from the aboriginal poetic form, made available in the aboriginal mythical source.[67] In the *Ring*, *Das Rheingold* will be the site for the presentation of that aboriginality.

In *Das Rheingold*, the originary moment is designated by music, not by drama. That is, the event generally thought to signify creation in *Das Rheingold* and to represent a point for which there is no prehistory—Thomas Mann's "primeval cell and ultimate beginning"—is decidedly and singularly musical.[68] The tale of creation "told" in the Prelude is not duplicated in the drama. The drama does not open at the beginning of time; instead, the music delivers us up to the opening of the drama. That delivery would seem to cover a great deal of time—not actual time in the theater (after all, the prelude is only 136 bars long), but signified time. In thus juxtaposing the expansive temporal coverage of the prelude with the limited temporal range of the drama, Wagner renders a temporal disjunction between the dramaturgical and dramatic referents at the outset of *Das Rheingold*. If the dramaturgical referent aspires to an allegorical rendering of the process of origination, the dramatic referent at the outset of the work refers to a moment that, even if it is historically vague, nonetheless occurs at a point much later than that purportedly alluded to in the music.

In beginning with music, and in beginning thus with a self-generating and repeating chord, Wagner does not return to the beginning of time (as many critics have supposed); instead, a careful reading of his theoretical writings would suggest that he returns, in the Prelude, to the beginning of language, language as *tönender Laut*, as melody. We can interpret the sustained E-flat chord—sounding as it does from the sonic depths, without a perceptible beginning and without any initial melodic or rhythmic inflection—as rendering the aboriginal tone (without melody or rhythm) of *Tonsprache* that Wagner describes in *Opera and Drama*. In this way, Wagner could be said to stage—albeit invisibly—his argument that in the beginning of language there was *Tonsprache*. At the same time, he takes us back to that beginning.

As the chord develops, it gains melody, which in turn gains gesture and rhythm. Here, the aboriginal scene is musical. To what end? We find a partial explanation in *Opera and Drama*, where music is assigned the task of resuscitating language:

> Science has laid bare to us the organism of language; but what she showed us was a dead organism that only the Poet's utmost Want can resuscitate: namely, by closing up again the wounds cut into the body of language by the anatomic scalpel, and by breathing into that body the breath that will animate it into self-movement. *But this breath is—Music.—*[69]

In resuscitating good language, Wagner does not necessarily dispense with bad language. Indeed, we can read the *Ring* as an allegory of the confrontation between the different linguistic modes set out in *Opera and Drama*, namely the (bad, corrupt, dissembling) modern language of culture, and the (good, pure, authentic) language of nature. Each of these modes receives its own particular agent: not surprisingly, the heroes (represented principally by Siegfried) speak good language, while the antiheroes (represented principally by Mime, Alberich, and Hagen) speak bad language. In reading the work in this way, we gain a stronger sense of what is at stake in Siegfried's death, which, as I suggested in chapter one, is a death produced at a highly charged scene of reiteration. Insofar as he is made to embody a linguistic practice, his death stages (and the tragedy is augmented by) the reemergence of the language of culture and, concomitant with that reemergence, what we might term the second death of natural language.

NARRATING SIEGFRIED'S ORIGINS: PITTING NATURE VERSUS CULTURE

Once the drama opens, the tale is already belated. *Das Rheingold* begins in a realm where events have already transpired and require recounting. This belatedness is the product of Wagner's own theories of representation, for he begins (and insists upon beginning) with an explicit instance of plasticity as opposed to narration. As a result, the scene necessarily bears a past. And yet that past is, or at least appears to be, lost, especially since it is unavailable for narration. That loss arouses a desire to recoup what has been lost; thence the return to (lost) origins, in order to compensate for that loss by gaining control over the scene of its production.

In a sense, the loss itself is also staged, if only indirectly, in the opening scene of *Das Rheingold*, where Alberich's robbery results in the Rhinemaidens' loss. In addition to the overt, dramatic terms of loss, what is also lost is a state of speaking: Woglinde's pure, unencumbered mode of senseless *Stabreim* presented at the outset of the drama. This scene could be said to dramatize the scene of loss that Wagner envisions in *Opera and Drama*, that moment when the connection between language and nature is broken, when word-language loses touch with its roots and the modern language of the intellect is born. Thus if the Prelude takes us back to the origins of *Tonsprache*, the opening scene dramatizes the Fall from linguistic grace. In the wake of the robbery, the Rhinemaidens' refrain serves as a nostalgic marker of their loss. But this nostalgia extends beyond its evident dramatic referent (loss of the gold) to encompass this loss on the level of language, the loss of the mode of prelapsarian (or pre-Alberichian) nonsignifying *Stabreim*. Their loss is ours, but only as we partake of the community which had a language to lose. And as we shall see, the scene serves to constitute this very community that thus loses together, a community established on the basis of a fundamental exclusion that takes linguistic form. Thus, the "we" that loses is only formed when there is a recognizable "they" that is understood to have inflicted the loss. This "they" will be the anticommunity of the Jew.[70]

If the music alludes to the beginnings of language, the moment of *Tonsprache*, the drama begins at a much later point, even if that point still represents an early point in the development of language. In starting out at this point—a point later than the music, but also, and more importantly, a point that is not recognizable as the beginning point of *Darstellung*—the drama starts too late, and much of the rest of the tetralogy is taken up with the need to redress its own belatedness. In this sense, the works could be said to start out from where they are headed: opening up with a clear indication of the temporal disjunction to which they will repeatedly return. Woglinde's protolinguistic opening lines—the "Weia! Waga! Woge, du Welle" and so forth—serve as a recurring and presumably unintentional trace of that belatedness, signifying what we might term an early-modern stage of a linguistic history that *has not been shown*, but a state that has, nonetheless, been lost.[71]

To the extent that her opening lines become the Rhine maidens' refrain, we could say that the maidens gain an additional role, serving as the representatives of this belatedness, recalling a linguistic moment of aboriginality that they themselves have passed beyond as well as a mode of expression that has been lost. This would add a significant linguistic dimension to their assigned function, which is to voice everyone's bad conscience in the *Ring*. That is, their repeated pleas reinvoke not just the originary injustice shown at the opening of the work—the robbery of the Rhine gold—but they unwittingly reinvoke as well the disjunction and loss that accompany it: the belatedness signaled by their own occasional recourse to the forgotten (or repressed?) *Darstellung* of linguistic origins as well as the loss occasioned by Alberich's larceny.

As the tetralogy proceeds, the need to redress a sense of belatedness and loss only increases, for characters in the *Ring*, like its composer, are continuously preoccupied by the past and intent upon recovering it.

This disjunction is consonant with (if not attributable to) the genesis of the works, which are produced in the course of a desire to recoup for (and as) the present a narrative past that inevitably proves elusive even as it bears with it a further past. The *Ring* repeatedly seeks to close the gap that it itself opens up. Later on in this chapter, I will seek to account for this disjunction with reference to the logic of *Nachträglichkeit*. But before doing so, let us examine how the notion of origins is played out within the tetralogy.

Having raised Siegfried in isolation, Mime has been able to exercise virtually total control over his access to narrative information. But as *Siegfried* opens, that control is evidently at risk. Unable to forge a sufficiently resilient sword for Siegfried, Mime is also unable to fashion a sufficiently compelling narrative of his origins. Instead, he merely repeats the same old story, or, in this case, the same old song, a tired account of the trials and tribulations of raising the young hero:

> Als zullendes Kind
> zog ich dich auf,
> wärmte mit Kleidern
> den kleinen Wurm:
> Speise und Trank
> trug ich dir zu,
> hütete dich
> wie die eig'ne Haut.
> Und wie du erwuchsest,
> wartet' ich dein;
> dein Lager schuf ich,
> daß leicht du schlief'st.
> Dir schmiedet' ich Tand
> und ein tönend Horn;
> dich zu erfreu'n
> müht' ich mich froh:
> mit klugem Rathe
> rieth ich dir klug,
> mit lichtem Wissen
> lehrt' ich dich Witz.
> Sitz' ich daheim
> in Fleiß und Schweiß,
> nach Herzenslust

schweif'st du umher:
für dich nur in Plage,
in Pein nur für dich,
verzehr' ich mich alter
armer Zwerg!
[*Schluchzend*]
Und aller Lasten
ist das nun mein Lohn,
daß der hastige Knabe
mich quält
[*Schluchzend*]
und haßt!

[From a suckling babe I brought you up, warmed the little mite with clothes: food and drink I brought you, and tended you as if you were my own skin. And when you grew bigger I waited upon you; I made you a bed so you'd sleep comfortably. I forged toys for you and a ringing horn. To make you happy, I was happy to work: with clever counsel I counseled you cleverly, with lucid lore I taught you wit. While I sit at home toiling and sweating, you roam around to your heart's content: suffering torment for you alone, for you alone I suffer affliction and wear myself out, a poor old dwarf! (*sobbing*) And that's my reward for the burdens I've borne, that the quick-tempered boy torments (*sobbing*) and abhors me!][72]

It quickly becomes clear that Mime's refrain is losing its appeal in the face of—what else?—nature. As Siegfried grows, he grows closer to nature, which in turn takes him farther from Mime and makes him less inclined to believe the dwarf's version of events. The terms of their rift become clear the moment Siegfried first appears. Bursting in from the forest "with sudden impetuosity" [*mit jähem Ungestüm*], he has a bear in tow, which he sics upon Mime. While Siegfried's alliance with the bear is brief—he sends it packing after terrorizing Mime for a few moments—his alliance with nature is permanent. Thus when he looks for a friend, he looks to nature, which proves to be a much better provider than Mime. Mime, for his part, would have Siegfried look—and listen— to him alone for guidance. "I put up with it happily when you bag a bear," Mime complains, "But what are you doing—bringing live bruins home?"[73] Siegfried's response is as unequivocal as it is suggestive:

Nach bess'rem Gesellen sucht' ich,
als daheim mir einer sitzt;
im tiefen Walde mein Horn
ließ ich hallend da ertönen:
   ob sich froh mir gesellte
   ein guter Freund?
das frug ich mit dem Getön'.

Aus dem Busche kam ein Bär,
der hörte mir brummend zu;
er gefiel mir besser als du,
doch bess're fänd' ich wohl noch . . .

[I was seeking a better companion than the one sitting here at
home; deep in the forest I wound my horn till it echoed far and
wide: would some good-hearted friend be glad to join me, I asked
by means of that sound. From the bushes came a bear which,
growling, gave me ear; I liked him better than you, but might
find better ones yet . . .][74]

This is only the first (and, dramaturgically, the least eventful) of several
instances where Siegfried will demonstrate an easy rapport with nature.[75] The scene of call and response will be repeated in act II, when
Siegfried attempts to speak with the woodbird by reproducing its call,
but instead succeeds at rousing Fafner. In both of these instances, Siegfried attempts to speak the language of nature. Given Wagner's polemical juxtaposition of linguistic modes in *Opera and Drama*, the opposition is familiar enough: Siegfried is naturally inclined to the language of
nature, while Mime would subject him to the language of culture.

   This opposition is put to active use in the first scene of act I, where it
becomes clear—to Siegfried and to us—that Mime's tale of Siegfried's
origins (the rearing song) relies on eminently unnatural claims. Siegfried
is able to tease out the unnatural basis of Mime's account thanks to his
naturally keen powers of observation and his close ties to nature. Those
ties produce an ostensibly natural antipathy toward his guardian, pitting
nature on one side against Mime on the other:

Alle Thiere sind
mir theurer als du:
Baum und Vogel,
die Fische im Bach,

lieber mag ich sie
leiden als dich:—

[All the beasts of the forest are dearer to me than you: tree and
bird, fishes in the brook, I like them more than I like you.][76]

Mime sustains the distinction by seeking to repudiate it, presenting his
own rules as the law of nature and demanding obedience to the latter in
order to gain compliance with the former:

Jammernd verlangen Junge
nach ihrer Alten Nest:
Liebe ist das Verlangen;
so lechzest du auch nach mir,
so lieb'st du auch deinen Mime—
    so mußt du ihn lieben!
Was dem Vögelein ist der Vogel,
wenn er im Nest es nährt,
eh' das flügge mag fliegen:
das ist dir kind'schem Sproß
der kundig sorgende Mime—
    das muß er dir sein.

[Whimpering, young things long for their parents' nest: love is
the name of that longing; so you, too, pined for me, so you, too,
love your Mime, so you *have* to love him! What the baby bird is
to the bird when he feeds it in the nest, before the fledgling can
fly, that, little offspring, is what wise and caring Mime is to you,
he *has* to be that to you!][77]

Mime hampers his cause by introducing nature into the equation, for
there is a stark gap between his version of natural reality and nature's
own testimony, which Siegfried has duly recorded and dutifully recites.
Thus, for example, Siegfried notes that while animals in the forest organize themselves in pairs, Mime remains unnaturally partnerless, and
Siegfried unnaturally motherless.[78] To make his point, Siegfried returns
to the familiar terms of the rearing song:

Das zullende Kind
zogest du auf,
wärmtest mit Kleidern
den kleinen Wurm:—

wie kam dir aber
der kindische Wurm?
Du machtest wohl gar
ohne Mutter mich?

[You raised the suckling babe, warmed the little mite with
clothes—but how did you come by the little mite? You made
me, no doubt, without a mother?][79]

Thus, Mime's somewhat implausible scene of domestic tranquillity
starts to unravel as Siegfried compares it more and more insistently to
the image of nature he himself has encountered, laying bare the discrepancy at its core: Mime is not Siegfried's natural father and Siegfried is not
Mime's natural son.[80] In what amounts to a desperate and symptomatically unnatural fantasy of polysexuality, Mime claims to be both Siegfried's father and mother, which Siegfried takes as proof that he is neither. Thus, when Mime insists—according to the stage directions, *"in
grosser Verlegenheit"* [with great embarrassment]—

Glauben sollst du,
was ich dir sage:
ich bin dir Vater
und Mutter zugleich!

Siegfried's response is abrupt and defiant:

Das lügst du, garstiger Gauch!—

["You have to believe what I tell you: I'm your father and mother
in one!" "You're lying, you loathsome fool!—"][81]

Siegfried's defiance here is grounded in a different scene, if also one provided by nature. Readers will recognize its affinities with a more famous
and more recent scene, described by Jacques Lacan in his essay on the
mirror stage.[82]

Wie die Jungen den Alten gleichen,
das hab' ich mir glücklich erseh'n.
Nun kam ich zum klaren Bach:
    da erspäht' ich die Bäum'
    und Thier im Spiegel;
    Sonn' und Wolken,
    wie sie nur sind,

im Glitzer erschienen sie gleich.
  Da sah ich denn auch
  mein eigen Bild:
  ganz anders als du
  dünkt ich mir da:
  so glich wohl der Kröte
  ein glänzender Fisch,
doch kroch nie der Fisch aus der Kröte!

[That the young look like their parents I've luckily seen for
myself. When I came to the limpid brook, I glimpsed trees and
beasts in its glassy surface; sun and clouds, just as they are,
appeared in the glittering stream. And then I saw my own
likeness, too, quite different from you I thought myself then: as
like to a toad were a glittering fish, though no fish ever crept
from a toad!][83]

The scene described here is extraordinary for its availability to psychoanalytic interpretation, even by Wagnerian standards. Above all, it
serves to crystallize Mime's function as a sort of dumping ground for
disavowal. That is, by interpolating Mime into this scene, Siegfried is
able to fob off onto him the status (and origin) of his experience of not
belonging, of splitness, that would otherwise underlie the scene of mir-
roring described here. In this admittedly belated mirror-scene, Siegfried
does indeed recognize himself as split—not psychically split from or
unto himself, but physically or biologically split from Mime. Thus, the
moment at the brook, which is, after all, a moment of communion with
nature, sparks Siegfried's enthusiasm for a game of ancestral "Memory,"
where the imperative of natural correspondence impels him to look elsewhere for his correct ancestral match.

   In order for Siegfried to make that move, he has to come to recognize
the falseness of Mime's narration. That recognition is methodically
staged in the first scene of the first act. Thus Siegfried proclaims:

Sieh'st du, nun fällt
  auch selbst mir ein,
was zuvor umsonst ich besann:
  wenn zum Wald ich laufe,
  dich zu verlassen,
wie das kommt, kehr' ich doch heim?

Von dir erst muss ich erfahren,
wer Vater und Mutter mir sei!

[You see, now I realize of my own accord what I've long pondered
in vain: when I run off into the forest to leave you, how it is I still
come home: first I must learn from you who my father and
mother are!][84]

The realization is significant for our purposes as well. For in the course
of their confrontation, Siegfried and Mime have not merely been speaking two different languages—the language of nature and the language of
culture—but the structure of their exchange brings with it a significant
and by now familiar substitution: over the course of this scene, narration
in the form of Mime's rearing song is replaced by Siegfried's demand for
proof in the form of *Darstellung*. This shift is prefigured in the terms of
Siegfried's determination to discover his proper heritage: namely, his demand to *learn* or *experience* it (from the verb *erfahren*: "I must first *learn*
[or *experience*] from you who my father and mother are"). This "erfahren," as will soon become clear, involves an explicit and thoroughgoing suspicion of narration. And suddenly we find ourselves in familiar
biographical territory, reencountering some familiar terms from Wagner's own dilemma in preparing the *Ring*. That is, the positions staged in
this scene of *Siegfried* offer a vivid dramatization of positions about
dramatization, positions presented in Wagner's writings from the Zurich
period.

As Mime stands by his irrelevant story, he comes to stand for the
grounds of its irrelevance: his song tells more than an implausible tale of
Siegfried's origins, it bespeaks the unreliability of telling *per se*. As a
document of individual vision, it is warped by virtue of its idiosyncratic
individualism; removed from the collective, living out in the woods in
willed isolation, Mime's mode—of life and narration—bears no connection to the *Volk*. (Mime is, of course, an excellent agent of a loathsome
aesthetic principle since he is presented as so loathsome.) Insofar as it is
introduced in full and then repeated *ad nauseam*, we might think of
Mime's rearing song as taking the form of a counter-*Ring*, a nightmarish
vision of narration left to its own individualistic devices, independent of
nature and *Darstellung*.

As we have noted, Mime is presented—and presents himself—as singularly incapable of doing what has to be done and, at the same time,
single-minded in his commitment to talking others into doing those

things for him. (The two most prominent examples both involve Siegfried, who will forge the sword Mime cannot forge and kill the dragon he cannot kill.) In this way, we can understand Mime as an agent of narration, who, symptomatically, reforges the account of Siegfried's past in place of any real capacity to reforge the sword. By contrast, Siegfried, the quintessential man of action, functions as an agent of *Darstellung* whose impatience with narration is presented as well-founded by years of disinformation, and whose demand for a new, alternative mode is presented as the natural outgrowth of his affinities with nature.

The turn to *Darstellung* occurs when Siegfried can no longer tolerate the discrepancies between Mime's two accounts of the young hero's past: the old one, represented by the "rearing song," and the new one, which Siegfried forces him to reveal along with the fragments of Siegmund's sword. The new account, like the old one with which it competes, features information about Siegfried's heritage (in this case, Sieglinde's death and Siegfried's birth) that we have not previously seen. Both accounts offer instances of narration independent of any previous *Darstellung*, precisely what Wagner sought to eliminate in the *Ring*. At first, Mime seeks to forge the two accounts together, attaching extended passages from the rearing song to his recitation of the newer, presumably truer version of Siegfried's past. Thus, for example, when Siegfried asks whether Sieglinde ever mentioned his father's name, Mime's response is split between two tales and two tunes in contrasting meters, tempi, and musical textures:

> Erschlagen sei er,
> das sagte sie nur;
> dich Vaterlosen
> befahl sie mir da:—
> rund wie du erwuchsest,
> wartet' ich dein';
> dein Lager schuf ich,
> daß leicht du schlief'st'є. . .

> [That he'd been slain, was all she said; and to me she
> commended the fatherless child:—"And when you grew
> bigger I waited upon you; I made you a bed so you'd sleep
> comfortably" . . .][85]

The first section of the response offers Siegfried new narrative information and new musical material; the second section, however, is easily recognizable as another in a series of quotations of the earlier, entrenched version of the tale (indeed, the quotation is marked *with quotation marks* in the libretto and the score[86]). At the very moment Siegfried is intent upon garnering new narrative material, Mime is stalling. His familiar chorus is tantamount to an aesthetic anthem, singing the praises—here inflected as the eminently *false* praises—of narration.

Confronted thus with two conflicting versions of his past, Siegfried is presented with a choice between a relatively new tune (offering new information) and the same old song (communicating the same old story). In opting for the new tune, Siegfried insists upon a new mode. Thus, he first explicitly rejects the old song, and then demands a new form of proof for Mime's revised version of events:

> *Siegfried*:
>   Still mit dem alten
>   Staarenlied!—
> Soll ich der Kunde glauben,
> hast du mir nichts gelogen,
> so lass' mich Zeichen seh'n!
>
> *Mime*:
> Was soll dir's noch bezeugen?
>
> *Siegfried*:
>   Dir glaub' ich nicht mit dem Ohr',
>   dir glaub' ich nur mit dem Aug':
>   welch' Zeichen zeugt für dich?
>
> [*Siegfried*: Stop that old birdsong! If I'm to believe your account,
>   if you haven't lied to me, then let me see some proof!
> *Mime*: What else would prove it to you?
> *Siegfried*: I don't believe you with my ear, I only believe you with
>   my eye: what proof will back you up?][87]

Here, in Siegfried's rejoinder, we encounter the turn away from narration (suggestively metonymized by the ear) toward *Darstellung* (metonymized by the eye). According to the new terms that Siegfried imposes upon Mime, seeing, not hearing, will be believing.[88] (Indeed, seeing arguably enables this turn from narration, in that Siegfried sees himself as not-Mime, or not *of* Mime, in the brook.)

In the course of a spirited polemic concerning the importance of vision—and particularly, mirrors—in the elaboration of Wagner's racism,

Marc Weiner cites a key passage from "Was ist Deutsch?," another of Wagner's notoriously xenophobic pamphlets: "thus we see an odious travesty of the German spirit upheld today before the German *Volk* as its imputed likeness. It is to be feared that before long the nation may really take this false image for its mirrored image; then one of the finest natural dispositions in all the human race would be done to death, perchance for ever."[89] Weiner suggests that in Wagner's argument, it is the (Jewish, foreign) artwork that would distort. We can usefully apply the logic and terms of this argument to the case at hand. In the relationship between Siegfried and Mime, the false image that risks being mistaken for the mirror image is very often narration itself. And in the scene of Siegfried's confrontation with Mime that we have been considering, Siegfried will arrive at precisely the sort of recognition that Wagner envisions in the essay: that is, he will recognize the distortion and demand real, material (and visually verifiable) proof. Mime's preferred mode of distortion, of course, is narrative and thus, the move toward what Weiner astutely characterizes as an occularcentric regime is also a move away from a false narrative regime.[90]

Be it in the form of the flimsy swords he has previously presented to Siegfried, or the "one" sword that he has been hiding, the scene of presentation is unusually fraught for Mime. We can trace the problem, at least in part, to Mime's name: viewed with a skeptical eye, he might be seen—and indeed, *will* soon be seen—to be dissimulating.

In acceding to Siegfried's demand for proof, Mime retrieves not just the fragments of the shattered sword, but the plasticity that Wagner prefers in his highly charged, Manichaean dramaturgical aesthetics. Siegfried immediately recognizes the shattered sword as his proper inheritance, and, as such, his ticket out of this *faux* foster home; at the same time, we can recognize it as a ticket to a different narrative mode. If Mime's rearing song serves as an anthem for the regime of bad faith narration (whose primary accomplishment was negative: impeding Siegfried's access to his "proper" inheritance), the fragments of the sword offer Siegfried an entirely new refrain, one ostensibly of his own making. But we ought to examine the precise logic underlying Siegfried's acquisition of Nothung, for the fragments of the sword serve as a bidirectional (i.e., retrospective and prospective) relic, evincing a past regime of deeds as well as a future one, one that will soon avenge the bad faith of narration.

ORIGINS AS WILL AND IDEA: HOW SIEGFRIED
REFORGES HIS HERITAGE

We have considered several examples of Wagner's preoccupation with origins, his determination to gain access to and control over them. The theorization of linguistic origins in *Opera and Drama* and the impetus toward origins in the conceptualization of the *Ring* are two prominent examples I have discussed here. But how is this preoccupation expressed in the *Ring*? Mime's determination to instill into Siegfried his own narrative—as content and form—is the first scene we have encountered. It is, of course, just the beginning.

George Bernard Shaw was not the first, but he was probably the funniest critic to note that there are an incredible number of occasions when characters review their origins in the tetralogy.[91] We can attribute some of those instances to the requirements of such a massive work, where the need to establish and reestablish character encompasses the need to elucidate the character's heritage. But the preponderance of such scenes goes beyond the simple need to orient the audience, suggesting a recurring thematic interest in origins. Indeed, it seems as if the narration of origins often provides the unwitting focus for Wagner's preoccupation with narration. Thus, when a character narrates in the *Ring*, that narration often centers around origins, whether in the most familiar sense of personal heritage (such as Siegmund's account of his past in act I, scene ii of *Die Walküre*) or the prehistory of an event (as in Wotan's account of the past to Brünnhilde in the famous act II monologue of *Die Walküre*).

The preoccupation with origins is not merely a recurring moment or scene in the *Ring*, it is also at the heart of the dilemma confronting its principal protagonists. Thus, as the work progresses, it becomes clear— even to characters within the work—that the crisis confronting Wotan is bound to his origins. Indeed we could say that the crisis inheres in his *being bound* to his origins. Of course, what Wotan wants and needs is someone to do his bidding who is as unbound as he himself is bound by familial, historical, and contractual ties; a figure who bears the proper heritage and destiny but does not know it, a self-made man. Thus, he envisions a man who will act in his—Wotan's—interests but independent of his narrative limitations.

Wotan's predicament not only produces Siegfried, it also signals the ongoing vitality of a dubious visionary rhetoric in the *Ring*, a rhetoric of predetermination. As I hope to suggest, that rhetoric signals a conflict between narration and action, where the latter is continuously dogged by the former. How so? Wotan's narrative entanglements lead him to wish for a figure who will—independently—do his bidding. As I suggested in the introductory chapter, this fantasy involves an element of freedom (the character will act independently of Wotan's will) and an element of prescription (in so doing, he will fulfill Wotan's will). We might say that Wotan, in his monologue with Brünnhilde, makes the self-made man by dictating his qualities. Significantly, he does so through narration. In acceding to his calling, Siegfried must assume and erase the traces of this narrative prescription. In the following, I propose to examine the lexical traces of this process.

Let us begin with the rhetoric of predetermination, which goes beyond the expression of mere sentiments ("we need someone to set things right") or vague presentiments ("someone will set things right") to offer a scenario of predetermination ("only one man can set things right"). In act II of *Die Walküre*, Wotan uses the following terms to describe what he has in mind:

> Nur Einer könnte
> was ich nicht darf:
> ein Held, dem helfend
> nie ich mich neigte;
> der fremd dem Gotte
> frei seiner Gunst,
> unbewusst,
> ohne Geheiss,
> aus eig'ner Noth
> mit der eig'nen Wehr
> schüfe die That,
> die ich scheuen muss.

> [One man alone could do what I myself may not: a hero I
> never stooped to help; who, unknown to the god and free of
> his favors, all unwitting, without prompting, by his own need
> alone and with his own weapon would do the deed which I must
> shun . . .][92]

Here we have a succinct statement of the paradox of Wagner's rhetoric of predetermination, for Wotan prompts the figure who will be "without prompting" and arms the man who will act "with his own weapon." Of course, he does not do so in a literal sense (as he did with Siegmund). Or rather, he does so literally, which is to say figuratively—through narration. In order to demonstrate this, I propose an intricate surveillance, attending to the often minute lexical traces of Siegfried's accession to his narrative predetermination. I will thereby track Siegfried's journey to what Wotan describes as "his own weapon."

Wotan's incapacity to bear out this rhetoric of predetermination—since he cannot make the self-made man—is the product of his past willingness to do so. Earlier he had delivered on his promise to provide Siegmund with a sword in his hour of need. Although we do not witness the promise, Siegmund recalls it in act I of *Die Walküre* when he breaks into his desperate and pompous refrain, "ein Schwert verhieß mir der Vater, / ich fänd' es in höchster Noth.—" [My father promised me a sword: I'd find it in direst need.—][93] Of course the sword *is* waiting for Siegmund, but Sieglinde discovers it before he does. And in realizing that the sword was destined for him she also realizes that they are destined for each other. Thus she points out the weapon and its destiny:

> Eine Waffe lass' mich dir weisen—:
> O wenn du sie gewänn'st!
> > Den hehr'sten Helden
> > dürft' ich dich heißen;
> > *dem Stärk'sten allein*
> > *ward sie bestimmt*

> [Let me show you a weapon: O if only you could win it! As the noblest of heroes I could proclaim you; *for the strongest alone it was intended.*][94]

In both of these instances, the action is not just anticipated, it is foretold; and in this scene, as will be the case later in the tetralogy, the predicted moment is one of patrilineal transmission. But whereas Wotan had Siegmund in mind when he placed the sword into the tree trunk, the "one hero" he longs for in his monologue with Brünnhilde is left unnamed, unembodied. At this point, he has a destiny, but no name.

In *Die Walküre*, the patrilineal transmission from Wotan to Siegmund backfires, since Fricka sees through Wotan's transparent attempt to steer the illicit course of his illegitimate offspring. But as it backfires, Brünn-hilde assumes responsibility for embodying Wotan's desire, not by be-coming the anticipated hero, but by saving and naming him. In the course of doing so, Brünnhilde comes to employ the rhetoric of predeter-mination. When Sieglinde insists, in act III of *Die Walküre*, that she would rather die than flee, Brünnhilde informs her not just that she's pregnant but that she will bear the greatest of heroes (and as she speaks, the Siegfried motif sounds for the first time in the orchestra):

> *Brünnhilde*:
> den hehrsten Helden der Welt
> 　hegst du, o Weib,
> 　im schirmenden Schooß!—
> [*Sie zieht die Stücken von Siegmunds Schwert unter ihrem
> Panzer hervor und überreicht sie Sieglinde*]
> 　Verwahr' ihm die starken
> 　Schwertes-Stücken;
> 　seines Vaters Walstatt
> 　entführt' ich sie glücklich:
> 　der neu gefügt
> 　　das Schwert einst schwingt,
> den Namen nehm' er von mir—
> 'Siegfried' erfreu' sich des Sieg's!
>
> [the world's noblest hero, o woman, you harbor within your
> sheltering womb!—(*She brings out the fragments of Siegmund's
> sword from under her breastplate, and hands them to
> Sieglinde.*) For him keep safe the sword's stout fragments; from
> his father's battlefield I haply took them: let him who'll wield
> the newly forged sword receive his name from me—may
> 'Siegfried' joy in victory!][95]

Thus, Wotan's "Einer" gains a name and a more specific destiny, to swing the reconstructed sword. At the same time, Brünnhilde stands in for Wotan's desire to steer the course of events: like a super-sonogram *avant la lettre*, she can tell it's a boy, and more than that, it's a hero; and the orchestra joins in to tell us it's Siegfried.[96]

Brünnhilde's prediction differs slightly but significantly from the wording of the stage directions. While Brünnhilde envisions Siegfried swinging *the* reconstructed sword, the stage directions have her handing the remains of *Siegmund's* sword to Sieglinde. The transition from the paternal possessive (Siegmund's sword) to the neutral definite article (the sword) anticipates a significant erasure of heritage that will be staged in *Siegfried*. This erasure will mark Siegfried's reappropriation of the sword. In remaking the sword, Siegfried will remake his identity in accordance with Wotan's prediction in *Die Walküre* that he would be a self-made man.[97] Siegfried—much like Parsifal, who will also be raised more or less storyless—embodies the promise of a new hero, free of narrative binding, a paradoxically pre-scribed *tabula rasa*, an unwritten if already pre-scripted tale. To the extent that his destiny is thus preformulated, his self-madeness is made by others: by Wotan, Sieglinde, and Brünnhilde.

We have seen that Mime, of course, has very different (if similarly self-serving) plans for Siegfried, and formulates a different account of his origins: if Wotan would have Siegfried be self-made, Mime would have him believe he was Mime-made. Eventually, of course, Siegfried will go about making himself. The scene of his self-making is set at Mime's anvil, and the sword Nothung serves as the lexical and physical marker of the process: in recasting the sword's origins, Siegfried effectively recasts his own.[98] Although the sword first appears on stage quite late in the first act of *Siegfried*, it is invoked at the very outset of the opera. Mime's intense agitation as the opera begins—the "punishing torment" and "toil without purpose" that plague him—are a direct consequence of his inability to create a proper sword for Siegfried.[99] His predicament is, in a sense, born of the overdetermination of the envisioned act: Mime knows that any sword he forges will not do for Siegfried, and, at the same time, he knows that he cannot forge the only sword that *will* do.

> Es giebt ein Schwert,
> das er nicht zerschwänge:
> Nothungs Trümmer
> zertrotzt' er mir nicht,
> könnt' ich die starken
> Stücken schweißen,
> die meine Kunst
> nicht zu kitten weiß.
> Könnt' ich's dem Kühnen schmieden,
> meiner Schmach erlangt' ich da Lohn!

[There is one sword that he'd never shatter: Nothung's
fragments he'd not defy, could I but weld the mighty shards
which no art of mine can piece together. If I could only forge it
for that hothead, I'd find a due reward for all my shame!][100]

Whence this knowledge? How has Mime come to speak the rhetoric of
predetermination, exemplified by the recurring notion that Nothung is
the one sword that Siegfried will not destroy, that the young hero is
destined to swing the sword, and that he, Mime, cannot forge it?[101]

We could invent an explanation since the work does not provide one:
we could assume that Mime has been told—as Sieglinde was in act III of
Die Walküre[102]—that Siegfried is destined to carry his father's sword;
and we could further assume that, after several attempts, Mime has
come to realize he is incapable of forging the sword himself. And yet this
explanation would suture what remains a noteworthy gap in the work.
We might better account for the gap by examining its function. Thus we
can explain Mime's position and his relation to it in terms of a certain
compliance with the preformulated terms of the narrative. In his opening remarks, Mime not only transmits vital narrative information—that
he has raised Siegfried, that Fafner is hoarding the gold, that he is plotting to use Siegfried to get the ring for himself, etc.—but he also estab-
lishes his own subordination to the rhetoric of predetermination introduced in *Die Walküre*. He does so by serving as its carrier, reiterating the
terms introduced in the earlier work.

At the same time, Mime is plotting against the very plot toward which
he exhibits such compliance, aspiring to manipulate the narrative and
thus control it (in order, as he reasons, to gain control of the world). How
so? Mime envisions his power resulting from a strategic, surgical intervention in the tale. Allowing that Siegfried must gain the sword in order
then to fulfill the further task set for him, to kill the dragon, Mime seeks
to produce an unforeseen swerve in the hero's—and the narrative's—
preordained path: as Siegfried's guardian, Mime intends to murder him
and filch the ring once Siegfried has killed Fafner. But if the opening of
the opera shows Mime at an impasse, by the work's conclusion it will
become clear that the impasse was he: by hoarding the pieces of
Siegmund's sword, he keeps Siegfried from his preordained inheritance,
but by complying with the rhetoric of predetermination, he insures that
the delay will be merely temporary.

At the outset of the opera, Mime notes that his "Kunst" or "art" does not extend to repairing Nothung.[103] Just what is Mime's art ? Although he is a blacksmith by profession, his name obviously designates a form of artifice (miming) as it locates him at a remove from nature (as in the Greek stem, mime). As Jean-Jacques Nattiez suggests, "Mime embodies and synthesizes all those artists who are incapable of creating a unitary work of art. The image of shards and fragments is one that Wagner uses to describe those artists who are condemned to a certain impotence."[104] Indeed, it is not just that Mime is an impotent artist, but as I hope to show later in this chapter, his is the art of impotence.

Although it is clear that Siegmund owned the sword Nothung previously, it is not entirely clear where Nothung came from.[105] In the course of his confrontation with the Wanderer in act I of *Siegfried* (which is, after all, a scene around and about narrative recapitulation), Mime relates that

> in einer Esche Stamm
> stieß es Wotan:
> dem sollt' es geziemen,
> der aus dem Stamm es zög'.

> [Wotan drove it into the trunk of an ash tree: it was meant for the man who could draw it forth from the trunk.][106]

Mime goes on to recount that Siegmund alone was able to pull the sword from the tree, and that he carried it in battle, "bis an Wotans Speer es zersprang" [until it snapped on Wotan's spear].[107] This historical narrative duplicates what we have been told and shown in *Die Walküre*.

> Nun verwahrt die Stücken
> ein weiser Schmied;
> denn er weiß, daß allein
> mit dem Wotansschwert
> ein kühnes dummes Kind,
> Siegfried, den Wurm versehrt.

> [A wily dwarf now keeps the fragments; he knows that only with Wotan's sword will a certain foolish and foolhardy child, Siegfried, harm the dragon.][108]

Here Mime merely repeats information he has revealed at the very outset of the opera as he reiterates his compliance with the rhetoric of predetermination: he is hoarding the fragments of the one sword with which Siegfried will be able to kill the dragon. But it is not referred to as just "the sword," nor is it called "Siegmund's sword"; instead, Mime labels it "the Wotan-sword."

As the pieces of Wotan/Siegmund's sword are reforged, so too is the sword's character; that is, changes in the physical disposition of the sword are associated with changes in its name. The first act of renaming occurs when Siegfried dismisses Mime and heads toward the fireplace in which he will reforge the sword:

> Her mit den Stücken!
> Fort mit dem Stümper!
> *Des Vaters Stahl*
> fügt sich wohl mir:
> ich selbst schweiße das Schwert!

> [Here with the fragments! Away with the bungler! For me my father's blade will doubtless fit together: I'll forge the sword myself!][109]

In reforging the sword, Siegfried effectively "resurrects it." The young hero's characterization of this resurrection suggests an indirect resurrection of Siegmund, whereby the dead father is juxtaposed to the living son through the re-creation of the sword:

> Dem sterbenden Vater
> zersprang der Stahl,
> der lebende Sohn
> schuf ihn neu.

> [The steel sprang apart as my father died; his living son has made it anew][110]

We hardly need to explore the phallic resonances of this claim: they are clear enough. Siegfried sustains the ambiguous reference and the image of resurrection when he greets the sword "back to life:"

> Nothung! Nothung!
> Neidliches Schwert!
> Zum Leben weck' ich dich wieder.
> Tot lag'st du
> in Trümmern dort,
> jetzt leuchtest du trotzig und hehr

[Nothung, Nothung, fearsome sword! I've wakened you to life again. You lay there, dead, in ruins; now you glisten, defiant and glorious.][111]

Beyond its obvious overdetermination, this resurrection is also a historical reinscription: Siegfried creates the old sword anew, searing it of its historical antecedents. In reforging the pieces, the sword becomes whole, and wholly Siegfried's. ("Warst du entzwei, ich zwang dich zu ganz" [Though you were broken in two, I've restored you to wholeness.][112]) It is noteworthy that Siegfried heats the flames of historical reinscription with the marker—arguably the erstwhile repository—of the sword's history: the ash tree serves as the source from which Wotan derives his power and garnered his spear, and it serves as the site into which Wotan placed, and from which Siegmund pulled, the sword. By burning the traces of its history, Siegfried constitutes the sword as the locus of his heritage and his future. Indeed, in the second act of *Siegfried*, the sword gains an agency of its own when Siegfried asks Nothung to "lead" him.[113] Thus in addition to being "called back to life," the sword will also *direct* and thus wield Siegfried as Siegfried directs and wields the sword.

As we have seen, in burning the ash tree and recasting the fragments, Siegfried melts down the sword's odd history and its ambiguous origins as well. In reclaiming or literally reforging his own heritage, Siegfried would effectively erase the material and lexical traces of the sword's heritage. Both Mime and Siegfried accordingly recast their characterizations of Nothung. What was, according to Mime, "the Wotan-sword" ("das Wotansschwert") is now Siegfried's "own weapon, that he won for himself"[114]; and what Siegfried had referred to as his father's sword, he now refers to as his own. Pouring the glowing contents into a mold, Siegfried addresses himself to Nothung: "soon I'll wield you as my sword."[115] Indeed, he swings Nothung into action almost at once. The famously raucous line that concludes act I at once christens the sword—now fully Siegfried's—and celebrates the destruction of the site of its production:

Siegfried:
   Schau, Mime, du Schmied:
   [*Er holt mit dem Schwert aus*]
   so schneidet Siegfried's Schwert!
   [*Er schlägt auf den Amboss, welchen er von oben bis unten
   in zwei Stücken zerspaltet, so dass er unter grossem Gepolter
   auseinander fällt*]

[See, Mime, you smith: (*He raises the sword to strike a blow*)—this is how Siegfried's sword cuts! (*He strikes the anvil, which splits from top to bottom and falls apart with a loud crash.*)][116]

The transaction between fusion and fission is complete: the sword, fused anew in name and in deed, splits the anvil—the site of its fusion—in two. In doing so, Siegfried stages, with a characteristic, if nonetheless startling, violence the destruction of origins that he has heretofore effected upon the ash tree and at the level of the signifier: having burned the ash tree in order to melt away the sword's heritage, Siegfried destroys the site of the sword's reproduction. The act of erasure and reinscription thus comes full circle: first, the anvil is heated by the ash tree, whose status as a historical marker thus turns to ash; then the sword is recast and its heritage erased; finally, the sword can be put to use smashing the anvil, thus destroying the site of its material reproduction. In order for the sword to become truly Siegfried's, it has to "cut" thus, and in cutting thus, it supposedly becomes truly Siegfried's.

Here, then, is a typically Wagnerian *coup-de-theatre*. The conclusion of the act is a fittingly conclusive act, one that appears to present a conclusion of and to narration. That is, we can read Siegfried's grand gesture in stark and violent juxtaposition to the opening of the act (and the work), where Mime was shown bemoaning and recounting his fate. If the outset of the work was marked by Mime as an agent of and captive to narration, then the conclusion shows us Siegfried as very much the man of *Darstellung*. The transition from one mode to another involves a particularly ironic instance of citation. Siegfried's exultant cry, "Bald schwing ich dich als mein Schwert!" [Soon I'll wield you as my sword!][117] echoes the prediction it fulfills: Brünnhilde's announcement in act III, scene i of *Die Walküre* that Siegfried will be the one "der neu gefügt, das Schwert einst schwingt" [who "will forge (the sword's fragments) anew and one day wield (it)"].[118] In thus searing the sword of its origins, Siegfried enters into the path that he has been preordained to forge: in this way, the moment of ostensible liberation becomes a moment when he accedes to his pre-scription. The irony here is that Siegfried acts out of a fundamental misapprehension of his situation, for in swinging his father's sword as his own and smashing the means of its production, Siegfried is utterly bound and at least unconsciously coerced. To the extent that he assumes this tale as his newfound inheritance, Siegfried enters into a narrative economy over which he has no control, one that has already assigned him a precise place.

THE *DARSTELLUNG* OF CULTURAL LANGUAGE

The transition between regimes takes place at the seat of Mime's power, the anvil: Siegfried installs himself as the master forger while Mime becomes (and duly notes that he has become) his veritable—if still scheming—slave.[119] Siegfried's first deed is duly spectacular: he accomplishes what Mime, his former master, precisely could not do, he reforges the sword. His next deed is equally spectacular: he destroys the anvil—what we might describe as a metonymic throne of narration—and moves on. But while Mime's workbench is smashed in act I, the abuses of power for which it stood are left unavenged until act II.

The wisdom of Siegfried's skepticism toward Mime's words is borne out quite graphically in act II, scene iii. If the repetition of the rearing song throughout act I represents a nightmarish account of narration left to its own individualistic devices, then act II, scene iii of *Siegfried* represents a *Darstellung* of that nightmare, a vivid dramatization of the mendacity of the language of culture. Thus, Mime is made to speak the truth, but not by speaking the language of truth (i.e., the language of nature). Instead, nature itself constrains him involuntarily to speak the true mendacity of the language of culture. He does so as a direct consequence of an event that most closely approximates the linden-leaf episode. We should briefly review the plot before proceeding.

After repeated attempts to talk with the animals, Siegfried finally succeeds in doing so just after he kills the dragon, that is, at a point where we would expect the linden-leaf episode to occur. In the course of pulling the sword Nothung from Fafner's breast, Siegfried stains his hand with a smattering of the dragon's blood. As a reflex, he licks the blood off his finger. Suddenly, he senses that the birds whom he had been trying to address when he inadvertently awakened Fafner are now addressing him:

> Ist mir doch fast—
> als sprächen die Vög'lein zu mir:
> nützte mir das
> des Blutes Genuß?—
>
> [It's almost as though the woodbirds were speaking to me: was this brought about by the taste of the blood?—][120]

The voice of the woodbird responds (from a linden tree, according to Wagner's stage instructions), urging Siegfried to retrieve the magic cap and ring from Fafner's cave.[121] When Siegfried returns from the cave with these items, the voice of the woodbird speaks again:

> Hei! Siegfried gehört
> nun der Helm und der Ring!
> O traute er Mime
> dem Treulosen nicht!
> Hörte Siegfried nur scharf
> auf des Schelmen Heuchlergered':
> wie sein Herz es meint
> kann er Mime versteh'n;
> so nützt' ihm des Blutes Genuß.

> [Hei! Siegfried now owns the cap and the ring. Oh let him not trust the treacherous Mime! Were Siegfried to listen keenly to the rogue's hypocritical words, he'd be able to understand what Mime means in his heart; thus the taste of the blood was of use to him.][122]

At the very same moment, Mime is hatching his own plan of dissimulation: he plans to kill Siegfried and take the gold, the magic cap, and the ring:

> Zwiefach schlau
> sei nun der Zwerg:
> die listigste Schlinge
> leg' ich jetzt aus,
> daß ich mit traulichem
> Trug-Gerede
> bethöre das trotzige Kind!

> [Let the dwarf be doubly sly: I'll set the most cunning snare now and fool the defiant child with falsely friendly words!][123]

This "snare" will, of course, take linguistic form: that is, he will attempt to talk Siegfried into his own death. In so doing, Mime will seek to exploit the space of duplicity suggested in his determination to be doubly sly: but, as we will see, while Mime plots to double (or split) intention and meaning, nature plots to rebuff him by reconnecting them. We should note that Mime does not even plan to kill Siegfried; instead, he will convince him to imbibe the potion with which to dispatch himself.

The plan does not merely confirm Mime's status as an agent of narration; beyond that, it is the product of his determination—discussed above—to manipulate the narrative to his advantage: here is where Mime hopes to produce the swerve in the narrative. But rather than producing it in his interlocutor (the Freudian model), he will produce it for and by himself: that is, he himself will produce the rift in the tale, at once producing the "initial version" (what he means) as well as its revision (what he says). Mime's fantasy is one of linguistic manipulation: he seeks to forge a malleable bond between signifier and signified where language would respond to his own devices. And yet, Wagner's writings make it clear that Mime's devices are nothing more than the devices of culture, and these devices are, in turn, responsible for the very rift that Mime would single-handedly suture. Mime's incompetence as a smith who cannot reforge the fragments of Siegmund's sword extends to his plot to reforge language. Thus, what Mime had envisioned as a spectacle of his mastery over language ends up as a spectacle of his own unwitting subjugation to it. This inversion deserves our attention.

Nature anticipates Mime's plot, if only to override its intended effect: his words are revealed for what they "really" are, false speech. The process of dramatizing this moment is more complicated than it seems, for Wagner has to distinguish between the signifier and its inversion in Mime's intention. As it turns out, Siegfried (along with us in the audience) is not just able to understand what Mime means despite what he supposedly says; in fact, he hears what Mime means *as what he says*; that is, he hears—and we hear—his intention as his words. In this way, the scene stages Mime's extraordinary isolation, for everyone *except Mime* hears the words describing his underlying intention. Thus the scene renders a spectacular rift between intention and meaning at the very moment where Mime would redress that rift. Following is an example. To the most saccharine orchestral accompaniment, Mime explains to Siegfried:

> *Mime*:
> Siegfried, hör' doch, mein Söhnchen!
> Dich und deine Art
> haßt' ich immer von Herzen;
> [*Zärtlich*]
>> aus Liebe erzog ich
>> dich Lästigen nicht:
> dem Horte in Fafner's Hut,
> dem Golde galt meine Müh'.

[*Als verspräche er ihm hübsche Sachen*]
   Giebst du mir das
   gutwillig nun nicht,—
[*Als wäre er bereit, sein Leben für ihn zu lassen*]
   Siegfried, mein Sohn,
   das sieh'st du wohl selbst—
[*Mit freundlichem Scherze*]
   dein Leben mußt du mir lassen!

Siegfried:
   Daß du mich hassest,
   hör' ich gern:
doch auch mein Leben muß ich dir lassen?

Mime: [*ärgerlich*]
   Das sagt' ich doch nicht?
   du verstehst mich ja falsch!

[*Mime*: Siegfried, sonny, listen to me! You and your kind I have
   always hated with all my heart; (*tenderly*) it was not out of
   love that I brought you up, you nuisance. My efforts were
   aimed at the gold, at the hoard in Fafner's safekeeping. (*As
   though promising him pretty things*) If you don't give it up
   willingly to me now (*As though he were ready to lay down his
   life for him*), Siegfried, my son, you can see for yourself (*With
   amiable jocularity*), you must yield up your life to me!
Siegfried: That you hate me I'm glad to hear: but must I also
   yield up my life to you?
Mime: (*angrily*) Surely I didn't say that? You've understood me
   all wrong!][124]

   Nature thus not only produces the voluptuous rift between what
Mime wants to say (dissimulative words of love) and the words he actually produces (transparent words of hatred), it also erases the lexical
traces of that rift. It is as if we had suddenly landed back in a linguistic
Garden of Eden, where nature's power over expression is so great that no
one could dissimulate even if s/he wanted to. Of course, only Mime and
his kind would want to dissimulate. Nature, however, intervenes forci-
bly if invisibly, short-circuiting his plot to manipulate language, and reforging the natural link between signifier and signified.[125]
   The space that opens up between Mime's words and intention is pre-

cisely the space that Freud would open up to the analytic process. In this case, Siegfried's response to Mime's perjury is extremely aggressive—he kills his erstwhile guardian by stabbing him in the throat (we will examine this scene in more detail shortly).[126] Siegfried kills Mime for the discrepancy between an old story (the rearing song, but also the sweet tale that Mime intends to tell Siegfried) and a new one (the bald statement of Mime's underlying intentions)—which is, in the end, not all that new as a story, since it merely literalizes the sentiments that were barely repressed in the previous tellings. In failing to reforge language, Mime actually serves to forge a community, indeed, one that closely resembles what Wagner had hoped to create in Bayreuth: the audience and Siegfried are one in their recognition of Mime's villainy. I will examine the politics of this community-formation later in this chapter. For now, it is important to note that Mime dies when he perjures himself, or more precisely, when nature perjures him.

What are we to make of this? What is the relation between the protection afforded by the blood of the dragon in the *Ring* and the *Nibelungenlied*? In the latter, the hero's body gains protection; here, the protection is much more abstract. This may in part be because Brünnhilde assumes the function of dispensing invulnerability in the *Ring*, rendering Siegfried invulnerable by blessing his body.[127] If the woodbird can be said to provide any protection at all, it is protection from Mime's language, the language of culture. Here, then, we have a utopian moment in Wagner's polemical aesthetics, a kind of *Darstellung* of language. Mime's growing frustration at the rift between his intention and Siegfried's understanding dramatizes the rift that bifurcates the modern language of culture (and, by extension, the narration produced by that language). But the fact that Mime is suddenly if unconsciously rendered incapable of reproducing that rift means that the scene also dramatizes the overcoming of that rift, the return of an ostensibly uncorrupted, natural language.

What the woodbird offers is due cause for Siegfried to kill Mime: the lurid rift between Mime's statement and intention invites retribution. But what the woodbird does not offer is a lesson in hermeneutics, which is, in a sense, what it promises. Siegfried does not have to "listen keenly" (which is what he's instructed to do): insofar as Mime speaks his "true" intention for all to hear—in an unwitting and unwittingly literal fulfillment of his intention to engage in "deceptive-speech"—his supposedly dissimulating speech becomes "true," and we and Siegfried have to *infer* its status as false. Thus, nature does all the work, and Siegfried, whose ear could have used the additional training in discerning "false speech," is left without substantive protection from subsequent dissimulators. It would have been different had Siegfried (and we) heard what Mime *meant to say* rather than what he meant, for then Siegfried would have had to develop an ability to discern the rift between signifier and intention. As it stands, nature heals that rift before it reaches his and our ears.

Does Siegfried benefit when he speaks with nature? Put in the woodbird's terms, "what was the use of tasting the blood"? In the short term, he gains due cause for disenchantment with his guardian (a disenchantment to which Siegfried lends a personal, if by now predictable, expression by murdering Mime). Having thus stood in the way of the "only one" and having sought to manipulate his predestination for personal gain, Mime is made to "taste" the sword he could not fix and whose transmission—from Wotan, Siegmund, Brünnhilde, and Sieglinde to Siegfried—he impeded. As he kills Mime, Siegfried gives due expression to the odd mixture of linguistic and phallic terms characterizing their confrontation: "Schmeck' du mein Schwert, / ekliger Schwätzer!" [have a taste of my sword, you loathesome babbler!][128]

It is important to note that at that moment, Mime is not and has not been babbling, but speaking the truth. This is significant in that it anticipates the terms of Siegfried's eventual undoing. For this scene leaves Siegfried no less vulnerable to just such dissimulation in the future. Protected on this one occasion when dissimulation is simply suspended, Siegfried is left unprotected against its effects. In the *Ring* as in the *Nibelungenlied*, Siegfried will be the victim of narrative manipulations.

But how so? In the *Ring*, narration frequently takes the form of a ring, moving off in order to loop or swing back to where it started from. So, for example, just after Siegfried has killed Mime, he lies down and formulates a quick life story, one that takes him on an accelerated narrative trip from the present back to his beginnings, and from there back to the present:

> Doch ich—bin so allein,
> hab nicht Brüder noch Schwestern;
>   meine Mutter schwand,
>   mein Vater fiel:
> nie sah sie der Sohn!—
>   Mein einz'ger Gesell
>   war ein garst'ger Zwerg;

Güte zwang
uns nie zu Liebe;
listige Schlingen
warf mir der Schlaue:—
nun mußt' ich ihn gar erschlagen!—

[But I am so alone, have no brothers or sisters; my mother died,
my father was slain: their son never saw them!—A loathsome
dwarf was my only companion; kindness never led to love; he
slyly set me cunning snares:—now I've had to slay him!—][129]

Although Siegfried's tale is one among many in the *Ring*, in another
sense, his story is quite singular—because, for the longest time, he has
been quite story-less. As I have indicated, that state of story-less-ness
itself forms another important story in the *Ring*, since Wotan has specifically planned to produce just such a story-less hero.

At the point when Siegfried lies down to formulate his impromptu
autobiography, his tale is skimpy, his family—parents and guardian—are
all dead, and having grown up in seclusion in the woods, he has not
much more to tell. Act I of *Siegfried* does not *show* us Siegfried's history;
instead, it shows us his determination to discover it. Siegfried's movement away from Mime's cave and into the world is accompanied by
a corresponding movement from autobiographical dearth to autobiographical plenitude. He starts with very little, and soon, he is a man with
a story, with a past, with connections. That movement from narrative
rags to riches will ultimately be Siegfried's undoing.

Hagen and the Culture of Dissimulation

When Siegfried exultantly declares his determination to
abandon Mime's cave for "the world" he perceives himself to be radically unbound:

Aus dem Wald fort
in die Welt zieh'n:
nimmer kehr' ich zurück.
Wie ich froh bin,
daß ich frei ward,
nichts mich bindet und zwingt

Mein Vater bist du nicht,
in der Ferne bin ich heim;
dein Herd ist nicht mein Haus,
meine Decke nicht dein Dach.

[Go forth from the forest into the world: I'll nevermore return.
How glad I am to have gained my freedom, nothing binds or
constrains me! You're not my father, my home's far away; your
hearth's not my house, nor your roof my shelter.][130]

When Brünnhilde finally meets Siegfried and tells him his story (in act III
of *Siegfried*), she loads him with narrative baggage: no longer "bound and
constrained by nothing," he is at once free and bound by his newly acquired tale, a dualism suggested by his determination to leave just as he
has arrived. When he heads off "zu neuen Thaten" [to new deeds] at the
conclusion of the Prologue to *Götterdämmerung*, he is no longer simply
bound for his narrative but also bound by it. Thus when he enters the
society of the Gibichungen, there is an ironic ring to his claim that he has
nothing to offer Gunther as a token of friendship: "nicht Land noch
Leute biet' ich, / noch Vaters Haus und Hof: / einzig erbt' ich / den
eig'nen Leib" [I can offer you neither lands nor men, nor a father's house
and court: I inherited only this body of mine].[131] That is not quite true,
for in addition to his own body, he has—and Hagen *knows* he has—acquired the well-formed body of his own narrative. Thus, Hagen's immediate response to Siegfried's claim is culled from his command of that
narrative:

> *Siegfried*:
>   nur ein Schwert hab' ich,
>   selbst geschmiedet—
> hilf, mein Schwert, meinem Eide!—
> das biet' ich mit mir zum Bund.
>
> *Hagen*:
> Doch des Nibelungen-Hortes
> nennt die Märe dich Herrn?
>
> [*Siegfried*: I've only a sword, which I forged myself—by that
>   sword I swear this oath! With myself I present it as part of the
>   bond.
> *Hagen*: But the tale names you lord of the Nibelung hoard.][132]

Hagen will educe the mark of revision from the body of that tale, just as, in the *Nibelungenlied*, it is grafted upon Siegfried's garment. And that is enough to form the outlines of a plot: an auto-narrational plot, and a plot to betray that narration. Here, then, is where Siegfried's lack of training in critical listening becomes significant: for in *Götterdämmerung*, nature will not intervene to articulate Hagen's mendaciousness as it did with Mime in the second act of *Siegfried*.[133] When Hagen manipulates Siegfried's narrative, he succeeds where Mime failed.

In the *Ring* as in the *Nibelungenlied*, Hagen bears an extraordinary control over narrative information. While Mime is eventually unmasked—by and in nature—as an incompetent agent of narrative manipulation, Hagen is shown to be its more sinister master. (And to this end it is only fitting that he exercises that mastery at the Gibichungen court, which is, until the final conflagration, clearly beyond nature's immediate sphere of influence.) Thus, in the first lines of the first act of *Götterdämmerung*, Gunther addresses Hagen as a kind of pollster, one who can tell the king where he stands in the public eye.[134] But Hagen's knowledge is not merely passive and political, it also involves a good deal of insider information. Thus, in the course of briefing Gunther, it becomes clear that Hagen knows about Brünnhilde and, more interesting, that she is reserved for Siegfried. In addition, he is fully—if rather mysteriously—informed about Siegfried and envisions him as a husband for Gutrune, the king's sister.[135]

Hagen will continue to exercise a kind of mastery over the narrative until the very end of the work, when he tries and fails to take possession of the ring. Most important for our purposes is the control he exercises over the scene of Siegfried's death. As in the *Nibelungenlied* and the Nibelungen film, Hagen stages the scene. But unlike the *Nibelungenlied*, Hagen has been shown to be staging scenes from the start. That is, in *Götterdämmerung* he does more than narrate past events, he directs current events—such as suggesting that Gutrune employ the *Minnetrank* and supervising its presentation, suggesting that Siegfried win Brünnhilde for Gunther, and instructing the Gibichungen vassals on how to receive Brünnhilde. Not surprisingly, the scenes he sets repeatedly feature narration—not just as a mode but as a dramatic focus. Thus, when he emerges from among the Gibichungen masses upon Brünnhilde's arrival, he directs them to pay careful attention to Brünnhilde's lament; when he has Gutrune serve the *Minnetrank* to Siegfried, it is in order that the latter will forget his past; and when he himself serves an antidote to Siegfried in act III, it is in order that he will remember.[136] But whence Hagen's particular and thoroughgoing association with narration?

To answer this question we must consider the social milieu of *Götterdämmerung*. In the final work of the tetralogy we have entered a very different world—a social world on the earth's surface, a world, then, most like Wagner's own.[137] This has famous compositional consequences—it offers the first appearance of a chorus in the tetralogy. But beyond that it has linguistic consequences. Here we need to keep in mind Wagner's account of linguistic development in *Opera and Drama*—or rather, his account of its ostensible devolution. According to Wagner, language went farthest astray in advanced society: here the need for designation multiplies in proportion to the complexity of life, while the association with the "soil" that produces and sustains linguistic roots decreases precipitously. The language of modernity is the language of the cities—a cosmopolitan, civilized language, which is, in the Wagnerian lexicon, a corrupt, unnatural language. This is not always the case: as we saw, those in touch with the land are in touch with the language. But Gunther, Gutrune, and Hagen are hardly presented as inveterate salt of the earth. From the very outset of *Götterdämmerung*—from the words "nun hör', Hagen!" [So listen, Hagen!]—it is clear that this is a linguistic setting where language has been functionalized. Or, to mingle Marxist and Wagnerian terminology, we could say that this is a linguistically alienated society.

And Hagen, as we have seen, is a master of, if not vaguely responsible for, this alienation: he manipulates language with no apparent heed to its natural reference and with every attention to his personal gain. Thus, he can conjure truth out of perjury (by making Siegfried enter into sworn agreements having forgotten about Brünnhilde) and then conjure perjury out of truth (by making Siegfried violate those sworn agreements when he is made to remember Brünnhilde). This does not simply render Hagen a villain in the dramatic constellation of the work, it locates his villainy in a specific culturo-linguistic register. In thus wielding language in such a masterful fashion, he exploits its lack of reference and contributes to it. If Mime narrated repeatedly and somewhat foolishly, we should note that Hagen operates on a more advanced level—and for Wagner, linguistic advancement is tantamount to the advancement of corruption, debasement, and selfishness. In the next section of this chapter, I will attempt to account for the terms of this linguistic corruption, arguing that it marks Hagen and Mime as foreigners and, by implication, as Jews.

The point has to be emphasized. For while innumerable characters in the Wagnerian cosmology narrate, many do so with good intentions and to good effect. If we consider, for example, Gurnemanz and Parsifal, Tristan and Isolde, even Wotan and Waltraute, each resorts to narration with a clear mimetic aspiration, one that imparts and in turn produces what we might, echoing James Treadwell, characterize as a communitarian spirit. The recurring instances of monologue create an audience as community, an audience that is bound into an impromptu—but politically and aesthetically very significant—union by the mechanics of address and identification. As we have seen, this fact contradicts one of Wagner's principal aesthetic tenets: that the dramatic experience depends for its proper effect upon the dramatization—and not the narration—of events. Mime and Hagen represent a perfect foil for Wagner's dramaturgical dilemma, for their form of narration is demonstrably bad: it is calculating, selfish, and manipulative, born of conscious and cultural aspirations rather than unconscious and natural ones.

Thus, it is not surprising that Hagen's scheme would focus on Siegfried's suggestively anachronistic capacities to converse with nature, since in Wagner's eyes, nature is most threatened by—and most threatening to—culture's manipulations. Siegfried's exchange with the woodbird in act II of *Siegfried* occurs at the moment we would expect the linden-leaf episode to occur. And in a sense, the linden-leaf spot materializes here in act III, when Hagen stages the scene of reiteration, educing the spot of narrative difference and acting out the aggression that it authorizes. For Siegfried is rendered particularly vulnerable here: as in the Nibelungen film, he is shown to be oblivious to the manipulations of his culturally adept enemies. Thus, Hagen exploits Siegfried's obvious affinity for nature and the naiveté to which it testifies.

We need to examine the plot in more detail to see how this is so. When Siegfried arrives empty-handed at the hunting feast, Hagen recounts a familiar tale, a tale of the tale's familiarity: "Ich hörte sagen, Siegfried, / der Vögel Sanges-Sprache / verstündest du wohl: / so wäre das wahr?" [Siegfried, I've heard it said you can understand the language of birdsong: can it be true?][138] By failing to perceive the manipulation underlying the question, Siegfried implicitly attests to his ongoing affinity for the language of nature. For Wagner this failure is, of course, a charming and noteworthy quality, one that marks his hero as a bit of a *reiner Tor*, a pure fool. But beyond that it will kill him. For the fact is, Siegfried did not learn his lesson when the woodbird alerted him to the deceptions of Mime's language in the second act of *Siegfried*. And by failing to learn his lesson in hermeneutics Siegfried is vulnerable to the recurrence of that scene.[139] It is a point that is made rather obliquely in the course of Siegfried's account here. He agrees to provide a bit of entertainment to Gunther and the assembled hunters by recounting his past adventures. When he arrives at the point in the tale when he would recount the woodbird's warning, he garbles it. It is, to use the Freudian insight, a telling revision. According to Siegfried,

> Ring und Tarnhelm
> hatt' ich gerafft;
> da lauscht' ich wieder
> dem wonnigen Laller;
> der saß im Wipfel und sang:—
> rHei, Siegfried gehört nun
> der Helm und der Ring:
> o traute er Mime, dem treulosen, nicht!
> Ihm sollt' er den Hort nur erheben;
> nun lauert er listig am Weg:
> nach dem Leben trachtet er Siegfried—
> o traute Siegfried nicht Mime.Є

> [Ring and Tarnhelm I'd gathered up; then I listened again to the wonderful warbler; it sat in the treetop and sang:—"Hey, Siegfried now owns the helm and the ring: oh let him not trust the treacherous Mime! He only wants him to win him the hoard; now he's craftily lying in wait and seeking to take Siegfried's life—oh let him not trust Mime."][140]

This is partially correct. Siegfried's recollection is flawless as far as the first refrain is concerned: he repeats the precise terms of the woodbird's warning. But then the account, when repeated, changes. According to Siegfried, the woodbird warned him of Mime's physical disposition and his intentions (he's craftily lying in wait and seeking to take Siegfried's life). But in fact, the woodbird issued a different warning, one focusing on Mime's linguistic disposition:

> Hörte Siegfried nur scharf
> auf des Schelmen Heuchlergered':
> wie sein Herz es meint

kann er Mime versteh'n;
so nützt' ihm des Blutes Genuß.

[Were Siegfried to listen keenly to the rogue's hypocritical
words, he'd be able to understand what Mime means in his
heart; thus the taste of the blood was of use to him.][141]

The taste of the blood, it seems, was of only limited use to him, since the
memorable lesson is one that Siegfried forgets. It is a telling error, a
hermeneutic oversight; indeed, an oversight of a command to hermeneutics. In failing to attend to the command, Siegfried is easy prey to
Hagen's sophisticated manipulations. The rest of the scene moves like
clockwork: Siegfried recounts how he killed Mime, and then, following
the woodbird's recommendation, stepped through the fire and awakened
Brünnhilde with a kiss. The ostensibly shocking revelation horrifies
Gunther; more important, it enables Hagen to avenge Siegfried's apparent perjury by stabbing him in the back (where else?). In the following,
I will be less interested in the spectacle of Hagen's violent betrayal than
in the logic that informs it. Indeed, the woodbird's missing command,
embedded within the work, is what we must attend to. For an uncritical listening undoes Siegfried here. And, we need to note, the same sort
of uncritical receptiveness accounts for the ostensible predominance of
Jews in Germany.[142]

I want to consider Wagner's relationship to narration in light of his
relationship to alterity in general and Judaism in particular. In doing so,
I shall explore the dramaturgy of disavowal introduced in the preceding
chapter. I hope to suggest how narration foils Siegfried's project as well
as the ambitions of the *Gesamtkunstwerk*. At the same time, I want to
suggest that Wagner's writings on the Jews are best read as a kind of
"working out" of principles that motivate the dramaturgical logic of his
music-dramas.

THE *GESAMTKUNSTWERK* DOES NOT EXIST, AND
NARRATIVE IS ITS SYMPTOM

In the *Ring*, Mime and Hagen do double duty, standing in as
the embodiment of language gone astray *as language* (that is, language
that has lost touch with nature) and, at the same time, language gone
astray *in the Gesamtkunstwerk* (where language ought to be in the

service of *Darstellung*). How and why would this be the case? As it turns out, the concentration in these figures of these two qualities of language gone awry alludes to a familiar, if highly controversial, position in Wagner's aesthetics.

In *The Sublime Object of Ideology*, Slavoj Zizek makes a point about the operations of ideology, and he puts it bluntly: "Society doesn't exist, and the Jew is its symptom."[143] Zizek's assertion offers a useful way of thinking about ideology; more important, it allows us to make better sense of Mime's function in the *Ring*.

Traditional ideological critiques of anti-Semitism have helped to show us how the Jew is made to stand in for something threatening. Thus the Jew often occupies a position within a fantasy, or even a series of contradictory positions: for the Nazis, the Jew was a Bolshevik and, at the same time, an industrialist; impotent and a seducer.[144] But while a good deal of work has been done to identify and interrogate these fantasies, the question still needs to be addressed, how and why would one figure come to occupy such contradictory positions and, more vexingly, what is at stake in assigning the Jew to them? In Zizek's argument, the Jew does not merely stand in for something, instead, he stands in for nothing. Traditionally, the Jew has enabled and sustained a fantasy of fullness or completion, in this case, a fantasy of social cohesion, by serving as the embodiment of not-belonging. In this way, the social body can be designated as whole to the extent that it defines itself as wholly not Jewish.[145]

According to Leon Botstein, Jews have figured in a cyclical scenario of social cohesion and dissolution since the Middle Ages: "In the eyes of the majority, Jewish participation in culture and business constituted a danger that could be eliminated without any detrimental effect. On the contrary, it was thought that such an act would salvage the unity and health of the nation." Botstein goes on to make an economic comparison between American and German racism:

> In America after 1860—let alone in the time of slavery—the substantial economic role of the black population and their absolute numbers (in the 20th century, the influx of Spanish-speaking minorities add to this figure) were such that the notion of eradicating them or returning them to Africa was never either plausible or practical. The fact that those who were hated were always necessary inevitably impeded the racist movement despite all of its brutality. These restrictions, however, never applied to European anti-Semitism, since the notion of a

world without Jews was the product of a desire to eliminate a danger-
ous competitor.[146]

I think we gain a sharper sense of the Jew's function in constituting society by reformulating Botstein's argument, for it is not just that the Jewish contribution to society can be removed without posing a danger, but
that a greater danger to society arises when there are no "Jews" to remove, when there are none who, in being removed, can produce the society that removes them. Rather than formulating the argument in
terms of a traditional sense of economic needs, we can reformulate it in
terms of an economics of desire that underlies the operations of social
identity. In this economics, the hated are, as Botstein says, "always necessary," if for very different reasons than those he cites. According to
Sander Gilman, they are always necessary in order to embody their societal superfluity, to fulfill society's desire for an embodiment of not-
belonging.[147] That desire is all the more pressing since, in Zizek's argument, the very notion of social or national status is itself the product of
a related fantasy.

"Fantasy," Zizek writes, "is basically a scenario filling out the empty
space of a fundamental impossibility, a screen masking a void."[148] According to Zizek, the most fundamental ideological fantasy is that of
society as an organic whole, what he terms the "Society as a Corporate
Body."[149] The Jew can serve as the structural guarantor of this fantasy. By
occupying a position on the outside, the Jew serves to constitute an in-
side outside of which he has been positioned. "In short," Zizek writes,
"'Jew' is a fetish which simultaneously denies and embodies the
structural impossibility of 'Society': it is as if in the figure of the Jew this
impossibility had acquired a positive, palpable existence—and that is
why it marks the eruption of enjoyment in the social field."[150] The notion of society as a whole, as an intact and seamless fabric, only comes
into existence when this other element, this flaw to the fabric is both
fantasmatically introduced and expelled. Thence the pithy formula: society doesn't exist, and the Jew is its symptom.

Does Zizek's thesis still hold if the fantasmatic totality in question is
a metonymy for society rather than society itself—especially if, as he
argues, the notion of the society is itself a metonym for fantasmatic
wholeness? That is, how can Zizek help us consider the function of the
Jew in the *Gesamtkunstwerk*? And how does the Jew's role in the *Gesamtkunstwerk* relate to his role in Wagner's aesthetics and, much more
particularly, to the juxtaposition of narration and *Darstellung* in the

Ring? To consider these questions, we must examine one of Wagner's most infamous tracts, the essay "Judaism in Music," first published in 1850.[151]

Anti-Semitism has always assumed an overdetermined and invariably unsettling role in Wagner's work; attempts to account for it have often seemed equally overdetermined.[152] In the years following World War II, critics spent a good deal of time arguing about the shape of the line leading from Wagner to Hitler, quibbling, often with fervor, about whether it should be seen as straight, circuitous, or broken. Historically, work on the subject has not won many awards for subtlety: one camp reads Wagner's works as programmatically anti-Semitic, while the other camp (the more prominent and socially presentable of the two) finds no relationship between Wagner's racism and his works for the stage. Some more recent criticism seeks to read the aesthetic traces of Wagner's anti-Semitism: Philippe Lacoue-Labarthe's *Musica Ficta* and Marc A. Weiner's *Richard Wagner and the Anti-Semitic Imagination* seem especially provocative in this regard. Indeed, if we are dissatisfied with the notion that Wagner's anti-Semitism results in a programmatic determination to present (and, more important, discredit) particular Jews as Jews on stage, and if we are likewise dissatisfied with the claim that there are no traces of anti-Semitism in Wagner's stage works, then how might we go about defining the place of anti-Semitism in the works?

I propose that we seek out the traces of anti-Semitism in the aesthetic register rather than the political or biographical.[153] I suggest that we can define an *aesthetics* of anti-Semitism in Wagner, a recurring gesture by which Wagner invests certain characters not just with vile qualities but also with vile *aesthetic practices*. Thus, the mark of the Jew in Wagner's works is, in the end, less physiognomical or social (although it is these things too) than it is aesthetic. The formula is rather straightforward: Jews in Wagner's works are dogged by aesthetic qualities that the composer loathed. Wagner seems to introduce Jews as the carriers of those qualities, if only in order to expel them. For in thus dispensing with them, Wagner's works also dispense with the aesthetic qualities they embody.

One of the critics who have come close to this sort of analysis is Theodor Adorno. In his monograph on Wagner, Adorno points out that anti-Semitism is essential to the social character of Wagner's work. But in what sense? Adorno formulates a few important theses: first, for Wagner, Jews satisfied a "sadistic desire to humiliate," an impulse that found expression in his day-to-day life (for instance, in his interactions with the conductor Hermann Levi) and in his writings (for instance, in the pamphlet "Judaism in Music"); second, as a victim himself, Wagner tended to despise other victims, especially Jews.[154] And finally, to return to an observation quoted in the previous chapter, "All the rejects of Wagner's works are caricatures of Jews—the gold-grabbing, invisible, anonymous, exploitative Alberich, the shoulder-shrugging, loquacious Mime, overflowing with self-praise and spite, the impotent intellectual critic Hanslick-Beckmesser."[155] Surprisingly, Adorno does not have much of an explanation for this phenomenon—he associates Wagner's anti-Semitism with that shared by "other representatives of what Marx called the German Socialism of 1848."[156] In order to explain its virulence beyond that, Adorno suggests only that Wagner hated what he most feared in himself.

The critical (and, for that matter, the uncritical) literature has argued the biographical dimension of Wagner's anti-Semitism in some detail.[157] Throughout his life, Wagner was purportedly unsure of his paternal heritage, specifically, whether his father was a Jew. Nietzsche was one of the first to raise the question, in typically oblique fashion. Here, again, is the famous quotation from "The Case of Wagner," where Nietzsche commingles ornithology with a sly innuendo:

> Was Wagner a German at all? There are some reasons for this question. It is difficult to find any German trait in him. Being a great learner, he learned to imitate much that was German—that's all. His own nature *contradicts* that which has hitherto been felt to be German—not to speak of a German musician.—His father was an actor by the name of Geyer. A *Geyer* [vulture] is practically an *Adler* [eagle].—What has hitherto circulated as "Wagner's Life" is *fable convenue*, if not worse. I confess my mistrust of every point attested to only by Wagner himself. He did not have pride enough for any truth about himself; nobody was less proud. Entirely like Victor Hugo, he remained faithful to himself in biographical questions, too—he remained an actor.[158]

Since then, scholars have argued the same point with predictably contradictory results. Jacob Katz dismisses the notion out of hand, while Peter Burbidge takes it quite seriously.[159] Barry Millington and Stewart Spencer offer a judicious and sober view when they note that

> it will probably never be established definitively whether Wagner's father was the police actuary Carl Friedrich Wagner or the actor-

painter Ludwig Geyer. . . . What is important is that the boy himself was never to know the truth. He was loved by his adoptive father and took his name until some years after Geyer's death, but he suffered from a lifelong, tormenting suspicion (in fact groundless) that Geyer was of Jewish birth. The fear of belonging to a race considered almost universally at the time as inferior . . . was aggravated by the awkward facts that he was born in Brühl, the Jewish quarter of Leipzig, and that he had the prominent nose and high forehead generally associated with the Jewish physiognomy.[160]

But where can we locate the aesthetic traces of that fear? Marc Weiner locates them at the very center of Wagner's artistic production. According to Weiner, "Wagner's preoccupation with the uncertainty of his father's identity, laden with racial implications, is still discernible in virtually all his most celebrated music dramas."[161] Adorno's argument is less sweeping but no less controversial. In a famous passage, he focuses on the *Ring*, noting the startling affinities between the character of Jewish language as described in Wagner's essay, and Siegfried's characterization of Mime:

> Siegfried says to Mime: "when I see you standing, shuffling and shambling, weak-kneed and nodding, blinking your eyes, I long to seize the dodderer's neck and finish off the filthy twitching creature!" . . . This is reminiscent of the description of Jewish speech in the essay on Judaism and leaves no doubt as to the source of such monstrous beings as Mime and Alberich: "What strikes our ear as particularly odd is a hissing, buzzing, humming and growling sound that is typical of the Jewish way of speaking: a use of inversion that is utterly uncharacteristic of our own national tongue, and the arbitrary way in which the Jew twists words and constructions gives his pronunciation the unmistakable character of an intolerably confused babble of sounds . . ." However, this idiosyncratic hatred is of the type that Benjamin had in mind when he defined disgust as the fear of being recognized by the object of disgust as indistinguishable from that object.[162]

But just what is this object? Adorno's analysis is on the right track, but it rushes past an important point: Jewish speech is not only Jewish, it is also speech. In this sense, we ought to consider the extent to which what Wagner hates is not just his inner Jew (or for that matter, his inner Mime[163]), but the *speech* within these works. Wagner associates the two—and then ascribes to the Jew the unsavoriness of speech. As a result, the Jew becomes doubly loathsome, a pariah for biographical and aesthetic reasons, and the necessity of his expulsion becomes all the more pressing.

"Judaism in Music" was first published pseudonymously in 1850 and republished in Wagner's name in 1869; it is a relatively brief and extremely vitriolic pamphlet that seeks to explain how and why Jews have no place in music. The essay's biographical genesis—Wagner's repeated failures in Paris, his intensely felt, unilateral estrangement from Meyerbeer (who was particularly successful in Paris), and the paranoia that followed—has been discussed extensively elsewhere.[164] But there is more to the essay than an excessive slander of a former benefactor. Wagner also rehearses several important aesthetic tenets introduced in his earlier writings and discussed above: the origins and situation of language, the limits and possibilities of representation, the need for social change. But the context is different in this essay, for it turns out that Jews are not only "in" music, they are also in language, on stage, in society; and Wagner is intent upon removing them.

Wagner's main argument is astonishingly stubborn: Jews do not belong to the community of the people, the *Volksgemeinde*.[165] This leads to a slew of significant exclusions: since artistic expression is born of an intimate connection to the people, and the Jew supposedly has no such connection, then the Jew is incapable of artistic expression. Since language is produced only through an unconscious, deep and lasting tie to the community, and because the Jew supposedly has no community, then the Jew has no mother tongue and speaks all languages as a foreigner.[166] These terms may seem familiar; do they not correspond largely to the description of speech's errant ways in *Opera and Drama*?[167]

Wagner's remarks on the connection between language and the community read like an addendum to his remarks in *Opera and Drama*:

> A language, and its manner of expression and continued development, is not the work of individuals, but of an historical community: only the person who has grown up unconsciously within that community can take part in what it creates. The Jew, however, stands outside this community, stands alone with his Jehova as part of a fragmented and soil-less tribe [*bodenloser Volksstamm*] that was prevented from evolving internally. . . . Now, it has never so far proved possible to

write *true* poetry in a *foreign* language, even to geniuses of the highest
rank. Our whole European art and civilization, however, has remained
a foreign tongue to the Jew . . .[168]

The passage creates the unity of the community ("our whole European art and civilization") at the very moment that it excludes the Jew
from that community ("has remained a foreign tongue to the Jew . . .").
The question is whether the claim to wholeness (doubled in the "our"
and "whole" of "our whole European art and civilization") does not require the inclusion of the Jew on the outside, the inclusion, that is, of an
exclusion.[169] Read in light of the *Ring*, this passage helps to explain the
emphatic quality of Siegfried's communion and communication with
nature: Wagner has to show him speaking with nature from the start in
order to cultivate Siegfried's claim to belonging to the right (i.e., natural)
community and to prepare his escape from the prison house of Mime's
(read: Jewish) language. After all, if Siegfried did not speak with the animals, he would end up speaking only with Mime, thus forming a community with one who has none. Since Siegfried is shown to be on such
friendly terms with nature at the outset (as in his jocular comment to the
bear in act I, "Lauf' Brauner: / dich brauch' ich nicht mehr!" [run along,
brown fellah, I don't need you any more!][170]), he can grow up in communion with nature while resisting the false communion with Mime.
The situation is dramaturgically precarious, for in having Siegfried com-
mune thus with nature, he essentially becomes a Jew to Mime's false
community, with one crucial difference: Siegfried separates himself
from such a community *in order to be in communion with nature*, unlike the Jew, who in Wagner's formulation stands "solitary with his Je-
hova in a splintered, soil-less tribe."

Read in light of *Opera and Drama*, the passage suggests a slight but
significant revision in Wagner's earlier position on language, art, and
modernity. In *Opera and Drama*, Wagner argued that the language of
modernity was hopelessly severed from nature and that any work of art
created under its influence was tainted. According to this view, farmers
were the only group that spoke the language of nature, and only a distant
offspring of it, at that. In "Judaism in Music," the offending party is
much more narrowly defined (the Jew, rather than everyone who is not
a farmer) and the pool of good art is much broader (encompassing anything produced by one who possesses—and properly possesses—the na-

tive tongue). Rather than arguing that true art can hardly be produced by anyone, Wagner now argues that it can never be produced by a Jew.

If we look closely at Wagner's claims about the place of "Jews" in music, we find that they repeatedly bear an element of desire. Thus, for example, in the pamphlet "Judaism in Music" Wagner writes, "no matter which European nationality we belong to, [the Jew's outward appearance] has something about it which is foreign to that nationality, and which we find insuperably unpleasant: *we wish to have nothing to do with such a person (wir wünschen nicht mit einem so aussehenden Menschen etwas gemein zu haben).*"[171] I am interested in the furious ambivalence of this desire *not* to have anything to do with the Jew. In order for this wish to take shape, as it does throughout Wagner's works and writings, the Jew must constantly be seen—in order to be seen as that with which the community does not want to be seen, which in turn enables the community to take shape.

"This is very important," Wagner writes,

> a person who, by dint of his very appearance we must consider incapable of any artistic expression—not as this or that character but, collectively, in terms of his race—must be deemed equally incapable of the artistic presentation of pure humanity in general.
>
> Incomparably more important, however, indeed of crucial importance here, is the effect which the Jew produces upon us by virtue of his *method of speaking. The Jew speaks the language of the country in which he has lived from generation to generation, but he always speaks it as a foreigner.* The first point to make is the general one that the Jew speaks the modern European language in question not as a native but only as something learned, a circumstance which is bound to exclude him from any ability to express himself with any character and independence in that language . . .[172]

Here again we encounter unity by fiat: whence this single "modern European language"?[173] And as the Jew embodies the failure of artistic expression, his presence on stage enables Wagner to label the failure of representation as Jewish, and with his passing, or rather, with his expulsion, the community is at once created and saved while representation is fantasmatically freed.

What happens if we apply some pressure to the notion of the Jew representing linguistic foreignness, always speaking as an "Ausländer"?

Could he not be understood to be acting then as an undocumented alien, albeit a planted one, embodying the foreignness of language within the territorial confines of the *Gesamtkunstwerk*? In this way, Mime could be seen as recognizably not belonging, not just as a Jew, but also as a narrator. After all, in Wagner's argument, the Jewish tongue is always only foreign. Thus, when a Jew speaks in society, he speaks as a foreigner. Could it be that when a Jew speaks in the *Gesamtkunstwerk*, he embodies the foreignness of narration itself?

Here Zizek's argument seems particularly compelling. Given Wagner's commitment to the *Gesamtkunstwerk*, to a program of seamless aesthetic totalization, the Jew functions as the structural guarantor of that totality by representing, within the work, that which does not belong, which must be exorcised. In this way, the Jew would function to shore up dramaturgical and aesthetic unity: the other elements are united in being not Jewish. How are they thus united? By a process of aesthetic separation, whereby the evil narrators and narratives—characterized by selfishness, calculation, and consciousness—are inflected as Jewish while those heroes and their heroic narratives—committed to an aesthetics of *Darstellung*—are inflected with a form of positive negation as not Jewish. The separation is even staged in the work, where the Jewish figures are shown to be willfully separate from the society: Mime lives off in the woods, apart from the community; while Hagen, who lives amid the community, repeatedly demonstrates and declares his separation from it. Their relationship to narration represents an aesthetic correlative to that willed separation.

Jews, then, are the "I don't" that guarantees a series of polygamous unions—the reconciliation of language and nature in non-Jewish speech, the union of the arts in the *Gesamtkunstwerk*, even the union of Siegfried and Nothung, and later, Siegfried and Brünnhilde, whose union is thus repeatedly—if only temporarily—marred by what must nonetheless be seen as its guarantor. This formal guarantee can be seen on the level of dramaturgy as well, for the introduction and subsequent expulsion of Jewish characters seems to guarantee the bond binding the rest of the characters, many of whom, not so coincidentally, end up being naturally related.

Wagner's commitment to the *Gesamtkunstwerk* was not limited to his music-dramas. Indeed, his extensive writings on social and political matters establish a broad scope for his narrow-minded vision of how society and the arts should interact. Essentially, and this is a point that

Wagner makes with numbing frequency, they should be one. That is, in a recurring gesture of consolidation, Wagner sought to unite disparate elements—and at various points in his program of unification, the Jew serves as the foil to that program—which is to say, the Jew serves as its guarantor.[174] The pamphlet "Judaism in Music" is the most explicit statement of this program, although it finds repeated expression in Wagner's music-dramas.

In the course of a spirited account of the strange character of Wagner's politics, Wolf Rosenberg points out that Wagner always needed an embodied enemy, an image of his opponent.[175] In this, Wagner anticipated Freud, who admits to the very same need in *The Interpretation of Dreams*. While Rosenberg's point is directed to Wagner's politics, I think we can extend it to his aesthetics as well. The Jews are not merely conceived as a threat to the society and to Wagner's aesthetic production, but this threat is desirable and necessary to the identity that it threatens. Thus we might say that the *Gesamtkunstwerk* does not exist, and the Jew is its symptom.

Let us conclude by returning—in a patently Wagnerian gesture—to Carolyn Abbate's account of the "great paradox in the *Ring*'s history, and what many consider to be the great flaw in its text: that the narratives, despite Wagner's glee over their elimination, were kept . . ."[176] Abbate's wording is absolutely on target, if unwittingly so, for the great flaw in the text of the *Ring* turns out to be the great flaw in its hero's armature, the *missing* "great flaw": in place of the *Lindenblattstelle*, the incidental mark of nature, we have the flaw of narration, grafted upon the body of Siegfried's story. Within the work, Hagen is able to capitalize on this great flaw, to educe it and then assassinate Siegfried for it. Wagner, for his part, is able to project that flaw onto Mime and Hagen, who are—in different ways—made to speak the flawed language of culture as they stand in for the flaw of narration in the *Gesamtkunstwerk*. In this sense, we can observe how the "great flaw" is quite literally *in the text* of the work, in its ambivalent propensity toward narration.

Chapter Three

Viewing with a Vengeance

THE DRAMATURGY OF APPEARANCES IN

FRITZ LANG'S *SIEGFRIED*

I N AN ARTICLE published in February of 1924, shortly
before the premiere of *Siegfried*, the first part of the two-part film *The
Nibelungen*, Fritz Lang suggests that the project was conceived in terms
of what it was not: "in the case of *The Nibelungen*, the point was not to
make a film in the American style, with an eye to all possible secondary
aims. Here the only thing that mattered was the work."[1] Thus Lang juxtaposes his own single-minded dedication to the calculating and distractible mindset in Hollywood. A bit further along in the same essay,
Lang invokes the same binary terms to praise his set designers Otto
Hunte and Erich Kettelhut:

> [Hunte and Kettelhut] constructed the German cathedral and the Ger-
> man forest on the studio grounds at Babelsberg. Not in the American
> style. And yet, I would be so bold as to claim that the spirit that per-
> vades the Nibelungen sets has more of the breath of universality than
> has ever arisen from the grounds of Los Angeles, since it stems from
> the original essence of a great nation . . .[2]

America/Germany; Hollywood/Babelsberg—the bald terms of opposi-
tionality are not new to the discourse of Weimar film in the mid-1920s.[3]
What makes them interesting for our purposes is their repeated reference
to a scene of vision. In Lang's eyes, the Americans are distracted and
distractible: in place of his own steely resolve, the Americans issue

"side-glances"; while Lang's eyes are firmly locked on a cultural prize, the Americans are keeping an eye out for special effects. This traffic in clichés concerning the visual attributes of cultural difference is not limited to Lang's public statements about the project; indeed, it forms a conceptual motor driving the film.

The avowed purpose of the *Nibelungen* film was twofold: first, to outwit (or better, to out-culture) Hollywood by exploiting the Germans' purportedly superior cultural tradition and, through it, their privileged access to the universal; then to make the results available to the German public at large. The first component of the project would distinguish this film from the undistinguished (because uncultured) glut of Hollywood product that had been overrunning the German market since the early twenties. Of course, the determination to make the film available to a mass audience would in turn distinguish this remake from the mass of Nibelungen remakes that had been crowding the German cultural scene since the middle of the nineteenth century. Lang alludes to this second component of the project in the program book to the film:

> we are not dealing with just any old filmic adaptation of a work that already exists in some other form. Rather, what we're dealing with here is the spiritual shrine of a nation. Thus our task with the Nibelungen project was necessarily to create a film in a form that would not banalize its sacred-spiritual aspect; a film that would belong to the *Volk* and not, like the *Edda* or the medieval German epic, belong to a relatively small number of privileged and cultivated minds.[4]

Given the ferocious popularity of the medieval epic and its central role in the consolidation of German national identity since the early nineteenth century, it seems especially surprising that Lang would choose to bash it as elitist. In doing so, he seems to be clearing out a space for his own project. Just as American cinema supposedly occupies the cultural low ground, appealing to the basest aesthetic sensibilities, here Lang situates the epic in the cultural stratosphere; that is, in a place accessible only to "a few cultivated minds"; an obscure, inaccessible, cerebral space; the province of intellectuals. As a result, the middle ground becomes available, a place where German culture can meet the German masses. This is the place that the Nibelungen film will seek to occupy.

In producing a new German vision of an *Ur*-German saga for a mass German audience, the film also presents a vision of vision itself. Thus, character traits are inflected in terms of vision and important dramatic events are organized around it. Hagen, for example, embodies a dispassionate and perspicacious mode of viewing while Siegfried's gaze is enthusiastic and naive. Likewise, the film plays out the relationships between protagonists in terms of vision: thus, for example, Alberich seeks to blindside Siegfried and, in a very different register, Siegfried and Kriemhild fall in love with each other at first sight. Each of these instances contributes to the film's dramaturgy of vision, its recourse to vision as a means of condensing and expressing an interrelated set of concerns about how one ought and ought not to look. Embedded within the dramaturgy of vision is an allegory of power. Those characters who look properly look powerfully, while those who look naively—no matter how powerful they are in body or political/social standing—are lost. Thus, Siegfried's demise becomes a drama of visual subordination: he dies not because he looks bad (indeed, he looks great), but because he does not look intelligently.

The dramaturgy of vision is not restricted to the film's narrative level. In a self-referential register, the film formulates an implicit statement of where film should be going as well as an allegorical account of whose hands it is in. On the level of spectatorial identification, the film portrays the need to exert and maintain careful control over appearances and demonstrates the perils of losing (or failing to gain) that control. And thus we are returned to the terms of Lang's article from February of 1924: for just as Lang distinguishes between his view of the project (as a product of steely purposiveness) and an American view (which is subject to all sorts of distractions), so too will the characters within the film and the film's audience be distinguished along the same lines. In this sense, we might revise Raymond Bellour's claim, first published in *Critique* in 1966, that "from *Fury* onwards, both in his images and in the implications of his scripts, the focus of Lang's *mise en scène* is so often vision itself."[5] Here, ten years before *Fury*, Lang is already focusing upon vision, allowing it to organize the film's variegated concerns.

In the following pages I will examine how vision works in the film: how individual characters conceive of and relate to one another visually, how visibility and invisibility are deployed, and how we see that visibility and invisibility. In examining the film's dramaturgy of vision, I will suggest that the film erects an elaborate allegory of visual power. The film suggests that there is a right way to look in (and at) *Siegfried*, and a wrong way; a German and a foreign way; a strong and a weak way; an honorable and a dastardly way. How might we make sense of these views of viewing? And what do they tell us about this particular rendering of the Nibelungen material?

FROM *NIBELUNGEN* TO NUREMBERG

Rather than considering the dramaturgy of vision within the film, most critics have concentrated quite singly on the film's overall vision of its subject matter, largely regarded as a product of the film's architectural politics.[6] This is undoubtedly due to the lasting influence of Siegfried Kracauer's famous critique of *Die Nibelungen*, presented in *From Caligari to Hitler*.[7] Kracauer was particularly disturbed by the imposing, monumental sets and highly symmetrical arrangement of human forms in the film, arguing that they produced an insidious or-namentalization, reducing human beings to mere accessories. Since then, critics have tended to view the Nibelungen film in Kracauer's terms, arguing for or against his thesis that the film served as a kind of visual laboratory for a fascist aesthetics of the mass ornament.[8]

Although Kracauer did not review the film upon its release, it serves as a major point of reference in the account of German film history pre-sented in *From Caligari to Hitler*. His interpretation of the film is typi-cally unabashed and uncompromising: *Die Nibelungen*, he argues, pre-figures the spectacle of ornamentalization produced by the Nazis in their cinema and, more importantly and insidiously, in their politics.

> Absolute authority asserts itself by arranging people under its domina-
> tion in pleasing designs. This can also be seen in the Nazi regime,
> which manifested strong ornamental inclinations in organizing
> masses. Whenever Hitler harangued the people, he surveyed not so
> much hundreds of thousands of listeners as an enormous ornament
> consisting of hundreds of thousands of particles. *Triumph of the Will*,
> the official Nazi film of the Nuremberg Party Convention in 1934,
> proves that in shaping their mass-ornaments the Nazi decorators drew
> inspiration from *Nibelungen*. *Siegfried*'s theatrical trumpeters, showy
> steps and authoritarian human patterns reappear, extremely magni-
> fied, in the modern Nuremberg pageant.[9]

At the conclusion of his book, Kracauer returns to this argument, re-stating his view that Nazi culture realizes characters and situations first presented in Weimar film. In his conception, the *Nibelungen* is more important for its aesthetics than its characters. Thus, while other Weimar films present extraordinary characters who, in Kracauer's view, walk off the screen and into the new Germany, the *Nibelungen* sets the Nazi stage, the stage upon which the spectacle of National Socialist power was to be so artfully and convincingly arranged.[10] In this way, politics imitates art: the massive and monumental sets in the *Nibelungen* are but a miniature version of the settings for the Nuremberg Party Congress.[11] Kracauer's argument about the Nibelungen film reproduces in microcosm and with a particular architectural-aesthetic slant the larger trajectory traced in his book—the route from the *Nibelungen* to Nuremberg parallels the route from *Caligari* to Hitler.

A number of critics reject this position out of hand. According to Lang's official biographer Lotte Eisner, the monumental sets were necessary, required by the theme and befitting "the Germanic mind":

> Lang's theme necessitated the use of massive frescoes, for the composition of which he resorted to the monumental proportions seen as befitting the Germanic mind. Langbehn, the author of *Rembrandt als Erzieher*, had already held that German *Kultur* was wrought in granite, from which material it was impossible to carve anything but massive shapes, which was why the Germans' ultimate aim was to "monumentalize."
>
> The massive architecture in *Die Nibelungen* constitutes an ideal setting for the stature of its epic heroes.[12]

But ideal for whom? In Kracauer's mind, it constitutes an ideal and ideally oversized classroom for those who seek schooling in the aesthetics of totalitarianism. Furthermore, Kracauer would argue, it is those aesthetics (and not, as Eisner suggests, "Lang's theme") that "necessitate" or at least explain "the use of massive frescoes."

The problem with Kracauer's argument lies less in his conviction than in his roughshod analysis which tends to strong-arm the evidence at the expense of careful reading.[13] His unease with the monumentalism of the Nibelungen films is certainly justified, as is his impression that monumentalism plays a major role in establishing and sustaining the authoritarian tenor of *Triumph of the Will*. But the commutative character of monumentalism needs to be explained and the notion that monumentalism moves between these films should not substitute for analysis of its dramaturgical function.

In the wake of Kracauer's forceful argument for aesthetic teleology, the critique of monumentalism has itself become monumental. Thus, while numerous critics have considered the politics of the sets, few have proposed alternative ways of reading the film. Thomas Elsaesser's work offers a notable exception. Elsaesser formulates a thoroughgoing critique of Kracauer's analysis, paying close attention to the exigencies of visual pleasure in Weimar film: "Weimar cinema," he argues, "is of particular interest because the look is in some sense consistently privileged."[14] Elsaesser's modest summary of his argument is particularly apt for our purposes: "What can be said, in light of the general views presented here, is perhaps only to point out how often the look motivates the narrative (the act of narration, by way of the cut on the glance) in films as dissimilar as *Madame Dubarry* and *The Nibelungen, Phantom* and *Pandora's Box*."[15] My interest here involves a slight but significant modification of Elsaesser's point, for I will be centrally concerned with control over vision in this film—what we might term the look of and at the look.

READING SIEGFRIED SEEING

In *Siegfried* power is less a product of physical strength or political standing than visual acumen. During the course of the film, that visual acumen will be inflected allegorically. In order to understand how this is the case, we need to consider how the key characters in the film relate to viewing. Hagen, the man with the weakest eyes—indeed the man with only one eye—will be shown to have the strongest vision. The film will suggest that his gaze is the most powerful because it is properly strategic, properly savvy. Unlike those who see naively, Hagen sees critically; he reads what he sees. It is this practice of critical viewing that explains Hagen's position as the king's eyes and ears; and it distinguishes Hagen from Siegfried and the other figures at Gunther's court. Kriemhild's drastic transformation from a sweet, pretty maiden to a calculating, vindictive fury is played out in the visual register: she will thus be transformed from a woman who properly embodies all of the feminine attributes of viewing—what Laura Mulvey has famously termed "to be looked-at-ness"—to a woman who wields and controls an unambiguously if not unproblematically phallic gaze.[16]

If Kriemhild is introduced as a picture of feminine appeal, Siegfried is positioned as her proper mate: he does heroic things and he looks great

FIGURE 2. An image of who Siegfried is not: Mime admiring Siegfried's sword. Photo courtesy of the Film Stills Archive, The Museum of Modern Art, New York.

doing them. From the outset, the camera dotes upon his radiant mien and sculpted body.[17] And from the outset, he outshines his surroundings. Thus, our introduction to Siegfried in the film's first "song"—(the film is subdivided into *Gesänge* or songs)—also provides us with an elaborate and unintentionally comical view of who Siegfried is *not*. Put bluntly: Siegfried is not Mime. (Indeed, Mime in the film is not the same Mime as in the *Ring*: although he is still presented as an incompetent and scheming smithy, he is largely inconsequential to the narrative, disappearing from the film after the first "song.") Here in the first scene Mime functions as an implicit visual foil to the strapping hero: Siegfried is tall, Mime is a dwarf; Siegfried occupies the center of the screen, Mime and his assistant occupy its margins; Siegfried laughs, Mime scowls; Siegfried strides, Mime shuffles; Siegfried is trusting, Mime is a schemer; Siegfried is strong, Mime is weak; Siegfried has flowing blond hair, Mime's hair is wild and dark. Here, then, is a good object of identification—offset, presumably to underscore his appeal, by a bad object. Later in the film we will reencounter this binary dramaturgical logic. But if Siegfried appears as the positive term in contradistinction to the negative terms that surround him, it will soon become clear that appearances can deceive. For Siegfried acts the way he looks. That is, his visual appeal will not translate into visual authority.

In the first scene of the film, Siegfried is sent home by Mime, who claims that there is nothing more that he can teach the youth. But rather than head home to his father in Xanten as Mime suggests, Siegfried heads off to Burgundy. He does so only because he has a vision, and significantly, that vision is not his own.[18] As Siegfried wanders out of Mime's grotto, he overhears one of Mime's cronies addressing a small group: his tale provides Siegfried—and us—with a vision of Kriemhild and life at the Burgundian court. As the film presents that vision it also presents Siegfried's response to it.

Siegfried hears about this picture-perfect queen, and, in a conflation of the traditionally active role of the phallic screen hero with the passive role assigned to the cinematic audience, he sets off to get her. Thus, from the very outset of the film Siegfried distinguishes himself as a naive viewer, one whose investment in the image is so complete that he announces his intention to win the heart of its leading lady. Siegfried's pompous response is laughable to the storyteller and his audience, all of whom have presumably mastered the operations of narrative identification: after all, a tale is supposed to arouse desire in its audience, but that desire is supposed to be subject to the laws of sublimation. Siegfried, it turns out, may have mastered the art of forging swords, but he has a lot to learn when it comes to sublimation. Indeed, his over-investment expresses itself as intemperance: when the storyteller and his assembled audience of lackeys laugh at Siegfried, he threatens to kill them.

Siegfried's intense identification with the image enables his quest and the film's adventure to take off, but also renders them somewhat foolish and naive. This is part of the film's pathos, for in thus inflecting the figure, it evinces a nostalgia for an older, purer, less complicated time—in German history but also and more specifically in the history of spectatorial identification. The film will not simply wallow in that pathos, it will go on to portray its perils, for Siegfried will die as a result of Hagen's machinations, and Hagen's brutal shrewdness centrally involves vision. Hagen's gaze is diametrically opposed to Siegfried's: where Siegfried's is transparent, naive, and exuberant, Hagen's is dark, calculating, and restrained. This becomes clear in their first meeting.

Upon arriving in Burgundy, Siegfried applies for an audience with King Gunther, but Hagen counsels Gunther to deny Siegfried admission to the court. When Gunther rejects that advice and receives Siegfried, Hagen's disapproval of the guest is clearly registered in his penetrating stare.[19] And just as power in this film will be expressed in terms of vision, so too will conflict take that form: Hagen evidently does not like the looks of Siegfried, and will employ visual machinations to dispense with him. Siegfried, for his part, does not see what is happening. The difference, in the end, will be decisive.

Siegfried announces his intentions without much fanfare: he has come to ask Gunther for the hand of his sister Kriemhild. Hagen, ever the wily strategist, quickly intervenes, suggesting to Gunther that before giving away Kriemhild, it might be wise to have Siegfried assist the king in getting a wife of his own. Gunther and Siegfried are both annoyed: Gunther because he has been reminded that he has his eye on a woman whom he knows he cannot get; Siegfried because he has never served any king and is sure he never will. The dispute escalates rapidly: Siegfried is offended by Hagen's suggestion, and Hagen is offended that he is offended.

In the first "song" we saw how Siegfried was stirred into action by viewing the image of Kriemhild conjured by the storyteller at Mime's grotto. But if viewing can readily arouse Siegfried, it can also subdue him. Thus, just as Siegfried and Hagen (and their respective forces) are about to do battle, Kriemhild steps into view. It is love at first sight. Or rather it is love at first live sighting—for each of them has already fallen in love with the image of the other, an image transmitted on the one hand by the storyteller at Mime's grotto (considered briefly above) and on the other hand by Volker, the Burgundian court minstrel (we will examine this scene in detail below). Both of these previews prove to be accurate: thus, Siegfried as sung by Volker and envisioned by Kriemhild corresponds to the Siegfried who, shortly thereafter, appears at Gunther's court; similarly, Kriemhild as described by the confabulator at Mime's cave and envisioned by Siegfried corresponds to the figure he encounters upon his arrival. In this sense, the narrators come to stand in for the film's project: namely, to produce a compelling and properly mimetic vision of the (ancient) tales told in the Nibelungen material.

The alliance is reciprocal, for the film also allies itself with the ancient tellers and the ancient tales, lending vision to their vision. The film's vision is framed in archaic terms: the titles of the "songs" into which the

FIGURE 3. Siegfried arrives at Gunther's court and makes his desires known. Photo courtesy of the Film Stills Archive, The Museum of Modern Art, New York.

film is subdivided are printed in archaic German script, as are the intertitles. But beyond the will to anachronism on the level of form, how is archaism played out on the level of content? Not surprisingly, it is a principal feature in the film's dramaturgy of vision and visual technology, where an old-fashioned, unappealing, but perspicacious form of viewing—embodied by Hagen—is juxtaposed to a more modern, distractible, and naive form, embodied by Siegfried. At the same time, the film will present the character of Alberich as a bad object, one whose sinister ambitions are bound up with his peculiarly cinematic powers.

We can locate the origins of this division of visual power (between the perspicacious and the naive) in the scene of Siegfried's arrival at the Burgundian court. Upon Kriemhild's entrance, calm—indeed, love prevails. It is a scene whose overdetermination is laughably transparent. The switch from combat to love involves a simple substitution: in turning to

Kriemhild, Siegfried lowers and resheaths his large sword. His melodramatic decision to make love and not war does not go unobserved. The following scene of Siegfried and Kriemhild staring long and lovingly into each other's eyes is interrupted by a shot of Hagen staring at them staring at each other. (It is the only shot that interrupts the binary exchange between the would-be lovers.) The film shows us that Hagen not only sees their love but envisions its implications. Thus, he steps over to Gunther: "Prepare yourself for your wooing expedition, King Gunther, because Siegfried, the strong hero, will win Brunhild for you."[20] This will be the film's preferred metaphor for Hagen's character: his loyalty and power centrally involve his ability to see and foresee all.

Hagen's association with vision is not restricted to the film. In the fall of 1923, some six months before *Siegfried* was released, Thea von Harbou published *Das Nibelungenbuch* [The Nibelungen Book], a prose vehicle designed to publicize the film. In the book, Harbou—who also wrote the screenplay—repeatedly flags the visual source of Hagen's authority and the metaphysical quality of his vision. Thus, for example, Hagen explicitly claims—and is shown—to see better and more than his stereoscopic master: "'Gunther, King Gunther!' he whispered. 'I have only one eye; rip it out of its socket—I don't need it! Even without it I would see more than you!'"[21] Insofar as Hagen's power is visual, his vision is political: thus, he claims that he would be able to see what transpires behind the scenes even if he could not actually see. And while everyone else at court sits around and waits for things to happen, Hagen watches and acts.[22] In this particular scene in the film, he watches Siegfried and Kriemhild and then acts to bind Siegfried as the king's emissary. Thus captivated by Kriemhild, Siegfried will agree to Hagen's proposal and Hagen knows he will. As a result, Siegfried will appear to be tainted (I examine this scene in some detail below).[23]

And yet, the point that marks Siegfried's downfall, or at least, the real possibility of that downfall—occurs much earlier than the moment he appears, unseen, at Gunther's side on Brunhild's battlefield. Almost immediately after Siegfried's arrival at court, Hagen has pegged the young hero as a naive viewer. Hagen does not just read Siegfried correctly, he reads his vulnerability correctly, and that vulnerability will be a product of Siegfried's mode of vision. For here the defiant hero becomes a compliant stooge when distracted by a "pretty picture."[24] This moment of viewing, the moment Siegfried lowers his sword to stare openly, longingly, publicly at Kriemhild, signals the genesis of his undoing. In staring thus at Kriemhild and resheathing his sword, Siegfried openly expresses male vulnerability in the face of desire. Hagen embodies a very different relationship to desire. In looking out for Gunther (whose fearfulness is immediately legible in his face), Hagen serves as a kind of watchman for and from a male psychic citadel: his is a teutonic poker face. Thus, the grimness that has traditionally characterized Hagen is here associated with his viewing practices—how he sees and how he looks. In the end, Siegfried will be punished for letting his libidinal cat out of the bag; to the end, Hagen will never do so.

Of course, the dramaturgy of vision in this scene is not limited to Siegfried and Hagen: the scene also fixes Kriemhild's subordination in visual terms. As the film progresses, she will abandon the visual subordination implied in her status as "a pretty picture." At the conclusion of *Siegfried*, she is physically and dramaturgically positioned to reanimate Siegfried's gaze. Significantly, her attempt to do so is motivated by the experience of deprivation: she would assume the gaze that she has been deprived of, both structurally (as a woman embodying a pretty picture) and narratively (as a wife deprived of her super-hero husband). The film shows us the implications of that attempt. Baldly, unabashedly, Kriemhild is transformed from a textbook example of a desirable, good object (i.e., one who has assumed the proper—because properly disempowered—feminine relationship to viewing) into a textbook example of a bad object (one whose aspirations to authority and control take her far beyond her assigned place). The film marks the black-and-white transformation in black and white: in *Siegfried* she wears only white, in *Kriemhilds Rache* [Kriemhild's Revenge] she wears only black.[25]

Siegfried is subject to no such transformation, although the terms of his appearance are similarly overdetermined: he is and remains a naive viewer. And that naiveté extends to Siegfried's relation to visual technology, embodied here in the *Tarnhelm* or magic cap. In order to dispense with him, Hagen will set about manipulating that naiveté. How does he do so? Although the negotiations are not shown on film, Siegfried, Hagen and Gunther evidently agree to terms whereby Siegfried will assist Gunther, enabling him to win Brunhild by deceit. Thus, Siegfried will render himself invisible by donning the magic cap, procured from Alberich, king of the Nibelungen. That cap will prove especially important to my argument since it condenses a number of the

FIGURE 4. Kriemhild as good object: a pretty, immobile picture. Photo courtesy of the Film Stills Archive, The Museum of Modern Art, New York.

film's concerns about visibility and power. For now I simply want to note that when Gunther takes on Brunhild, he will have Siegfried, unseen, at his side.

The details of this arrangement are not made explicit in the film, although they are presented in *Das Nibelungenbuch*. In the book, Hagen proposes the arrangement to Gunther immediately upon suggesting that Siegfried might assist him in gaining Brunhild: " 'Well,' said Hagen with a thin smile, 'Siegfried is the strongest—invulnerable thanks to the dragon's blood. He's got the magic cap under his belt. If he were to battle Brunhild disguised as you—it would be a cinch for him who swings the sword Balmung to conquer a defiant woman!' "[26] In the *Nibelungenbuch* we are told that Hagen organizes this deception and, in doing so, organizes Siegfried's visual appearance (which is to say, his disappearance); we can assume, if only by implication, that he does so in the film as well. In the film, Siegfried does not end up fighting Gunther's fight as Gunther; instead, he simply acts as an invisible aide. But how are we to understand the deception enacted here? According to most writers—including a number of critics as well as the set designer Erich Kettelhut—the deception lies in the sinister plot to deceive Brunhild.[27] And yet that deception crucially involves visual manipulation: in order to deceive Brunhild, Siegfried will have to become invisible. It is this visual deception—its terms and implications—that we need to consider.

ORGANIZING THE APPEARANCE OF VICTORY

When Siegfried intercedes invisibly in Gunther's battle, he enables the king to vanquish the threat posed by Brunhild's explicit (and explicitly matriarchal) challenge to male power. The terms of that challenge are especially lurid: when Siegfried originally introduced Gunther as the combatant for her affections, Brunhild stepped over to the king and warned him that by the time their contest was over, his "broken weapons" would join the host of others adorning her palace walls.[28] In the end, she and her realm of female warriors[29] are defeated only because Siegfried assists Gunther in his contest with her; and Siegfried is able to do so because he renders himself invisible.

Here, then, we encounter a fantasy that we might term the *hero behind the back*, which refigures the equally resonant fantasy of the "stab

in the back": rather than the hero being stabbed from behind by a supposed ally (which will, of course, be Siegfried's fate), the invisible hero
props up the embattled and evidently powerless king. This particular
incarnation of the fantasy has a strong filmic resonance. For rather than
having Siegfried appear as Gunther (which is how the scene is described
in the screenplay and in Kettelhut's memoirs), the scene shows us the
"real" Gunther engaged in the tests of prowess assisted by Siegfried,
whose invisibility is marked by flickering, occasional glimpses of his
presence. Thus, after Brunhild heaves a huge stone across the court-
yard and jumps an impressive distance, we see glimmers of Siegfried behind Gunther reassuring the king, throwing the stone on his behalf,
and adding tremendous force to his jump. (Indeed, in a scene that is inadvertently comical, the hero jumps with the king, essentially and im-
probably carrying him through the air.) The final test is also the most
overdetermined: Siegfried, still invisible on the battlefield but partially
visible to us, is able to help Gunther fend off Brunhild's javelin and in
turn throws Gunther's javelin with such might that it shatters her
shield.

The implications of the scene are not especially subtle. Taken together, the swords, broken weapons, and javelins piercing female shields
offer a graphic account of the threat of castration. In the end, Brunhild's
overt claim to the phallus is vanquished by a wily (but no less transparent) strategy, one that renders the phallus covert. When Siegfried
(dis-)appears as Gunther's invisible aide, the film prefigures the literal
terms of Lacan's famous claim that the phallus can only play its role
when veiled. Here the phallic claim is issued in its withdrawal: it would
appear that Gunther is powerless, but the phallus—in its new, improved,
invisible form—is with him. And that is the problem, for although the
phallus is with him, it is not his to wield. In thus gaining Brunhild for
Gunther, Siegfried rescues phallic authority, both in the particular (and
particularly emasculated) form of King Gunther, but also in the more
general sense of regaining the phallus for men.[30] Despite Gunther's apparent victory—or because it is merely apparent—the king's claims to
Brunhild and his authority over her are hardly legitimate: she will challenge them soon enough.

The victory opens up an ominous gap between the king's public and
private bodies. Gunther's apparent power (which was just displayed on
the battlefield) is juxtaposed to his real weakness (which is about to be
revealed in the ship's master bedroom). Of course, this gap did not sim-

FIGURE 5. Siegfried helps Gunther shatter Brunhild's shield. Photo courtesy of the Film Stills Archive, The Museum of Modern Art, New York.

ply materialize by accident. Instead, Siegfried was made to embody the difference that produced the gap, by providing the essential invisible assistance. Later in this chapter, I will examine the genesis and exigencies of this ability; for now I want to concentrate on its location. For while Siegfried would seem to exercise that magic capacity, he does so under Hagen's supervision and control. Siegfried is the actor under Hagen's direction.

More precisely, the magic cap permits Siegfried to become a special effect: we see traces of his body (his hand assisting Gunther in tossing the javelin; his face as he whispers into Gunther's ear), while Hagen and Gunther can see only his shadow, and the rest of the characters at Brunhild's court see no traces of Siegfried's presence at all. On an immanent level, this opens up a further space between Siegfried's apparent body (which is down at the ship preparing for Gunther's imminent departure) and his real body (which is here invisibly assisting Gunther). Siegfried's real body is here shown to be especially apparent by virtue of its invisibility. In a broader sense, Siegfried's appearance as apparent is produced under Hagen's direction: the scene's director is also the special-effects coordinator.

Hagen's plot involves a crucial division of visual power: Siegfried does the dirty work of dissimulation while Hagen shows himself to be merely watching from the sidelines. When Gunther appears on the battle-grounds in order to face Brunhild he is evidently seized by a wave of anxiety. Hagen steps forward to reassure the king, pointing out Sieg-fried's shadow (since Siegfried himself is invisible) on the ground adja-cent to them.[31] In the ensuing competition between Gunther and Brun-hild, the seeds of Brunhild's resentment toward Siegfried are being sown; and Hagen, who has overseen their cultivation, will reap the reward. The same structure will recur in the following "song" when Hagen again con-vinces Siegfried to don the magic cap on Gunther's behalf.

It is not long before Brunhild comes to suspect that the emasculated king is not the man he appeared to be—although in a certain sense he is precisely the man he appeared to be, since Brunhild immediately took him for a coward. Lang and Harbou spare Gunther the ignominy of being hung upon a nail in his bed chamber for the duration of the conjugal night (which is his fate in the *Nibelungenlied*[32]); instead, they insert a similar scene at an earlier moment. The shift in sequence is accompa-nied by a significant shift in dramaturgy.

In the epic, the ship is awash in "much merry-making," as Brünhild and Gunther sail back to Worms together.[33] The film offers quite a differ-ent view. Near the outset of the fourth "song," the ship has arrived at Worms and Gunther comes to fetch Brunhild in order to bring her to shore. As he approaches, Brunhild shoves him away violently, eventu-ally wrestling him to the ground and binding his hands with a belt, ask-ing, "Are you the man who defeated me thrice in battle?"[34] Hagen, who has been listening at the entryway to the bedroom, steps in and an ap-pearance of order—which is to say, the phallic order—is immediately restored: Brunhild jumps up and Gunther is able to free his arms from her belt. The scene duplicates the earlier scene of battle at Brunhild's court, except this time Gunther's assistant is visible and the visible as-sistant is Hagen, not Siegfried. Beyond suggesting that Hagen keeps care-ful watch over Gunther, the scene leaves Gunther indebted to him and not to Siegfried.

In the *Nibelungenlied*, Gunther convinces Brünhild to free him from his embarrassing and precarious perch before anyone will discover him

FIGURE 6. Hagen convinces Siegfried to alter his appearance and tame Brunhild. Photo courtesy of the Film Stills Archive, The Museum of Modern Art, New York.

thus compromised.[35] Then, later in the day, Gunther confides in Siegfried, who offers to "tame" Brünhild secretly and invisibly on Gunther's behalf. Siegfried himself hatches and announces the plot: "Tonight, Lady Brünhild must become your woman. I shall enter your chambers in my magic cloak so secretly that none shall perceive my wiles."[36] Thus, in the epic, Siegfried is entirely in control of his own disappearance: he suggests and executes it on his own.

But when Hagen steps in during the fourth "song" of the film to discover Brunhild binding Gunther with the belt, he becomes the sole witness to Gunther's shame and the unsolicited interlocutor for his unwitting confession. As a result, Siegfried will not offer to "tame" Brunhild of his own accord; instead, Hagen convinces him to do so. Thus, later in the scene, Hagen confronts Siegfried, grabs the magic cap from his belt, and addresses him ferociously: "The magic cap transforms you as you wish. Turn yourself into Gunther and break Brunhild's defiance!"[37] After a series of refusals, Siegfried eventually agrees and heads off into the bedroom, donning the magic cap and assuming Gunther's appearance. In the meantime, the "real" Gunther remains in the anteroom, anxiously awaiting his surrogate's return.

In the course of his cameo appearance as Gunther subduing Brunhild, Siegfried grabs a bracelet from her arm and stuffs it into his pocket. It is a crucial and famous blunder, one with evidently disastrous consequences. Kriemhild eventually comes across the bracelet and wears it; Siegfried sees it and tells her how it came into his possession; she swears not to tell anyone and then, in the course of a terrible confrontation with Brunhild, shows her the bracelet and tells her how it came into her possession. Thus it comes out: Siegfried—not Gunther—ultimately vanquished Brunhild on the battlefield in Isenland and then again in the king's bedroom. What emerges in the process is the sense that Siegfried cannot keep his mouth shut. As Hagen puts it in a brief confrontation with Siegfried: "your big mouth, oh hero, was worse than a murder."[38] Siegfried's reason for pocketing Brunhild's bracelet is strangely undecidable, blending as it does questions of representational decorum with problems in character psychology and simple dramaturgy.[39] But more important than the notion that Siegfried cannot control his hands (when he "subdues" Brunhild) or his mouth (when he tells Kriemhild) is the recognition that Siegfried relinquished control of his appearance before he ever entered the bedroom.

In convincing Siegfried to don the magic cap and "break Brunhild's defiance," Hagen is not just plotting to avenge Brunhild's earlier transgression against Gunther. Beyond that, he is incriminating the appointed agent of retribution. In doing so, Hagen once again manipulates and exploits Siegfried's power of physical dissimulation. Why would this be? If Hagen's machinations in the *Nibelungenlied* and the *Ring* were primarily narrative, in the Nibelungen film they take visual form. Here and throughout the film, Hagen uses his visual mastery to protect his boss, rebuffing the immediate threat to Gunther's authority. Eventually, Hagen will use his mastery to hatch and execute a plot to kill Siegfried, capitalizing on the hero's willingness to relinquish control over his own appearance.

In a sense, the film has already done Hagen's work for him. At the end of the first "song" we were presented with the image of Siegfried bathing in the dragon's blood and the linden leaf falling upon his back. Thus, we witnessed the promise of Siegfried's invulnerability and the demise—or

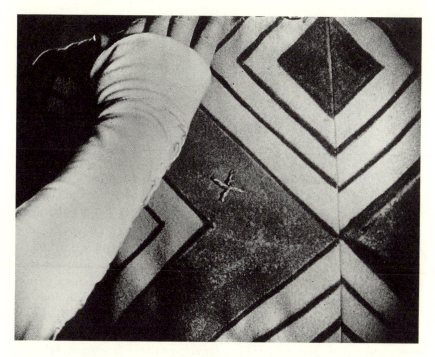

FIGURE 7. X marks the spot of Siegfried's vulnerability. Photo courtesy of the Film Stills Archive, The Museum of Modern Art, New York.

at least, the qualification—of that promise. The problem for Hagen is that he was not privy to the scene: his actions can be understood as an attempt to revisit it in order to locate the mark of vulnerability that it produced. That is, Hagen aims to see the scene that we saw.

The hitch in the plot to kill Siegfried is that no one except Kriemhild and Siegfried knows the precise location of the linden-leaf spot on Siegfried's back. (It is entirely unclear how Kriemhild comes to know the location of the spot and it is equally unclear how Hagen knows that she knows.) In order for Hagen to dispense with Siegfried, he will have to locate that spot, and in order to do so, he dupes Kriemhild into identifying it for him. In doing so, his mastery is as much visual as narrative: Hagen enacts an elaborate visual deception by placing himself where Kriemhild will see him and then feigning concern for her husband's welfare. Kriemhild is duly duped and suggests sewing the x to mark the spot on Siegfried's garment.

To the end, Siegfried remains ignorant: he is happily and remarkably oblivious to the plotting that surrounds him. If Siegfried is forever failing to notice, Hagen seems to see all. The juxtaposition of their viewing habits echoes certain recurring terms in the discourse of national cinemas in the Weimar Republic.

ALLEGORIZING VISION

In *Hollywood in Berlin*, Thomas Saunders charts the actual and imagined terms surrounding Hollywood's invasion of the German film market in the first half of the 1920s.[40] In 1924, Hollywood films were attracting German audiences in droves.[41] But according to a sizable contingent of German critics, Hollywood product was all action and no substance; it was spectacular and shallow, while German film was substantial and less flashy.[42] Thus, in the early 1920s, critics tended to juxtapose "American simplicity, naturalness, sensationalism, contemporaneity, and tempo" to "German fantasy, stylization, logic, historical sense, and profundity."[43] This rhetoric finds its way into Lang and Harbou's statements about their film. Of course these categories—already tentative and ephemeral—shifted over time. By 1924, when *Siegfried* premiered, critics in Germany had begun to augment the formulaic categories of "gloss, furious action, and happy endings" that characterized American film in juxtaposition to the "exotic, historical or mythical settings, exaggerated acting and ponderous tempos" of German film.[44] The point here is not to reify these categories but to attend to the echoes from the contemporary debate about national cinematic particularity that filter into the dramaturgy of the *Nibelungen* film, which was, after all, an explicit attempt at a national film epic. Those echoes resound in surprising ways, telling us about the conception of Siegfried's vulnerability and Hagen's strength within the film, and about the conception of cinematic vulnerability and strength in German film culture.

What would be the use of such an allegory? Why would the film adopt terms from that debate? In order to address these questions we need to recognize that the film seeks to win an audience not for itself alone, but for the cause of German film as well. Thus, it allegorizes the perils of naive viewing and a loss of control over visual representation—an allegory with obvious parallels to the ostensible risk Hollywood posed to the German film world. The threat of foreign film is grafted onto Siegfried (and not only him): his problems are less Germany's problems *per se* than Germany's problems with foreign film. Siegfried, after all, is a prototype of the German hero, specifically the *flawed* German hero. Both his heroism and the flaw that undoes him are characterized by the very qualities that attract German audiences to Hollywood films. Here is a German hero who can capture the attention of a German audience— whose attentions are otherwise dedicated in large measure to the imports. Thus Siegfried is quick, bold, daring, adventurous, romantic, unpredictable—all qualities associated with Hollywood films and Hollywood heroes in the first half of the 1920s. At the same time, however, he is flawed—and his flaw is crucially produced by the terms of his appeal. In this way, his flaw has a filmic resonance, for Siegfried does not exercise proper control over his magical (and properly filmic) powers. This becomes clear in the course of Siegfried's confrontation with Alberich in the film's second "song."

Siegfried's encounter with Alberich takes place in an eerie, misty, and barren landscape with "a knotted, crippled, grotesque tree stump" in the foreground. According to the screenplay, Alberich is "cowering" within the stump "as if he were a part of the tree itself."[45] So who is Alberich? Or rather, what is Alberich?

Alberich is king of the Nibelungs. But beyond that, he combines in exaggerated form the traditional and traditionally overdetermined qualities of the outsider with those of the cinematic insider. The film's vision of this character gives a surprising account of where cinema is and whose hands it is in; where and in whose hands it has been, where and into whose hands it is headed. At the same time, it suggests how and why Siegfried is vulnerable, providing a link between the linden-leaf spot and Siegfried's loss of control over his own appearance.

From the outset, nature is made to speak the truth about Alberich: the "crippled," "knotted," and "grotesque" quality of the barren stump matches the character and physique of the king cowering within it. When Alberich senses Siegfried's approach on horseback, he renders himself invisible by surreptitiously donning his magic cap (in fact, it looks more like a webbing than a cap, and it functions like a technologically retrofitted yarmulke). As the unsuspecting hero rides by, Alberich jumps him. Although momentarily disabled, Siegfried is able to wrestle his invisible assailant to the ground and is about to impale him. Suddenly Alberich and the magic cap materialize in Siegfried's hands. Alberich pleads desperately, pathetically with Siegfried, first begging him to

FIGURE 8. Siegfried wrestles his invisible assailant to the ground. Photo courtesy of the Film Stills Archive, The Museum of Modern Art, New York.

FIGURE 9. Alberich suddenly materializes in Siegfried's hands. Photo courtesy of the Film Stills Archive, The Museum of Modern Art, New York.

FIGURE 10. Alberich limps along, ushering Siegfried to the subterranean treasure. Photo courtesy of the Film Stills Archive, The Museum of Modern Art, New York.

spare his life in exchange for the magic cap (which, he explains, allows its owner to assume any form), then sweetening the deal by offering to give Siegfried the Nibelungen treasure as well.

To make good on his promise, Alberich ushers Siegfried from the forest deep down to the subterranean grotto where the Nibelungen treasure is displayed. Just before they descend, the Nibelungen king scurries into a hidden alcove and returns with a bright sphere that looks like a crystal ball and functions like a flashlight, lighting the path before them. At one point along the precariously narrow pathway down to the treasure,

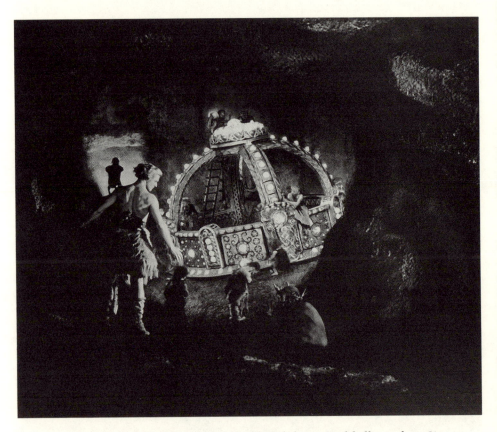

FIGURE 11. Alberich illuminates the wall with his crystal ball, much to Sieg-fried's amazement. Photo courtesy of the Film Stills Archive, The Museum of Modern Art, New York.

Alberich, who is a few feet ahead of Siegfried, directs the young hero's attention to a certain spot on the wall to their left. Holding the ball aloft between them, Alberich illuminates the wall. Suddenly, in a surreal moment reminiscent of Rabbi Löw's presentation to the court in Paul Wegener's *Der Golem* of 1920, an image appears on the wall: the rock has turned magically into a screen upon which Alberich magically projects a filmic image. Alberich informs Siegfried (and the intertitle informs us) that the Nibelungs are shown here, working on a crown for the king of the North.[46] There are two particularly interesting aspects to this scene. One involves the status of the projected scene as a film; the other involves Siegfried's reactions as a viewer.

The segment Alberich projects upon the wall is not of particular dramatic import: although there is plenty of action in the segment (the Nibelungs are shown scurrying about the massive crown), nothing particularly gripping "happens" in the scene (thus, for example, the crown is not suddenly stolen or destroyed). Presumably, this is because at this moment the medium is the intended message—the magic inheres more in the sheer production of the image than in its content. This assumption is borne out by the screenplay: Lang and Harbou intended for Alberich to render the wall transparent, and thus, Siegfried (and of course, we in the audience) would be treated to a view of the goings-on in his smithy behind the wall. And yet, the magic ends up on the wall and not behind it.

Here is how the screenplay describes the "behind the scenes" scene:

> Upon a heavy black anvil that occupies the entirety of the forge stands a gold crown that in turn occupies the entire surface of the anvil and almost extends to the top edge of the image. It is covered with an excess of ornaments and diamonds. Innumerable dwarfs are climbing about the crown, forging inside it, alongside it, all over it. Two of them are carrying a massive gem to the zenith of the crown where they are awaited by other dwarfs who receive the gem and struggle to roll it into place. Other dwarfs are sitting astride golden ornaments and hammering away at them. Everyone moves feverishly, engaged in this drudgery as if hounded by an invisible whip. The scene is lit by a fire in the forge-oven, which is serviced by other dwarfs, who stand nearby in order to fan the flames and man the bellows. The fire produces no smoke. Alberich observes the impression that the gold forgery makes upon Siegfried.[47]

After a few moments, the screened image disappears, and in an ostensibly charming mixture of wonder and bewilderment that marks him as the prototypical naive viewer, Siegfried rushes over and taps around on the wall where the image had appeared. There are no traces there of the crown or the Nibelungs; the image has vanished. When the image disappears Siegfried "seems to awaken out of a dream." In positing Siegfried as a quasi-dreamer, the film would seem to be enacting its own dream, conjuring up a nightmare in the eyes of German cultural nationalists: a scene depicting a cinema in the hands of this eminently unsavory character and a quintessentially German viewer enraptured by that cinema.

Siegfried's rapt absorption produces a certain vulnerability: easily distracted by the image, he is also unfamiliar with the rudimentary technical means of its production. This, then, is the second time that Siegfried has been portrayed as a naive viewer (the first was at Mime's grotto in the film's first "song"). The scene of naive viewing is a formative and recurring one in early silent film. One of its most famous and popular incarnations occurs in Edwin Porter's 1902 short *Uncle Josh at the Moving Picture Show*, a remake of Robert Paul's *The Countryman's First Sight of the Animated Pictures* (1901). In the film, Uncle Josh is a spectator in a cinema who mistakes the filmic image for reality.[48] Thus he rushes on stage to join a woman who is shown dancing on screen, but then flees when the film depicts a train rushing headlong toward the camera. As film historians have noted, these mini-scenes revisit important moments from the very earliest days of film.[49] Finally, Uncle Josh cannot contain himself: he attacks the screen and rips it down when the image depicts a man seducing a woman. In his determination to challenge the male suitor within the film, he instead encounters the projectionist behind the screen.

In each of these instances, Uncle Josh is shown to be a naive viewer, one who has not mastered the spectatorial economy of identification. His appearance as the subject of the film documents the wrong way to watch as it plays to the viewer—whom the film situates far beyond Uncle Josh's ostensibly primitive, ignorant viewing practices. While audiences in 1902 may have required further schooling in how to view a film, we can assume that the reintroduction of a scene of naive viewing in the Nibelungen film had little practical pedagogical value in 1924. Instead, the scene further crystallizes the distinctions between Alberich and Siegfried, relying, for that crystallization, on each character's radically different intentions—intentions encapsulated in their radically different relationship to film and viewing.

In attacking the man seducing the woman on screen (whom Miriam Hansen astutely labels his "paternal rival"), Uncle Josh discovers that there is no 'he' there, no materiality to the image, but that there is a projectionist behind the screen, standing in, so to speak, for Uncle Josh's projection.[50] In beating up the projectionist, Uncle Josh lends expression to the frustration attending the economy of mediation, a frustration that is integral to the position of the spectator—which Uncle Josh has evidently and explicitly not mastered. In *Uncle Josh*, the scene of revelation is aggressive and cathartic, for the apparatus finds its displaced embodiment in the man behind the screen, and Uncle Josh has the good fortune of finding him. In *Siegfried* the apparatus is foregrounded (in the crystal ball) and its source is embodied (in Alberich), but unlike Uncle Josh, Siegfried does not attack either of them; instead, he merely watches, transfixed, and eventually inspects the wall with childlike curiosity when the image vanishes. The image, it would seem, does not threaten Siegfried, on the contrary it seems to fascinate him.

The Jew and the Apparatus:
Whose Cinema?

In wielding the intended power to render the wall transparent, Alberich is invested with the power to project an image—the power, that is, of cinema. Thus, the view behind the scenes that Lang and Harbou provide is not as simple as it would appear. Intending to give us a glimpse of the Nibelungen behind the scenes, they end up giving us a glimpse behind the psychic and film-historical scenes of *The Nibelungen*. The scene being played out on-screen (or on-wall) enacts an important fantasy of cinematic self-definition, for here Alberich is shown to have the apparatus in the palm of his hand. Just as important (if less literally), he has Siegfried in the palm of his hand too, enraptured by the projected image.

We would do well to examine that hand—and indeed, the fingers surrounding the crystal ball are spindly and crooked, the hand itself is grubby, the arms too long, the shoulders stooped, the face deformed, the nose hooked, the eyes beady. Alberich embodies not only control over the apparatus, but he also embodies the Jew: his shiftiness, deformity, and scheming all correspond to reigning German stereotypes of the Jewish body and Jewish nature. In addition, his manner offers a remarkable visualization of Jewish *jammern*, a combination of cowering and pleading, flailing and grimacing, a visual loquaciousness that communicates all the more resonantly in its juxtaposition to the silence of the medium. For in the silence of Alberich's bombastic dissimulative excess, the viewer is implicitly invited to fill in the auditory blanks, to provide by projection the alternately pathetic or menacing sounds that form and fill the space of his pleas and curses.

Despite the overdetermined quality of Alberich's appearance, critics have paid scant attention to his dramaturgical function in the film. Kracauer presumably came closest to such a discussion: as I noted in chapter one, Lotte Eisner claimed that he was taken aback by the similarities between Alberich and popular anti-Semitic stereotypes.[51] But why would the film present Alberich thus? We can read the encounter between Alberich and Siegfried as an encounter between modes of cinematic power, where Alberich's cynical control is juxtaposed to Siegfried's pointed and thoroughgoing naiveté. That naiveté derives from a long-standing tradition whereby Siegfried is presented as fierce but naive—very mean in battle but very sweet, indeed too trusting in person. In this case, his good-hearted naiveté translates into a recurring naiveté vis-à-vis the filmic apparatus.

And yet it remains unclear why the film would inflect Alberich and Siegfried in these terms. A quick detour into recent scholarship on the rhetoric of national cinemas will help. In the course of an argument about the genesis of the monumental style in prewar Japanese cinema—a history that has much in common with the rise of an explicitly nationalist cinema in the Weimar Republic—Darrell William Davis argues that the most significant Other in the self-definition of the monumental style in Japan is Hollywood itself.[52] But not just Hollywood. According to Davis, "Hollywood is not the only Other, but it is the most universal. National cinemas react against other arts from the past, like the kabuki stage from which the earliest Japanese films emerged or disreputable ethnic ancestors from which a 'true' national cinema might wish to dissociate itself."[53] The Nibelungen film does both. At the outset of this chapter, we saw how Lang and Harbou situated the film against the agon of its epic and operatic precursors. The Nibelungen film reacts against Hollywood film while envisioning it in the hands of the Jew.[54] In the arithmetic of *völkisch*-nationalist cultural criticism in the mid-1920s, Hollywood is to German film what the Jew is to German society. Put in Davis' terms, as quoted above, both are just the sort of disreputable ancestor from which a "true" national cinema might wish to dissociate itself.

Here, the new national cinema involves a formative fantasy of itself and its hero in thrall to its ethnic and aesthetic Other. But why would this be? In short, because it provides a useful response to a riddle that haunts this and other Nibelungen works that reproduce both parts of the peculiar bipartite narrative of the *Nibelungenlied*. These works have to account for the fact that Siegfried, the hero of part one, is vulnerable and dies—killed by an unsavory figure, Hagen, who will, however, go on to become the hero of part two. How then can the bad guy of part one become the good guy of part two? Lang and Harbou inflect the problem—and its solution—in terms that are particularly resonant for cinematic, historical, and political developments in the mid-twenties. The scene in *The Nibelungen* rehearses anxieties about the dominance of foreign film and its lack of substance by showing us a spectacular (and obviously shallow) cinema in foreign hands—indeed, they are formulaically dirty, foreign hands. And while Alberich is the foreign film man, his product is foreign film: the segment that he screens for Siegfried—the Nibelungen scurrying about the crown—is not merely spectacular, it is the spectacle of wealth accumulating itself. As much as this is not the form and stuff of German film, it is a perfect condensation of the nationalist critique of Hollywood with the fantasmatic terms of Jewish cultural aspirations. At the same time, the scene shows us Siegfried enthralled by that very scene. What a dupe! As such, the scene makes dramaturgical sense in a number of registers: it lends credence to a xenophobic fantasy about Hollywood cinema while lending an interesting form to Siegfried's vulnerability. We need to consider the scene in a bit more detail in order to see how this is the case.

Once the image projected on the wall has disappeared and Siegfried has concluded his brief examination of the wall, he and Alberich proceed down to the Nibelungen treasure. The treasure fills the huge catacomb at the foot of the subterranean passageway: it is heaped high on a massive tablet that is supported by enslaved, enchained dwarfs. Kracauer was appalled by the scene: in his remarkably prescient analysis, the appearance of the dwarfs as "human ornaments" denoted "the omnipotence of dictatorship."[55] Siegfried does not take particular note of the dwarfs: he only has eyes for weaponry. Thus, after briefly rummaging about the treasure (and displaying no particular interest in the wealth on display), he happens upon Balmung, the wonder-sword. His excitement at the discovery demonstrates that his interest lies in swords rather than jewels or diamonds (let alone the liberation of the oppressed). As he swings the sword in evident glee, he turns his back upon Alberich, who slinks across the treasure and clumsily drapes a shawl over Siegfried's head and shoulders. Alberich's scheme is straightforward enough: he attempts to choke Siegfried when the hero's back is turned, first immobilizing and disorienting him with the shawl. Here as at the outset of the scene, the nature of Alberich's attack upon Siegfried suggests the nature of the dwarf's powers. Both of his attacks are designed to capitalize upon his invisibility—in the first case, he renders himself invisible with the magic cap, in the second, he renders himself invisible by (temporarily) blinding Siegfried with the shawl. In the second attack, Alberich marshals as many of cinema's resources as he can hold in two hands: the power to project (in the form of the crystal ball) in one hand, and in the other, the power to mislead, to disorient, to "put in the dark" (in the form of the shawl). When Alberich seeks to pull the wool over Siegfried's eyes this second time, Siegfried turns around, shakes off the shawl, and kills his assailant.

As Alberich expires, he turns himself and the Nibelungen to stone. Kracauer was appalled by this scene as well: in his view, the image of the Nibelungen gradually turning to stone represents "the complete triumph of the ornamental over the human."[56] But how are we to make sense of this spectacle of ornamentalization?

This final gesture further distinguishes Lang's Alberich from Wagner's, for in The Ring, Alberich cannot transform his subjects, he can only transform his own appearance—and that power wholly depends upon his control over the magic cap: once he loses the cap, he loses the power. In the film, Alberich's power over appearance evidently extends beyond his control over the cap. When he turns the Nibelungen to stone, he no longer possesses the cap: earlier in the scene he gave it to Siegfried who had, in exchange, spared the dwarf-king's life. So if Alberich's power to ornamentalize the Nibelungen is not derived from the cap, where does it come from? It derives from his posited alliance with the cinematic apparatus.

Alberich is not just a Jew on screen, he is a Jew who controls the screen. That is, his power extends beyond his own appearance and disappearance—the power bestowed by the magic cap—to encompass the power to produce visions upon command. Alberich controls the appearance of the filmic image on the wall as he and Siegfried approach the treasure; in addition, he rules over its depicted subjects: in screening the film he is the king of the cinema, while the images within that film remind us that he is king of the Nibelungs. Thus Alberich is in control of production on two fronts: the production of the image and the production displayed in the image. The two powers converge in the scene where the Nibelungs turn to stone: here, political authority takes visual form. Thus it is important to note that the scene of ornamentalization is not merely a suspicious ideological effect of the film, but is, as such, attributed to the suspicious repertoire of cinematic effects in Alberich's ever-so-Jewish hands.

In killing Alberich, Siegfried terminates his control of the medium, inheriting the Nibelungen treasure in addition to the magic cap. Siegfried will bring these inheritances to the Burgundian court: he will bestow the treasure upon Kriemhild as her "morning gift"—the gift given to the bride on the morning after the wedding night; and he (or, as we have seen, *Hagen*) will employ the magic cap to assist Gunther in defeating Brunhild. The treasure and the cap are clearly acquired from a dubious source: that is, the inheritance is tainted. Indeed, it was cursed by Alberich as he died. But beyond that, it is incomplete. For although he takes the cap and will later take delivery of the treasure, Siegfried ends up leaving Alberich's *laterna magica* behind, and thus his cursed inheritance is only—and significantly—partial.

It is not immediately clear why Siegfried leaves the crystal ball behind, especially since the screenplay envisions an entirely different conclusion to the scene in Alberich's cave. In the screenplay, the crystal ball mirrors Alberich's deteriorating physical condition: as he dies (with the crystal ball still in hand), its light begins to die out as well. While the Nibelungen turn to stone ("at the same rate as the light dissipates"), Siegfried is supposed to snatch the crystal ball from the ground (and Alberich's grasp) and swing it vehemently through the air. Thus, the scene of the transformation of the Nibelungen is supposed to be lit by Alberich's ball in Siegfried's hand. Here is how the scene is described in the screenplay:

> The crystal ball flares up and casts a long flash of light through the cave, but then once again immediately loses its light and becomes increasingly dim. Almost hastily, Siegfried begins to walk along the rim of the bowl [which holds the treasure]. (Camera on circular tracks.) He stares into the faces of the dwarfs and illuminates them with the crystal ball. They have turned to stone. Siegfried turns violently to the steps.[57]

In the screenplay, the crystal ball expires in Siegfried's hand, whereupon he flings it away, producing a general conflagration of Alberich's realm. This final conflagration includes a brief reappearance of the magic film image on the wall, which then simply fades to black; thus, the image disappears.

In the extant prints of the film, Siegfried never touches the crystal ball: it remains and expires in the Jew's hand. Similarly, the magic film image never reappears and there is no conflagration. The difference becomes significant if only because it elaborates Siegfried's relationship to the apparatus. In the screenplay, that relationship is characterized by an ambivalent fascination resulting in the twin acts of appropriation and destruction. Thus, Siegfried—like Uncle Josh—would display a violent sense of the crystal ball's powers and the threat that it poses. Significantly, the ball remains outside the frame in our last two glimpses of Alberich in the film—when he dies and when he has turned himself and the Nibelungen to stone. Unlike the scene described in the screenplay, Alberich's death in the film does not resolve an anxiety about Jewish power and control over the medium. The film depicts a victory of the bold blond warrior over the spindly, shifty Jew, but the status of the apparatus remains unresolved in the course of that victory.

If he does not gain control over the apparatus, what does Siegfried gain? His choice and his character are encapsulated in the final shot of the scene. Initially, he simply looks around at Alberich and the Nibelung slaves, all of whom have turned to stone. In doing so, Siegfried views the scene naively: reviewing the spectacle of the Nibelungen before him, he does not see what he should (the crystal ball in Alberich's hands). Nor does he remain a viewer for long; instead, he turns to histrionics. He suddenly juts his right arm into the air, holding Balmung aloft—a laughably pompous, melodramatic, heroic pose. The scene concludes with an iris-out upon Balmung's handle in Siegfried's grip. Thus, Siegfried has moved quickly from a position of the subject viewing (Siegfried gazing about the cave) to the subject viewed (Siegfried holding Balmung aloft—for all to see and admire). And yet, there is no one to see him: all of the eyes within the scene have turned to stone. The scene closes as the camera joins Siegfried in focusing upon his new acquisition: the sword.

How can we account for the scene's rather jarring and pompous conclusion? In a famous article entitled "Psychological Explanation in the Films of Lang and Pabst," Janet Bergstrom observes that in Lang's *M*, "detail shots enter into an elaborate system of clues or signs to be deciphered as opposed to providing indications of a character's emotional state."[58] In *Siegfried* they do both. That is, the iris-out on Balmung in Siegfried's hand registers his exultation as it provides us with a clue that he has left behind something far more significant than what he has

FIGURE 12. Siegfried enjoys a quiet moment with Balmung amid the just-calcified Nibelungen. Photo courtesy of the Film Stills Archive, The Museum of Modern Art, New York.

gained. For in thus celebrating Balmung, Siegfried fails to celebrate a much stronger weapon—indeed, the weapon that will undo him: the magic cap. Were he a savvier thinker, Siegfried would forego the heroic histrionics and forget Balmung (especially since the first "song" showed us that Siegfried already possesses a fantastically powerful sword). Were he even savvier still, he would appropriate the crystal ball. We might say that in taking control of the Nibelungen treasure, Siegfried fails to take control of the *Nibelungen* treasure—the treasure of cinematic representation itself. Instead of playing to the camera, Siegfried should have appropriated it. In acceding to a ready-made heroic pose, he leaves his newfound power to remake his image uncelebrated. More ominously, he leaves the power of cinema in the hands of the expired Jew. How can we explain this oversight? And how does it relate to the film's more general preoccupation with vision?

EXPLOITABLE EYES

I have already suggested that the film presents a hierarchy of visual authority, inflecting Hagen's vision as particularly sharp while the king's vision and that of the rest of the court is shown to be a good deal less acute. Siegfried's encounter with Alberich suggests that the strapping hero leaves plenty to be desired in matters of visual acumen. It turns out that the problem is not restricted to the characters on screen. That is, the hierarchy of visual authority shown on-screen parallels the purported situation of the film's audience.

According to Thea von Harbou, Germany's eyes in the mid-twenties were not what they used to be. In various writings accompanying the film's release, Lang and Harbou indicate that this *Siegfried* was primarily destined for the eyes. But not just any eyes. The eyes they had in mind were passive, exhausted, German eyes. Thus, Lang and Harbou distinguish between their own active vision—which they impart to the film—and the passive vision of their audience. Harbou accounts for the distinction by invoking contemporary political and social circumstances; Lang associates the active/passive split with the requirements of the apparatus.

In a 1924 article explaining how she and Lang transformed the *Nibelungen* epic into a film, Harbou argues that literature no longer allowed access to a place of fantasy and imagination. In her estimation, the great German *Volk* was so tired and overworked that no German worker could be expected to pick up and wade through a huge medieval epic: "after a long day of frazzling work, the *Volk* in its entirety—with but a few lucky exceptions cannot muster the spiritual fortitude to take up a thick book and read it with its own tired eyes."[59] And in an essay attributed to Fritz Lang but replete with the maudlin sentimentality that marks Harbou's prose, a similar claim is extended to the theater: "Who is capable of feeling the impact of a stage drama? Especially given the heaviness of theatrical language, the lifeless immobility of a stage, from which the key element—that which is mystically-magical—can only be recited?"[60] Thus, the people's need for adventure went doubly unfulfilled: absent from life, it was no longer accessible in art. Film—and more particularly, this film—would redress that need, providing a Nibelungen fix to the culturally strung-out *Volk*.[61] In doing so, it would resituate the place and quality of the Nibelungen tale, from a reader's private, solitary experience to a social and collective one; from the theatergoer's exclusive and privileged experience to one accessible to the masses. Thus Harbou and Lang envision bringing the tale to film and bringing the people to the cinema.

This last point is important to the extent that both Lang and Harbou expressed confidence that this film could produce the sense of wholeness that the people needed. Thus once again the *Nibelungen* material is called upon to suture the cultural identity of the *Volk*. It will do so by redressing a properly German desire for heroic adventure. According to Harbou, this desire "remains eternally vigilant" despite being "shackled"—presumably by economic and political conditions. The film would introduce and narrate a process of healing and unification:

> For this great, tired, and overworked *Volk* is full of longing for heroic adventures, a longing that once enabled it to become dangerous wanderers of the world, a longing that lies in shackles today and yet remains eternally vigilant. But after a long day of frazzling work, the *Volk* in its entirety—with but a few lucky exceptions—cannot muster the spiritual fortitude to take up a thick book and read it with its own tired eyes, constructing with its own worn-out brain a world that lies far beyond its normal faculties of visualization. The Nibelungen film is intended to serve this very German *Volk* as its singer, its storytelling poet of the self. Viewing calmly, the *Volk* should accept the gift, and in receiving it, should experience and thus regain what is for it—the *Volk* in its entirety—but a dim memory: a hymn in celebration of unconditional loyalty.[62]

It is hard to know where to start unraveling such overwrought and pandering claims. Let us begin with the notion of an enchained longing for adventure. As we have seen, this film presents the rise of an unabashed and uninhibited heroic adventurer—and yet it also presents his fall. The account of that rise and fall is prefabricated for visual consumption. That is, while the *Nibelungenlied* enabled (or, in Harbou's eyes, required) the reader to construct an image of its world and its inhabitants, the Nibelungen film does so on the viewer's behalf. The image comes ready-made because the audience is too exhausted to construct it. This visual exhaustion is at once a blessing and a curse. On the one hand, it means that the Germans are eager for visual stimulation, for heroic adventure. And yet on the other hand, their exhaustion leaves them open to exploitation, to an onslaught of outsiders or cinematic carpetbaggers who would take it upon themselves to exploit that weakness and dupe—even hoodwink—a vulnerable, enchained audience. Harbou makes clear that the Nibelungen film would never dupe its audience (after all, it's dedicated to the German *Volk*); instead, it will serve the people by providing them with the image they can no longer muster. But in the process, it will outline the perils of this loss of control over visual production, with Siegfried serving as the unwitting (because unwittingly disempowered) visual subject. Thus, the film allegorizes its own project, presenting its audience with an allegorical rendering of the perils of being provided with the image they themselves cannot muster. And yet in doing so, it is supposedly doing something else.

Harbou does not present the film as a gift of vision; instead, she presents it as a gift of national epic recitation: as she puts it, the film "is intended to serve this very German *Volk* as its singer, its storytelling poet of the self."[63] The film would occupy much more than the place of visual imagination; it would take on the role of speaking and singing for the people, and not just any people, but specifically the German *Volk*. But how would it do so, especially given the fact that it is a silent film?

Another article from 1924 offers a preliminary response. According to Lang, the language of the age is film: "Each century has possessed some sort of language in which the educated people of all lands could communicate. Film is the Esperanto of the entire world—and a great cultural tool. One needs no more than two open eyes in order to comprehend its language."[64] Part of Lang's polemic in this article has to do with an ongoing debate concerning the cultural aspirations of cinema: thus, he invokes "educated people" as film's implicit audience and describes film as a "great cultural tool."[65] But embedded within the claim to culture is a claim about film language. For Lang, to speak in film is to speak in images, and if a film is to speak for and to the people, it can replace words—the outmoded language of literature—with the modern syntax of images "spoken" in film. These images, as Lang suggests, are easily comprehended by anyone with two open eyes. But comprehension is not production: if film is the language of the world, who can *speak* it? And how is it spoken? In assuming the role of *singer* and *poet*, this film would become a visual spokesperson for the German people, envisioning on their behalf. In a narrow sense, the production process of film explains, even necessitates some form of split between active and passive vision: while everyone can understand the new language of film, only few can

produce it. But who is doing the producing? In the early 1920s, the nation's filmic storytellers and singers were not necessarily of the *Volk*, by
the *Volk*, and for the *Volk*. The Nibelungen film responds to this state of
affairs and makes it the stuff of representation.

CONTAINING FOREIGN FILM: VOLKER'S CINEMA

At various points, the notion of seeing in place of singing and
storytelling is transposed into the film itself. We have already considered
one such scene: in the film's first song, the storyteller at Mime's grotto
provided his cronies with a tale—and Siegfried with a vision—of Kriemhild and the Burgundian court. That story dissolved into and thus took
the form of a filmic image. In the following song, the listless court of
Burgundy hears the court singer Volker's song recounting Siegfried's exploits. I will examine the contents of this song in greater detail below; for
now I would like to focus on its form. The second song opens on the
Burgundian court, and when Volker begins singing *his* song (also *Ge-
sang*), the image dissolves into the contents of that song—a highly selec-
tive account of Siegfried's adventures following his impromptu shower
in the dragon's blood. Here, the filmic apparatus is structurally aligned
with Volker (who serves as the diegetic anchor for the image and appears
with his back to the camera[66]) and the viewer is aligned with the Burgundian nobility (who constitute the song's on-screen audience). Indeed, the
structural alignment is supplemented by an analogy on the level of representation, since the apparent exhaustion of the Burgundian nobility
could be said to mirror the exhaustion that Harbou attributes to the German *Volk*.

Dramaturgically, the scene represents a companion piece to the scene
of envisioning presented in the first song: while that first scene aroused
Siegfried's desire for Kriemhild, this one will arouse Kriemhild's desire
for him. Unlike the corresponding scene in the first song, which offered
a brief and unanchored snippet of life at the Burgundian court,[67] in this
scene the production of the image is firmly anchored and the tale is
much more fully fledged. That is, the events presented on screen are
explicitly linked to Volker's song and the song offers a rather elaborate
tale. Let us first consider the link between the scene and Volker's song.
The intertitle that bridges the dissolve from the Burgundian court (where

Volker sings) to the eerie, barren landscape of the tree where Alberich is hiding (the subject of his song) links the song to the image. The scene described in the song matches the scene we are given to see: "Then Volker sang. The violin resounded: the dragon-slayer, Siegmund's son, entered the realm of the Nibelungen. In battle he, the dragon slayer, won something unequaled on earth."[68] But what exactly does Siegfried "win"? The song will show us: he gains a victory over Alberich, plus the magic cap and the Nibelungen treasure. And yet we have seen how he gains much more and much less.

The scene's conclusion—the memorable iris-out on Siegfried pompously holding Balmung aloft—also concludes Volker's song: thus we are returned to the Burgundian court. This marks the conclusion of the *mise-en-abyme*—the film interpolated within the film. For its part, the mini-scene of Alberich's projection (within Volker's song) provides a *mise-en-abyme* within the *mise-en-abyme*. Volker's account opens the song, in turn dissolving into film, and in due course that film shows us Alberich's film magically projected onto the wall of the subterranean passage. Both of these sublevels are, of course, presented within the film, further redoubling the *mise-en-abyme*, for Lang's film shows us Volker's song on film of the Nibelungen king's account on film of the Nibelungen hard at work on a crown. What are the implications of these formal contortions?

From all we have seen of him, Alberich is the visual and dramaturgical opposite of Siegfried: Alberich is hysterical, Siegfried is calm; Alberich is scheming, Siegfried is naive; Alberich is weak, Siegfried is strong. Here again we encounter the binary formula that I noted earlier in this chapter. As in the first song, Siegfried's positive qualities are brought out in juxtaposition to a negative value: there it was Mime, here it is Alberich. And as in that earlier example, the appearance of greatness—encapsulated in Siegfried's emphatically heroic stance in the final shot of the scene—deceives. For Siegfried's attractive heroism is produced at the cost of visual acumen. In both scenes, his actions are the product of naive vision. Siegfried is both the hero who seduces and the naive viewer who is seduced. How can we distinguish between these roles? And how can we make sense of them?

In framing the scene of Alberich's magic projection within a further filmic frame, the film juxtaposes Alberich's corruption with Siegfried's naiveté, while it also juxtaposes Alberich's form of cinema with

Volker's. In this sense, Alberich's film (screened especially for Siegfried) will also serve to embody what Volker's film (featuring Siegfried's adventures) is not.

What distinguishes Alberich's film from Volker's? First, they are distinguished by different forms of narrative appeal. Alberich's film—generically, it would have to be called a 'short subject'—dazzles Siegfried, but the story it tells is of limited appeal: the Nibelungen are forging a crown. Here, the spectacle of the crown's production is not marshaled in the service of a narrative: the film does not tell a compelling story, it simply amazes Siegfried by appearing magically on the wall. Volker's account, on the other hand, has a clear narrative trajectory and a coherent purpose—in showing us Siegfried's exploits, it offers Kriemhild, the court, and us a sustained introduction to his accomplishments and his character. In filling the time (on what would appear to be a rather dull day at the Burgundian court) it fills in some of the narrative gaps between Siegfried's bath in the dragon's blood and his arrival at Worms.

At the same time, both films would appear to be organizing desire: Kriemhild thus desires the dashing hero at the conclusion of Volker's "film" while Siegfried ends up desiring . . . Balmung (in lieu of the apparatus). The rest of *Siegfried* will show us that Siegfried's desire was misplaced—or rather, flawed. The new German hero cannot simply be dashing and strong. He must be perspicacious, cultivating a gaze that is at once penetrating and impenetrable. There are two key components to the critical vision envisioned here (both of which happen to be embodied by Hagen). One involves erecting and maintaining a critical distance from profilmic events (the ability to control one's desire for the image). The other involves the ability to control one's own appearance (the ability to envision and maintain control over how one is seen).

This distinction between the two films becomes meaningful in the context of the discourse of national cinematic difference in the early 1920s, where American cinema is repeatedly accused of offering up unmotivated and senselessly lavish spectacle while the Germans are supposedly masters of character motivation and dramaturgical economy. Volker's film is a model of narrative clarity: it offers a coherent opening and closing, and a linear tale in between. The scene depicted in Alberich's film does not have a recognizable beginning, middle, or end. Indeed, nothing really transpires over the course of the film beyond the fact of the work depicted. In this way, the dramatic insubstantiality of the scene is doubled by its formal insubstantiality. Finally, as we have seen, Alberich's film seems unduly materialistic: it is not merely a lavish spectacle (which would be bad enough), rather it offers accumulated wealth or lavishness itself as spectacle.

This leads us to a second point of comparison between the two "films," their reception. The frame surrounding the two scenes of filmic production is comparable: we see the film itself, as well as the response of its audience. As we know, Siegfried is mesmerized by Alberich's brief snippet. Alberich observes Siegfried's naive distractibility and will try—unsuccessfully—to capitalize on it as soon as they get down to the Nibelungen treasure. We might say that Alberich produces the image in order to monitor its effects on Siegfried.

Volker's film is not produced for the same reason but it functions in the same way. The intertitle indicates that Volker's song is performed for Kriemhild.[69] Kriemhild is evidently moved by Volker's account—as a gesture of thanks, she gives the minstrel a lavish cloak she has been knitting. And although the song's intertitle informs us that Volker sang to Kriemhild, he did not sing for her alone. Thus we are shown Hagen's response as well: he glares at Kriemhild immediately before and after Volker's recitation. What are we to make of this? Kriemhild is presumably charmed by the depiction of Siegfried much as Siegfried was enchanted by the depiction of Kriemhild in the storyteller's account in the first song: both of them respond readily to the affective sweep of narrative. Hagen responds to the song quite differently: he monitors its effects on Kriemhild and is thus in a position to observe her budding interest in the romantic hero. In this sense, his mode of viewing could be described as functional and dispassionate. Instead of identifying with the image, Hagen identifies the traces of identification. And yet Kriemhild is not the only one to display traces of identification in this song. Any critical viewer of the scene of Alberich's projection—and the film presents Hagen as just such a viewer—will have observed that Siegfried is entirely too fascinated by the image. Like Alberich, Hagen will seek to capitalize on Siegfried's relationship to viewing and the apparatus; unlike Alberich, he will succeed. But Hagen does not merely take advantage of Siegfried's proclivities as a viewer. Beyond that, Hagen himself embodies a distinct and ultimately victorious alternative: a purposeful, grounded, perspicacious mode (that includes but is not limited to a mode of vision), one that serves as a model for *The Nibelungen* as well as the Nibelungen—for the film and for the Burgundians depicted within it.

HAGEN AND NATIONAL CINEMA

The distinction between Hagen and Siegfried is a distinction on the level of affect. According to the reigning discourse of appeal in mainstream film during the early- to mid-twenties, Siegfried is immediately legible as a seductive, appealing figure while Hagen is not. Indeed, Hagen looks much more like Alberich than like Siegfried, and yet his appeal is entirely different. For the film distinguishes between its bad objects: while Alberich is properly a bad object (embodying that which the film would disavow), Hagen is only apparently a bad object (embodying that which the film will ultimately celebrate). Indeed, Hagen will emerge as the precious kernel contained in a bad-object shell (along the lines of Clint Eastwood's Dirty Harry): he looks like a bad guy and acts like a bad guy, but in the end, he is shown to be a dedicated servant, the "truest of the true," as Kriemhild ironically labels him. But true to what cause? Obviously not to Siegfried. So how can Hagen emerge as the film hero, begrudged as he is? In order for him to do so, we have to swallow the lesson he embodies, the film's lesson in critical spectatorship.

On the most obvious level, Hagen serves as the embodiment of the principles that the film would celebrate: unconditional loyalty to his master. The film inflects this appeal in film-historical terms: insofar as Hagen's appeal is out of date, it is shown to have little currency—in being old-fashioned, he is a noticeably unappealing screen presence. In that sense, the oldest German values are rescued for the screen by being rescued from it: according to the logic of the film, the newfangled values, including the notion of screen appeal—formulated in Hollywood and embodied in its German incarnation by Siegfried—have great if superficial appeal. But the more lasting (German) values *predate* Hollywood's formula for cinematic appeal: their appeal resides in their refusal to yield to the dictates of appeal. Hagen, then, is appealing in part due to his marked lack of appeal: he looks scruffy, dark, and sinister. His actions are as unappealing as his looks: his plot to kill Siegfried is methodical and graceless. And yet, while the film inflects his famous stab in the back as a betrayal of Siegfried, it does not render Hagen a villain. Rather, in this work—as in a host of other renderings of the Nibelungen material, including, most famously, Hebbel's two-part play—Hagen acts in defense of his master's honor. The true German hero does what he has to do despite the fact that he may not look good doing it—indeed, he may not look good at all.

Here, then, we encounter a cinematic inflection of mid-twenties German nationalism: instead of outstripping Hollywood on its own turf, the film stakes out its own affective territory. A blond, strapping hero may be fine and good for all he's worth—and as long as the currency of Babelsberg is minted in Hollywood, he's worth a great deal—but in the end, (which is to say, in the battle to protect the king's honor—but also, in the battle to protect the honor of indigenous film) it is not looks but deeds and dedication that count. The law of the father has no need for niceties: it may not be pretty, but it is and remains effective. And as its first officer, Hagen is the privileged embodiment of its program. In this case, that program involves a platform of antiaffect that necessitates as it explains a practice of critical, dispassionate viewing. Put in terms of its pedagogical imperative, the film suggests that we must unlearn Siegfried's naive and seductive appeal—which is reiterated in his naive relationship to the image—in favor of that most unappealing (because long-established) of national virtues: critical distance and (what amounts to the same thing) upstanding, unquestioning, and unrelenting loyalty.

Marking Siegfried's Vulnerability

If the *Lindenblattstelle* is nature's mark of Siegfried's physical vulnerability, Alberich and his crystal ball mark his filmic vulnerability, embodying the fact of Siegfried's naive interest in the image and his lack of interest in gaining control over its production. As I have suggested, the two are related: as a naive viewer he shows himself to be easily manipulable by Hagen's stronger, savvier vision; in overlooking the crystal ball, he cedes control over the production of the image—and therewith his life—to Hagen. As a relentlessly astute viewer, Hagen sees through Siegfried's powers and will manipulate them with steely purposiveness—indeed, with the steely purposiveness of the new national cinema. And when Siegfried has been dispensed with, the film will record—and celebrate—the *Nibelungentreue* of his companions: the unyielding allegiance of the Burgundians to the cause of his defense.[70]

This recalls von Harbou's hopes for the film, expressed in her essay "Vom Epos zum Film." As she puts it, the people should receive the work as a gift, watch it calmly, "and in receiving it, the people should experience and thus regain what is for them . . . but a dim memory: the hymn of unconditional loyalty."[71] But unconditional loyalty to what? Most immediately, of course, she means the unconditional loyalty among the brothers of the Burgundian court. But the *Nibelungentreue* invoked here extends beyond loyalty in a familial or national sense to encompass loyalty to the vision of that loyalty. The unconditional loyalty to Hagen (who is, after all, the principal beneficiary of *Nibelungentreue* at the conclusion of *Siegfried*) could be said to extend beyond the diegesis to incorporate an unconditional loyalty to what he represents. Surely Hagen has done wrong in killing Siegfried (Gunther admits as much in the film's final song). But *Nibelungentreue* defends to the death the agreement among brothers. As Hagen embodies some key features of a new Germanic cinema, *Nibelungentreue* also comes to mean *Nibelungen-Treue*; that is, fidelity to the vision that he embodies. For his perceptions and actions have cinematic currency: in slaying Siegfried, he slays, in a sense, a *cinematic* half-brother—an all-too-powerful, attractive, appealing, and naive brother; one who gains his limited powers over appearance and disappearance from a dubious source and then proves all too willing to put those powers at the disposal of a more powerful figure.

In the previous chapters of this study, I sought to show how in other versions of the Nibelungen tale, the act of narration marks the hero's vulnerability, implicating the medium in the crime. Thus, for example, in the *Nibelungenlied*, speaking the tale was the project of the epic and the act that enabled the crime recounted there. In Wagner's *Ring*, the insistent return of narration dogs the tetralogy and ultimately undoes its hero. Here, the shift to film generates no less ambivalence about the project of recounting. Siegfried's confrontation with Alberich offers one instance of that ambivalence: a scene where the medium depicts itself in thrall to a character who is not merely unattractive, but who is plotting against the hero. As such, we might say that Alberich serves the film as Siegfried serves Hagen. While Siegfried repeatedly does the dirty work of dissimulation at Hagen's behest, Alberich does the film's dirty work, embodying control over a cinema that the film must project in order to disavow. If Alberich concocts a cinema of attractions, and Siegfried comes to the Burgundian court bearing some but not all of its means, then Hagen stands in for and defends a different, more turgid aesthetic identity: less spectacular but more methodical; less immediately appealing but more powerful in the end.

In having Siegfried walk away with the sword and without the crystal ball, the film opens up an explanation for Siegfried's fall, a way to trace his downfall back to the moment when, given the possibility of taking the genre into his own hands, he passed. That route would seem to lead to suspects still at large. For although Kriemhild will eventually avenge Hagen's treachery and Hildebrandt will avenge hers, the film hardly suggests that their vengeance is satisfactory. As I have argued here, Hagen's crime against Siegfried is not merely the result of a diegetic competition for standing and power. Instead, their competition allegorizes a larger and still unresolved competition, one that involves the merely implicit question of who controls appearance *in film*. Since the crystal ball was left in Alberich's hands in *Siegfried* and since all of the leading characters except Dietrich von Bern are dead by the conclusion of *Kriemhild's Revenge*, who is left to inherit the crystal ball? It is a question that the film leaves unresolved on the diegetic level; and yet, by implication, Siegfried falls not just at Hagen's hands, but at the hands of his wily proto-cinematic machinations. And those machinations deprive Siegfried of powers he himself bears—if only incompletely and unconsciously.

For when Siegfried wins the battle he loses the war: in vanquishing Alberich, he gains access to power over the apparatus, but fails to recognize that he has done so and thus fails to capitalize on the situation. At the same time the very qualities that make him desirable as a screen hero—his spirit of romance and adventure, his ready distractibility, his unabashed naiveté—will contribute to his undoing. Hagen is able to manipulate both—Siegfried's character traits and his powers over appearance. In the process, the vision that Hagen embodies—which is at once a vision of character and a vision of cinema—wins out. And Hollywood's loss is Germany's gain, for the Nibelungen, like *The Nibelungen*, are supposed to remain true to the very bitter end—true to each other and true to the cause of properly grounded character and a disciplined, unsentimental control over appearances.

Postscript

Disavowal and Figuration

THE NIBELUNGEN AFTER THE THIRD REICH

Disavowal ≠ Denial

In HIS 1927 PAPER ON "FETISHISM," Freud takes R. Laforgue to task for employing a new term—scotomization—where in Freud's eyes an old term would have done just fine. "It is necessary," he points out somewhat heatedly, "to introduce a new term when new developments warrant it: that is not the case here."[1] The "case here" involves the perception of lack and the need to differentiate between the psychic responses that it occasions. In order to clarify the problem, Freud invokes a compelling and familiar scene: the little boy who must come to terms with the lack that he perceives in the genital anatomy of the little girl. According to Freud, the boy's perception can produce a host of different responses, including differences in the register of affect and idea. Freud associates the affective response to the threat of lack with *repression*, while he links the idea or representation of lack with *disavowal*:

> If we want to differentiate more clearly between the vicissitude of the representation or idea [*Vorstellung*] in fetishism as distinct from the vicissitude of the affect in fetishism and reserve the term *Verdrängung* ("repression") for the affective component, then the correct German expression for the vicissitude of the representation would be *Verleugnung* ("disavowal").[2]

Freud's terminological self-assurance is somewhat disingenuous. While the term *Verleugnung* appeared with increasing frequency in his work beginning in 1923, its meaning did not stabilize for a few years. The confusion results in part from the conceptual proximity of disavowal to denial, a proximity that also, at times, produces a certain amount of overlap. Translations have tended to affirm the overlap by fudging the distinction: in some English editions of Freud's work, *Verleugnung* is translated as denial.[3] Not so in the *Standard Edition*. There, James Strachey consistently translates *Verleugnung* as disavowal, but this too leads to complications, since there are times, especially in the early 1920s, when Freud's inflection of disavowal encompasses some aspects of denial.[4] According to Michael Franz Basch, the term stabilizes by 1925. In Freud's paper "Some Psychical Consequences of the Anatomical Distinction Between the Sexes," published in that year, the same scene—of the little boy confronted by anatomical lack—seems to serve a similar purpose. Here, disavowal designates an operation of figuration, where the determination to overcome trauma results in a creative refusal: "when a little boy first catches sight of a girl's genital region, he begins by showing irresolution and lack of interest; he sees nothing or *disavows* his perception, he attenuates it, looks about for explanations so as to bring it into line with his expectations."[5] This recourse to creative figuration—encapsulated in the variety of responses Freud itemizes: seeing nothing, attenuating the perception, looking about for reassuring explanations—is an early and recurring attribute of disavowal, one of the means to distinguish it from simple denial in the Freudian lexicon.

In the preceding chapters, I have sought to take seriously the scenario of disavowal that Freud proposes: first, the recognition of lack and then the recourse to figuration that follows upon—and would compensate for—it. In the Nibelungen works we have considered and in Freud's various discussions of disavowal, a scene of perception—usually, a perception of lack—in turn produces a practice of compensatory figuration. Thus, in the above account, the little boy disavows the recognition of lack by constructing an alternative account.[6] The same is true for the fetishist: the absence is redeemed by an act of refiguration. In Wagner's tetralogy and Lang's film, the etiology of lack differs, but it finds expression in similar ways: in their works as in many of the scenes Freud recounts, the recourse to figuration involves an aesthetic process that in turn becomes the stuff of representation. That is, the disavowal does not just produce a simple figuration (such as the fetishist figures a nose or a foot), but the figuration is self-reflexive. It is a rather complicated point that deserves to be explained.

Consider the patient whose fetish takes the form of a "shine on the nose" [Glanz auf der Nase].[7] Freud famously reads the formulation as a bilingual allusion to the fetishist's original "glance" (an English homonym of the German Glanz) at the nose. For Freud, the fetish refigures—through the flimsiest of interlinguistic mediations—the glance by which the patient would disavow the revelation of lack.[8] The little boy, confronted with mother's genitals, gazed upwards to find the vision of fullness in—or more precisely, on the nose. This creative act of refiguration—where the nose comes to stand in for and relieve the traumatic perception of lack induced by the genitals—is then literalized, albeit cryptically, as an interlinguistic homonym. Thus, the disavowal takes the form of a figuration (in language) of a figuration (whereby the nose comes to stand in for the perceived lack). The fetishist's predilection for a "shine" on the nose re-marks the attributes of the fetish in language: it alludes to the physiological translation of the missing genitals into a nose, and then renders that translation in translation (naming the glance as a Glanz).[9]

The same process is at work in Wagner and Lang, although the figuration in their works is somewhat more elaborate. Thus, the disavowal in the Ring and in Lang's Die Nibelungen is not simply interesting for taking aesthetic form, but for the aesthetic form it takes. In both works, Siegfried, the flawed hero, is particularly flawed when it comes to the process of his self-figuration. In Wagner, Siegfried's relationship to narration reiterates a flaw in the work; in Lang, his relationship to vision and visual technologies dramatizes a flaw in contemporary cinematic culture. In both, the flaw figures the lack that haunts the work. But while disavowal in the case of the fetishist who treasures the glance on the nose produces a desired object to stand in for—and ward off—the traumatic recognition, the disavowal in Lang and Wagner produces a bad object, namely the Jew. As we have seen, that bad object embodies the bad aesthetic practices that the work seeks to dispense with.

If, within these works, Siegfried's flaw is educed in the service of a greater cause (such as King Gunther's honor in the epic and the film, or Hagen's plot in the Ring), we could say that the figure of the Jew is educed in the service of the work, in order to give material form to otherwise amorphous and invariably undesirable aesthetic positions. For the artist, the bad object is one that poses the threat of aesthetic dissolution or disintegration. This is why I have insisted that it is not enough to seek out the traces of aggression on the level of *content*: we need to account for the transposition of that aggression into aesthetics. For Wagner *the man*, there were plenty of—for us, familiar—objects of rage and aggression. For Wagner *the artist*, the objects of rage and aggression are less familiar: one of them, in the *Ring*, involves narration. Thus, Mime as Jew stands in as the embodiment of bad-faith narration, as its privileged agent, in order then to be expelled from the work along with his aesthetic baggage. For Lang as a filmmaker, the undesirable element involves control over visual production and identification. By presenting Alberich as Jew disposing over the medium and Siegfried as hero enthralled by Alberich's cinematic product, Lang poses the question of who controls the cinematic image and to what end. Here, Alberich's annihilation does not resolve the question. Indeed, in both works, the residual bad aesthetics of the expelled bad object continue to haunt the diegesis and eventually contribute to the hero's death. Thus, in the Nibelungen film, Siegfried is undone by Hagen's exceedingly acute vision, and in *The Ring*, Siegfried is killed when Hagen induces him to repeat his life story. In both cases, Siegfried is crucially shown to be subordinated to the means of his representation. The fantasmatic Jew is presented as the figure who exercises control over that representation.

The legacy of National Socialism has generated a heightened sensitivity to the politics of aesthetic fantasy in contemporary Germany. This is not to say that the fantasy of the Jew who appropriates and controls representation has disappeared in Germany (or, for that matter, in the United States). But the explicit terms of that fantasy have been largely forbidden and in its place other, less explicit scenarios have arisen. In recent years, the very notion of a single figure pulling strings has yielded to a more amorphous sense of representation as a kind of entangling force, a discursive webbing.

Thus, when Siegfried is presented as radically incapacitated in Frank Castorf's account at the Volksbühne, he is riven less by a Jewish figure pulling the strings behind the scenes than by a vague, anonymous force of representation that at once makes him and overwhelms him. Here, then, Castorf derives his dramaturgical orientation from Oliver Stone's rather pat critique of the mass media in *Natural Born Killers*. The television monitors on Castorf's stage do not simply appeal to the younger crowds and distract from Siegfried's predicament. In addition, they frame his disorientation in a nebulous realm of representation, situating him in a by-now formulaic, willfully postmodern space of mediation. Eventually, in Castorf's vision, Siegfried will die under the weight of his accumulated mediations. The figure of the Jew has disappeared here, and for obvious historical reasons. But it seems important to note that the logic that produces the Jew remains largely intact. Thus, while no single figure is behind the scenes, pulling the strings of Siegfried's mediation, Castorf's model of an anonymous, totalizing mediation does not foreclose the question of who—if anyone—controls that mediation: it simply leaves it unaddressed. The fact that the forces of mediation have been rendered anonymous does not render them any less problematic as an explanatory model.

There are alternatives. Indeed, a number of contemporary works have further retooled the Nibelungen material. They have often done so out of a sense that the celebration of German heroism is a dicey matter in the wake of the Third Reich. Thus, these works evince a determination not to reiterate—or, for that matter, simply invert—the structures of fascist hero worship. In closing, I would like to examine one such work, Michael Verhoeven's 1989 film *The Nasty Girl*.[10]

THE NASTY GIRL

Verhoeven's film begins rather abruptly, with a series of short sequences. After a brief initial scene of a drunken fellow swinging a beer mug and bellowing a football team cheer, we are presented with two brief texts on screen, introducing the film. The first is signed by the filmmaker, and alludes to the circumstances that led to the film's production; the second is read aloud by a woman who remains off-screen. Eventually, we will come to recognize the voice as that of Sonja Rosenberger, the heroine of the film.[11] The lines she recites are printed on the screen as she intones them. They are, by now, familiar:

> uns ist in alten mæren
> wunders vil geseit

von helden lobebæren,
von grôzer arebeit.
von fröuden, hôchgezîten,
von weinen und von klagen,
von küener recken strîten
muget ir nu wunder hoeren sagen.

[We have been told in ancient tales many marvels of famous
heroes, of mighty toil, joys, and high festivities, of weeping and
wailing, and the fighting of bold warriors—of such things you
can now hear wonders unending!]¹²

The recitation has a tinge of impish irreverence, a quality that will
mark the film in general and, more particularly, Sonja's character. The
irreverent tone is especially surprising since the film deals with extremely charged material: German history during and after National Socialism, the mass psychology of denial, and individual as well as collective responsibility for the crimes of the past. This is not normally the
stuff of light parody—certainly not in German film. Nor for that matter,
is it normally the stuff of the *Nibelungenlied*. It is, initially at least, hard
to "place" the *Nibelungenlied* in the film, hard to know how to read it.
If there has been a proper place for such a recitation since the middle of
the nineteenth century, it has been with the rather volatile forces of
right-wing German nationalism, forces that are embodied on-screen by
the beer-guzzling fan from the opening scene.

The stanza from the *Nibelungenlied* seems particularly apt since its
valence is initially so inscrutable. Thus the viewer is necessarily disori-
ented by the juxtaposition: whence the contiguity of the football fan and
the epic? And why the *Nibelungenlied*? The ambiguity of valence is re
inforced by an ambiguity of reference within the stanza: to return to a
question posed in the first chapter, what are the "earlier tales" alluded to
here? Two possibilities come to mind, one involving an ironization of
the epic, the other involving an updating of its tales. Let us begin with
the ironic reading. In the course of the film, the "ancient tales we have
been told" gain an apparent—and ironic—analog in the long-established
tales of heroism and resistance in the annals of Sonja's hometown during
the Third Reich.¹³ Sonja will interrogate and eventually debunk those
"ancient tales." In the process, she arguably debunks the use to which
the *Nibelungenlied* itself has so often been put—namely, to spur on defenders of the nation to imitate the deeds of heroism it depicts. She will

contest its traditional address by appropriating and recasting its message. Thus, the import of her purported "nastiness" becomes clear. In having her recite the national epic, the film figures the threat that she will embody: the threat to interrogate and recast signifiers of the nation's identity. In the process of ironization, the citation could be said to re-inflect and reinvigorate the epic. For thus retooled, the epic gains vi-brancy and relevance as an ironic commentary on its own claims.

But we can also read the citation in terms of the politics of its presen-tation: after all, it is recited here by the film's heroine. As the film un-folds, it positions Sonja as the subject of the exploits alluded to in the opening stanza. In this sense, the epic's vibrancy would derive from the recasting of its adventures in contemporary terms. The film will show a latter-day rendering of "many marvels," of "mighty toil," and of "weep-ing and wailing, and the fighting of bold warriors." So: an updating. But what would be the implications of such an updating? First, it suggests a structural similarity between Sonja's tale in the film and Siegfried's tale in the epic, insofar as she would emerge as the film's adventurer-heroine. But if she is aligned with Siegfried's heroism, how then does the film inflect her relation to representation? It is this analogy that I would like to explore.

It may be useful to recount the plot of the film. As a child, Sonja was a model student at school and a model daughter at home, and the film makes clear that her goodness at the time was even somewhat nauseat-ing. After winning a national high-school essay contest with what is pre-sumably a very "proper" essay on the topic of "Freedom in Europe," Sonja decides to enter a second essay contest, this time on the topic "My Town in the Third Reich." And although she sets out to document how exemplary her hometown of Pfilzing—and especially the church—was in resisting the Nazis, she very quickly runs into a massive and previ-ously invisible brick wall: none of the older people in her town can recall anything about the time, except that the former mayor, now deceased, had been an awful Nazi. The more resistance Sonja encounters, the more determined she becomes, and the more determined she becomes, the more resistance she encounters. Unable to get at the relevant files from the town archives or the newspaper archives, she sues in order to gain access to both. When she wins, she still can't get at the files; so she sues again and wins again, only to be told that the files are unavailable or too fragile to be viewed. Perceived as having declared war on her town's past, Sonja is the object of rage and resentment: she receives a slew of threatening phone calls, her apartment is bombed, masked men throw a brick through the back window of her car as she and her husband drive off from church after their wedding. Finally, through various ruses, Sonja gains fleeting access to some of the most damaging files, and eventually denounces Herr Juckenack, editor of the town's newspaper, who is also a history professor at the university where Sonja has recently enrolled.[14] When it becomes clear that the town is risking its reputation by continuing to ostracize and harass the young woman while defending Juckenack, the tide suddenly turns and he becomes the villain while she becomes the town hero, celebrated for her courage and perseverance.

SONJA AS REFUSENIK

As the film reveals Sonja's heroism, it ironizes it, through the sudden and repeated shifts in her fortunes. As a young girl in school, Sonja is a good object, repeatedly invoked by her grandmother and her teachers as a model worthy of imitation and praise. But when she persists in her determination to discover what transpired in Pfilzing during the Third Reich, she becomes a political and social pariah—a bad object. But then her status shifts again, from outcast and villain to heroine. Thus: once again, a good object. The film makes clear that there is an increasing level of hypocrisy and conceptual violence attending each of these identities. The process culminates in a scene set at the town hall where Sonja is celebrated and enshrined as the town turns again in her favor.

It is not especially surprising that Sonja rejects this enshrinement, although it is jolting to those who have to watch—that is, the film's two audiences, on-screen and in the auditorium. Her refusal, however, is particularly interesting for our purposes, as it crystallizes her relationship to the process of her own figuration, a problem encountered repeatedly in the production of the flawed hero in Wagner, Lang, and the medieval epic. To demonstrate how this is so, we may consider the film's concluding scene.

The town has commissioned a bust of Sonja, which is to be unveiled at a ceremony honoring her at the town hall. Everyone has turned out for the ceremony: Sonja's family is there—her parents and grandmother, her siblings, and her two daughters—as are many of the officials and citizens who had previously vilified her with such gusto. The mayor hosts the

event and the master of ceremonies is the new, young editor of the Pfilzing paper (Herr Juckenack, the former editor, has been sacked in the
wake of Sonja's revelations). When Sonja steps forward and unveils the
bust, the film suddenly veers from its naturalistic tracks. This is not the
first time it has done so: indeed, Verhoeven frequently resorts to a variety of comical Brechtian techniques, including especially a radical disjunction between foreground and background settings.[15] Here, however,
the disjunction is less comical than mimetic, figuring Sonja's alienation
from the events surrounding her. As she examines the bust, the film
shifts into slow motion and an exaggerated blue filter while the on-
screen audience's applause resounds jarringly and artificially on the
soundtrack. When, after a few moments, the film reverts to full color and
real time, Sonja turns on the assembled audience, insisting, with astonishing fury, upon her refusal: she will not allow herself to be muzzled by
their ceremonial celebration of her, she will not fall for it.[16] In a particularly harrowing scene, Sonja and the situation spin out of control: she
slaps her mother and swats at her grandmother, her father faints, her
daughters scream, the mayor storms out, and once again, the towns-
people curse her.

The terms of Sonja's harangue are particularly noteworthy, since they
bear upon the aesthetic and psychological politics of the Nibelungen
works we have been considering. In those works, Siegfried's pointed ig-
norance produces his unwitting subordination to his mediation. As a
result, he is easy prey for a master of mediation. In Verhoeven's film, on
the other hand, Sonja intervenes in order to block just such a subordination. To align her gesture with the citation of the *Nibelungenlied* from
the outset of the film, we could say that Sonja refuses to assume a place
as narrated object, except, of course, the place of that refusal. The scene
stages her attempt to wrest her status from the realm of lifeless aesthetic
reproduction (as sculpted bust) back to the realm of living person.[17] The
terms of the threat confronting Sonja arc clear: as sculpted heroine, she
will be silent and thus silenced, petrified and thus prettified. As unfixed
live person she can remain irritating because unpredictable and mobile.
Her status in the psychic economy of the town hangs in the balance as
well: as sculpted bust, she can resume her status as good object, whereas
her unpredictability renders her, once again, a bad object.

The Nasty Girl proposes a dramaturgy of disavowal in reverse. In Wagner and Lang, the aspiration to a totalizing representation produces the
need for an object that does not belong. In their works, the role of the

societal bad object is conflated with the role of the aesthetic bad object. That is, the scheming, unappealing character comes to bear aesthetic qualities that the work seeks to disavow. Sonja here produces *herself* as that bad object, insisting on the integrity of an identity as social pariah and the corresponding corruption underlying an identity as celebrated heroine. There is an aesthetic correlative to this refusal, as Sonja refuses her enshrinement as sculpted object. (The choice of sculpture is somewhat obvious, since it threatens to freeze her accomplishments and her persona *in stone*.[18]) But rather than lambaste that refusal of heroization and figuration, Verhoeven's film celebrates it, suggesting that the object of reverence is just as worthy of suspicion as the object of rage, that both serve as objects of projection and misrecognition. The work intervenes on behalf of the integrity of the bad object, in opposition to the production of the good object. If Sonja is the Enemy of the People as good object, then the bad object would have to be her sculpted bust as Town Heroine.

Sonja is presented as resisting her enshrinement within the work. In that sense, her intervention occurs on the level of figuration: in disallowing that enshrinement, she thematizes the danger of her reification through figuration. This sort of self-consciousness is never accorded Siegfried, who remains forever naive to the means of production through mediation, which is also to say—*his* production. In what is admittedly a slightly predictable valorization of transgression, Sonja emerges as heroic by virtue of her steadfast and savvy refusal of heroism. Sonja's resistance to her celebration and enshrinement inverts the scenario of Siegfried's naivete, for it zeros in on the moment of the hero's emergence and fixes it with a certain refusal. We might characterize this as a refusal of disavowal, a refusal of a reassuring refiguration that would render Sonja more appealing because less threatening. In the process, Sonja refuses a fantasmatic identity that contributes to the pathos of Siegfried's identity—namely, as a martyr to representation, which is also to say, a martyr to *her own* representation. Of course, Siegfried never accedes to this position of media consciousness. The tale of his subordination, told and retold in Wagner and Lang, is refigured in Verhoeven's film as an avowal of the political stakes of representation.

Notes

1. For a lavishly illustrated account of Gielen's work in Frankfurt, see Mara Eggert and Hans-Klaus Jungheinrich, *Die Oper Frankfurt: Durchbrüche*.

Chapter One

1. Hebbel's *Die Nibelungen* is divided into two parts: *Siegfried's Death* and *Kriemhild's Revenge*. Castorf's production consolidated the two into a single work.

2. See Helmut Brackert, "Nibelungenlied und Nationalgedanke: Zur Geschichte einer deutschen Ideologie," in *Mediaevalia Litteraria*, 343–64; Otfrid Ehrismann, *Nibelungenlied in Deutschland*; Otfrid Ehrismann, "*Nibelungenlied* und Nationalgedanke: Zu Geschichte und Psychologie eines nationalen Identifikationsmusters," in *Damals* 12 (1980): 942–60, 1033–46; and *Damals* 13 (1981): 21–35, 115–32; Otfrid Ehrismann, *Nibelungenlied: Epoche—Werk—Wirkung*; Werner Wunderlich, *Der Schatz des Drachentödters*; Wolfgang Frühwald, "Wandlungen eines Nationalmythos: Der Weg der Nibelungen ins 19. Jahrhundert," in: *Wege des Mythos in der Moderne*, ed. Dieter Borchmeyer, 17–40; Herfried Münkler and Wolfgang Storch, *Siegfrieden*; and Joachim Heinzle and Anneliese Waldschmidt, *Die Nibelungen*.

3. Two works that have by now become canonical in this regard are Benedict Anderson's *Imagined Communities* and Homi K. Bhabha's *Nation and Narration*. A more recent study is Anthony Julius, *T. S. Eliot, Anti-Semitism, and Literary Form*.

4. Philippe Lacoue-Labarthe, *Musica Ficta*, 17.

5. Friedrich Heinrich von der Hagen, *Der Nibelungen Lied*, xi; my trans.

6. See note 1, above. While most scholars—including, for example, Brackert, Ehrismann, and Frühwald—locate the high point of Nibelungen fervor in the nineteenth century, Günther Hess argues that the high point in the mythologization of the Siegfried material came during the decade from 1923 to 1933. See Günther Hess, "Siegfrieds Wiederkehr: Zur Geschichte einer deutschen

Mythologie in der Weimarer Republik," in *Internationales Archiv für Sozialgeschichte der deutschen Literatur* 6 (Tübingen: 1981): 112–44, especially 113 and 134.

7. On the importance of this date for the origins of German nationalism, see Michael Hughes, *Nationalism and Society*, chapter 3.

8. Among the many works that consider this question, see, for example, Wolfgang Storch, *Die Nibelungen*; Wolfgang Storch, "Körper und Panzer," in Münkler and Storch, *Siegfrieden*, 18–47; sections III and IV of Heinzle and Waldschmidt, *Die Nibelungen*; chapter 5 of Ehrismann, *Nibelungenlied: Epoche— Werk—Wirkung*; Werner Wunderlich's *Der Schatz des Drachentödters*; and the essay by Frühwald.

9. The sparse list of narratological works includes Harald Burger, "Vorausdeutung und Erzählstruktur in mittelalterlichen Texten," in *Zeitgestaltung in der Erzählkunst*, ed. Alexander Ritter, 247–77; Marie-Elisabeth Tisdell, *Studien zur Erzählweise einiger mittelhochdeutscher Dichtungen*; Sister Mary Frances McCarthy, "The Use of Rhetoric in the *Nibelungenlied*: A Stylistic and Structural Study of Aventiure 5," *Modern Language Notes (MLN)* 87 (1972): 683–700; and Edward Schweitzer, "Tradition and Originality in the Narrative of Siegfried's Death in the *Nibelungenlied*," *Euphorion* 66, no. 4 (1972): 355–64.

10. Here and in the rest of this book, I wish to distinguish between "Jews," those fantasmatically rendered by anti-Semitic stereotypes as bearing pronounced and infinitely unsavory physical and cultural traits, and Jews, those who belong to the Jewish faith. I cease the redundant quotation marks around "Jew" or adjectival derivations thereof after their first occurrences, but of course I always mean this discursively constructed "Jew" rather than real people.

11. *In Search of Wagner*, trans. Rodney Livingstone, 23. In German: "Der Gold raffende, unsichtbar-anonyme, ausbeutende Alberich, der achselzuckende, geschwätzige, von Selbstlob und Tücke überfließende Mime, der impotente intellektuelle Kritiker Hanslick-Beckmesser—all die Zurückgewiesenen in Wagners Werk sind Judenkarikaturen." *Versuch über Wagner*, vol. 13 of the *Gesammelte Schriften*, ed. Gretel Adorno and Rolf Tiedemann, 7–148, here 21. Hereafter, references to these works will be abbreviated *Search* and *Versuch*, respectively. Although Adorno wrote the study in 1937–38, it was not published until 1952. I will return to this quotation in the next chapter.

12. I am thinking here of books by Paul Lawrence Rose and Marc A. Weiner, as well as the polemical rejection of their—quite different—claims by Hans-Rudolf Vaget. Much of the furor on this topic has been aroused by the question of whether and how Wagner's anti-Semitism may have entered into his works for the stage. I explore some of the terms of this debate in the following chapter.

13. Eisner writes, "Kracauer alleged that Lang's Alberich has markedly Jewish features, and he reads into this a deliberate gesture of anti-Semitism" See Lotte

Eisner, *Fritz Lang*, 79. Kracauer's claim does not appear in the *Caligari* text, nor in any of his published film reviews.

14. A rather charged alternative to the term "dramaturgy of disavowal" would be the dramaturgy of ghettoization. Both terms share the same logic; I have opted for the former since it bears less historical baggage—although it is, for that reason, not as vivid or suggestive as the latter.

15. See Melanie Klein, "Notes on Some Schizoid Mechanisms," *International Journal of Psychoanalysis* 27 (1946): 99–110, and "On Identification," in Melanie Klein, Paula Heimann, R. E. Money-Kyrle, eds., *New Directions in Psychoanalysis*, 309–45; Hanna Segal, *Introduction to the Work of Melanie Klein*, esp. chapter 3. Hereafter, *Introduction*.

16. See Segal, *Introduction*, 26. This fundamental reasoning has been crucial to object relations in contemporary psychoanalytic theory. See, for example, the work of Otto Kernberg.

17. Here, I am seeking to apply to the aesthetic realm a by-now canonical insight about the Jew's role in the discursive consolidation of communities. As Sander Gilman puts it, "The Jew became inherently 'bad' as the image of those projected aspects of a world out of control and threatening to the integrity of the Aryan." See Gilman, *Freud, Race, and Gender*, 9. I will return to this argument later in this study.

18. The narratological impetus of my analysis is indebted to Gérard Genette's *Narrative Discourse: An Essay in Method*, trans. Jane E. Lewin.

19. Franco Moretti, "The Nibelung's Ring," in *Modern Epic*, trans. Quintin Hoare, 107. Hereafter, *Modern Epic*.

20. See in this regard Freud's "Analysis: Terminable and Interminable," in *Standard Edition of the Complete Psychological Works of Sigmund Freud*, trans. James Strachey, vol. 23, 209–53. Hereafter, *Standard Edition*.

21. See Thea von Harbou, "Vom Epos zum Film," in *Die Woche*, 6 (February 1924), 139; hereafter, "Vom Epos." Of course, Wagner's procedure in combining a host of sources for his version of the material does not differ greatly from Harbou's procedure. See, in this regard, Elizabeth Magee's encyclopedic *Richard Wagner and the Nibelungs*.

22. See chapter 6, "Phantasmagorie" [in English: Phantasmagoria], in Adorno, *Versuch* and *Search*. In the course of chapter 2, I will consider the function of narration—as *Erzählung*—in the production of the *Gesamtkunstwerk* as totality.

23. See chapters 5 and 6 of Abbate's *Unsung Voices*.

24. See Abbate, *Unsung Voices*, 160.

25. Roy Schafer, for example, has proposed a typology of Freudian narrative practices in the psychoanalytic scene, and Shoshana Felman has extended that typology to a more thorough consideration of Freudian and Lacanian models of narration. See "Narratives of the Self," in Schafer, *Retelling a Life*, 21–35; and

Schafer's "Narration in the Psychoanalytic Dialogue," in *On Narrative*, ed. W.J.T. Mitchell, 25–49, as well as Felman's *Jacques Lacan and the Adventure of Insight*, especially chapters 3 and 5. More recently, Mark Freeman has examined the psychology of narrative production in *Rewriting the Self*.

26. *The Interpretation of Dreams*, Vols. 4 and 5 of *Standard Edition*, here 5:524–25; emphasis appears in the translation, which has been slightly modified. In German: "Die Frage, ob jeder Traum zur Deutung gebracht werden kann, ist mit Nein zu beantworten. Man darf nicht vergessen, daß man bei der Deutungsarbeit die psychischen Mächte gegen sich hat, welche die Entstellung des Traumes verschulden. Es wird so eine Frage des Kräfteverhältnisses, ob man mit seinem intellektuellen Interesse, seiner Fähigkeit zur Selbstüberwindung, seinen psychologischen Kenntnissen und seiner Übung in der Traumdeutung den inneren Widerständen den Herrn zeigen kann." Sigmund Freud, *Die Traumdeutung*, 2: 502. Hereafter, references to the work will be abbreviated *Dreams* and *Traumdeutung*.

27. *Dreams*, 5: 515; trans. slightly modified. In German: "Ich pflege bei den Traumanalysen mit Patienten folgende Probe auf diese Behauptung nie ohne Erfolg anzustellen. Wenn mir der Bericht eines Traums zuerst schwer verständlich erscheint, so bitte ich den Erzähler, ihn zu wiederholen. Das geschieht dann selten mit den nämlichen Worten. Die Stellen aber, an denen er den Ausdruck verändert hat, die sind mir als die schwachen Stellen der Traumverkleidung kenntlich gemacht worden, die dienen mir wie Hagen das gestrickte Zeichen an Siegfrieds Gewand. Dort kann die Traumdeutung ansetzen." *Traumdeutung*, 2: 493–94.

28. See Mark Edmundson, *Towards Reading Freud*, 40.

29. Among the mountain of publications on Hagen's contradictory valence, see Ursula R. Mahlendorf and Frank J. Tobin, "Hagen: A Reappraisal," in *Monatshefte* 63, no. 2 (1971): 125–40; Hugo Bekker, "Hagen in Relation to Siegfried," in Bekker, *The Nibelungenlied*, 118–34; Harold D. Dickerson, Jr., "Hagen: A Negative View," in *Semasia* 2 (1975): 43 59; Holgar Homann, "The Hagen Figure in the *Nibelungenlied*: Know Him by His Lies," in *MLN* 97, no. 3 (1982): 759–69; Edward R. Haymes, "Hagen and the Heroic Tradition," in Haymes, *The Nibelungenlied: History and Interpretation*, 73–90; and Otfrid Ehrismann, "Strategie und Schicksal—Hagen," in Werner Wunderlich, ed., *Literarische Symbolfiguren*, 1: 89–115.

30. In this respect, Freud is arguably activating the dynamic implicit in his first name: Siegmund, of course, is Siegfried's father.

31. See, in this regard, Theodore Andersson's *Preface to the Nibelungenlied*.

32. Among the many works on this material, see Ehrismann, Münkler and Storch, Brackert.

33. Helmut de Boor, ed., *Das Nibelungenlied*, 1. In English: *The Nibelungenlied*, trans. A. T. Hatto, 17. Hereafter *NL*, and *NL-Eng*; translations will refer to this edition. Unless otherwise noted, references denote strophe numbers in the

de Boor edition and page numbers in the Hatto translation. Ehrismann offers a detailed discussion of the first strophe in *Nibelungenlied: Epoche—Werk—Wirkung*, 98–103.

34. *NL*, 87ff; *NL-Eng*, 27ff.

35. *NL*, 100; *NL-Eng*, 28; trans. modified.

36. This is not the case in the other works we will consider. In the *Ring*, Wagner eventually and famously decides to *dramatize* Siegfried's past rather than have it narrated; in Lang's film, the hero's past is alternately shown without further framing or told by Volker, the Burgundian court minstrel. We will explore these distinctions in the following chapters.

37. Thus Hagen launches into his account of Siegfried's life much as the narrative voice launched into the *Nibelungenlied*, addressing the assembled circle with the phrase "nu hoeret wunder sagen" [now hear tell of wonders], *NL*, 89.2; *NL-Eng*, 27; trans. modified.

38. *NL*, 875.4; *NL-Eng*, 118; trans. modified.

39. See *NL-Eng*, 118. Since Brackert's translation is based upon the Bartsch/de Boor edition, strophe numbers in the two versions are identical. See Helmut Brackert, *Das Nibelungenlied* Mittelhochdeutscher Text und Übertragung, 2 vols., 1: 875.

40. In the early moments of the argument, Kriemhild bids Brünhild to stop talking:

> "des wil ich dich, Prünhilt,   vil friuntlîche biten
> daz du die rede lâzest   durch mich mit güetlîchen siten."
> "Ine mác ir niht gelâzen," sprach des küneges wîp.
>
> ["I must ask you in all friendship, Brünhild, if you care for me, kindly to stop speaking." "I cannot," answered the Queen.] (*NL*, 822.3–823.1; *NL-Eng*, 112; trans. modified)

As the argument progresses, this claim recurs: thus Kriemhild snaps: "du solt mich des erlâzen,   daz ich von dir vernomen hân" [you must spare me such things as I have had to hear from your tongue], *NL*, 824.4; *NL-Eng*, 112, and, a bit later on, "kúndestu nóch geswîgen,   daz wǽré dir guot" ["It would have been better for you if you could have held your tongue," said fair Kriemhild angrily . . .], *NL*, 839.1–2; *NL-Eng*, 113–14.

41. *NL*, 845.3; *NL-Eng*, 114.

42. *NL*, 862; *NL-Eng*, 116.

43. In Jerold Frakes's reading, the scene shows Siegfried to be a batterer. I wonder how useful it is to apply such charged contemporary terminology to the work. Would it not be more useful—and less facile—to situate Siegfried in a rhetoric and culture of battery that appears frequently in the literature of the time? How can we account for his actions in those terms? See Jerold Frakes, *Brides and Doom*, 130–31.

44. *NL*, 898.4; *NL-Eng*, 121; trans. slightly modified.
45. Here again is the text of Hagen's introductory briefing to the court:

> Noch weiz ich an im mêre   daz mir ist bekant.
> einen lintrachen   den sluoc des heldes hant.
> er bádet' sich in dem bluote: sîn hût wart húrnîn.
> des snîdet in kein wâfen.   daz ist dicke worden scîn.

> [But I know more concerning him. This hero single-handedly slew a dragon and bathed in its blood, from which his skin grew invulnerable. As a result, no weapon will cut through it, as has been shown time and time again.] (*NL*, 100; *NL-Eng*, 28; trans. modified)

And here is the first stanza of Kriemhild's account to Hagen:

> Si sprach: "mîn man ist küene   und dar zuo starc genuoc.
> dô er den líntráchen   an dem berge sluoc,
> jâ bádete sich ín dem bluote   der recke vil gemeit,
> dâ von in sît in stürmen   níe dehein wâfén versneit"

> [My husband is brave and in addition very strong. When he slew the dragon at the mountain the gallant knight bathed in its blood, as a result of which no weapon has pierced him in battle ever since.] (*NL*, 899; *NL-Eng*, 121; trans. modified)

46. *NL*, 900–901; *NL-Eng*, 121; trans. modified.
47.   Dô sprach von Tronege Hagene: 'úf daz sîn gewant
>   næt ir ein kleinez zeichen.   dâ bî ist mir bekant
>   wâ ich in müge behüeten,   sô wir in sturme stân'.
>   si wânde den hélt vristen: ez was ûf sînen tôt getân.

> [Thus spoke Hagen of Tronje: "sew a little mark on his garment so that I shall know where I must shield him as we are engaged in battle." She fancied she was protecting the hero, yet this was aimed at his death.] (*NL*, 903; *NL-Eng*, 121)

48. Frakes argues that the society depicted in the *Nibelungenlied* is systematically misogynistic, denying women "significant forms of communication such as participation in financial affairs and verbal participation in public events." Frakes, *Brides*, 108–9.
49.   Dô sprach der künic Gunther: "wie möhte daz ergân?"
>   des antwurte Hagene: "ich wilz iuch hoeren lân.
>   wir heizen boten rîten   zuo uns in daz lant
>   widerságen offenlîche,   die hie niemen sîn bekant.
>   Sô jehet ir vor den gesten   daz ir und iuwer man
>   wellet herverten.   alsô daz ist getân,

sô lobt er iu dar dienen;   des vliuset er den lîp.
so ervar ich uns diu mære   ab des küenen recken wîp."

["How could the thing be done?" asked King Gunther. "I will tell you,"
replied Hagen. "We shall tell envoys to ride here to us in Burgundy to
declare war on us publicly, men whom no one knows here. Then you
will announce in the hearing of your guests that you and your men plan
to go campaigning, whereupon Siegfried will promise you his aid, and so
he will lose his life. For in this way I shall procure the brave man's tale
for us from his wife."] (*NL*, 874–75; *NL-Eng*, 118; trans. modified)

In the course of Hagen's plotting, Siegfried and Kriemhild are assigned their
respective roles: when he hears of the attack on Gunther, Siegfried will surely
volunteer to fight; and when she hears that he has done so, Kriemhild will volunteer to talk.

50. *NL*, 874.1–2; *NL-Eng*, 118; trans. modified.

51. Although as Theodore Andersson points out, the ultimate motivation
for the plot to assassinate is rather opaque in the epic. See Andersson, *Preface*,
139–40.

52. Here is the passage in the epic:

Des ándérn morgens   mit tûsent sîner man
reit der herre Sîfrit   vil vroelîchen dan.
er wând' er solde rechen   der sîner vriunde leit.
Hágene im réit sô nâhen   daz er geschouwete diu kleit.
Als er gesach daz bilde,   dô schiht' er tougen dan,
die sageten ander mære,   zwêne sîner man:
mit vride solde belîben   daz Guntheres lant,
und si hete Liudegêr   zuo dem künige gesant.

[The next morning, lord Siegfried set out happily with a thousand of his
men, imagining he would avenge his friends' wrongs. Hagen rode so
close to him that he was able to survey his clothes. *And when Hagen
had observed the mark he secretly dispatched two of his men to tell a
different tale*—that Liudeger had sent them to King Gunther to say that
Burgundy would be left at peace.] (*NL*, 907–8; *NL-Eng*, 122; trans.
modified, emph. added)

53. Here is the passage in the epic:

dô reit er [Siegfried] zuo dem künige;   der wirt im dánkén began:
"Nu lôn' iu got des willen,   vriunt Sîfrit.
daz ir sô willeclîche   tuot des ich iuch bit,
daz sol ich immer dienen,   als ich von rehte sol.
vor allen mînen vriunden   sô getrûwe ich iu wol.

Nu wir der herverte   ledic worden sîn,
sô wil ich jagen rîten   bérn únde swîn
hin zem Waskenwalde,   als ich vil dicke hân."
daz hete gerâten Hagene,   der vil ungetriuwe man.

[When Siegfried rode back to the King, the latter thanked him: "May Heaven reward you for your good intentions, friend Siegfried, and for being so ready to meet my wishes. I shall always seek to repay you, as I am bound to do, and put my trust in you before all my friends. But now that we have been spared this campaign I intend to go hunting the bear and the boar in the forest of the Vosges, as I have so often done." The traitor Hagen had advised this.] (*NL*, 909.4–911; *NL-Eng*, 122)

54. Here is the passage in the epic:

Dô sprach der degen küene: "noch wil ich iu mêre sagen
allez mîn gewæte   wil ich mit mir tragen,
den gêr zuo dem schilde   und al mîn pirsgewant."
den kocher zuo dem swerte   vil schier' er úmbé gebant.

["And I will tell you what more I shall do" [replied brave Siegfried], "I will carry all my equipment with me, my spear and my shield and *all my hunting clothes*." And he quickly strapped on his quiver and sword . . .] (*NL*, 975; *NL-Eng*, 130; emph. added)

55.   Dâ der herre Sîfrit   ob dem brunnen tranc,
er schôz in durch daz kriuze,   daz von der wunden spranc
daz bluot im von dem herzen   vaste an die Hagenen wât.

[Then, as Siegfried bent over the brook and drank, Hagen hurled the spear *through the cross*, so that the hero's heart's blood leapt from the wound and splashed against Hagen's clothes.] (*NL*, 981.1–3; *NL-Eng*, 130; trans. modified, emph. added)

56. See Hatto's commentary, where he attributes the absence of the spot to the poet's carelessness. "An Introduction to a Second Reading," *NL-Eng*, 304.

57. In "Bourgeois Opera," Adorno waxes uncharacteristically lyrical about Siegfried's encounter with the woodbird, citing it as "the loveliest point in Wagner's *Ring*." For Adorno, that song presents singing as "the utopia of prosaic existence" and stages "the memory of the pre-linguistic, undivided state of Creation." How odd for Adorno to fall so uncritically for Wagner's rather transparent ploy. See "Bürgerliche Oper," in Adorno, *Gesammelte Schriften*, vol. 16 (Musikalische Schriften I–III), ed. Rolf Tiedemann, 24–39; here 35. In English translation: "Bourgeois Opera," in David J. Levin, ed., *Opera Through Other Eyes*, 25–43; here 39.

58. Here is the text of Brünnhilde's revelation to Hagen, from act II, scene v of *Götterdämmerung*:

> *Brünnhilde*:
> Nicht eine Kunst
> war mir bekannt,
> die zum Heil nicht half seinem Leib'!
> Unwissend zähmt' ihn
> mein Zauberspiel,
> das ihn vor Wunden nun gewahrt.
>
> *Hagen*:
> So kann keine Wehr ihm schaden?
>
> *Brünnhilde*:
> Im Kampfe nicht:—doch—
> träf'st du im Rücken ihn.
> Niemals—das wußt' ich—wich' er dem Feind,
> nie reicht' er fliehend ihm den Rücken:
> an ihm d'rum spart' ich den Segen.
>
> [*Brünnhilde*: Not a single art was known to me that did not help to keep
> his body safe! Unknown to him, he was tamed by my magic spell
> which wards him now against wounds.
> *Hagen*: And so no weapon can harm him?
> *Brünnhilde*: In battle, no! But—if you struck him in the back. Never, I
> knew, would he yield to a foe, never, fleeing, bare his back; so I spared
> it the spell's protection.]

See *Wagner's Ring of the Nibelung: A Companion*, full German text with a new translation by Stewart Spencer, 53–372; here 327. Hereafter, *Ring* (Spencer).

CHAPTER TWO

1. The term is relatively easy to translate; thus I have chosen to use "narration" in place of *Erzählung* throughout this chapter. On the other hand, the companion term to *Erzählung* in Wagner's idiosyncratic dramaturgical lexicon—*Darstellung*—is far more difficult to translate and, for that reason perhaps, far more common (as a kind of terminological import) in English-language literary and cultural criticism. I have chosen to retain the word *Darstellung*, while seeking at times to clarify its meaning for Wagner. For recent accounts of the history and philosophy of *Darstellung*, see Martha B. Helfer, *The Retreat of Representation*, and Christiaan L. Hart Nibbrig, ed., *Was heisst "Darstellen."*

2. Uhlig (1822–53) was a violinist in the Dresden Opera Orchestra as well as a composer and critic. In addition to preparing the piano reduction of *Lohengrin*, he served during the early 1850s as Wagner's secretary in Germany during the composer's exile in Switzerland.

3. *Selected Letters of Richard Wagner*, trans. and ed. Stewart Spencer and Barry Millington, 223; trans. modified. The German text appears in Richard Wagner, *Sämtliche Briefe*, Gertrud Strobel and Werner Wolf, eds., 4: 43. Hereafter, references to these two editions of Wagner's letters will be abbreviated "Wagner, *Letters* [Spencer & Millington]" and "Wagner, *Briefe* [Strobel & Wolf]."

4. See, for example, Wagner's comments about the project in "A Communication to My Friends" (1851): "I had sketched and executed my poem of 'Siegfried's Death' solely to satisfy my inner promptings, but in no way with the thought of a production in our theaters and with the extant means of presentation [*die vorhandenen Darstellungsmittel*] which I could not but hold in every respect unsuitable for the purpose." *Richard Wagner's Prose Works*, trans. William Ashton Ellis, 1: 267–392, here 377–78; trans. modified. In German: "Eine Mitteilung an meine Freunde" (1851) in *Gesammelte Schriften*, 4: 230–344, here 330. Hereafter, references to this English edition of Wagner's works will be abbreviated *PW*; references to this German edition will be abbreviated *GS*. In addition, references to this essay will be abbreviated "Communication" and "Mitteilung," respectively. Wagner makes very similar points in *My Life*, ed. Mary Whittall, trans. Andrew Gray. In German: *Mein Leben*, ed. Martin Gregor-Dellin. See, for example, *My Life*, 377–78 and 380–81; *Mein Leben*, 390–91 and 393–94, where Wagner bases his skepticism concerning the feasibility of the project on the audiences and production values of the day. The "Communication" was written in June and July of 1851, a few weeks after Wagner's letter to Uhlig, and thus during the time when he was working on the texts for the *Ring* (before he had written drafts and texts for *Das Rheingold* and *Die Walküre*); Wagner did not begin *Mein Leben* until almost fifteen years later; it was dictated between 1865 and 1880.

5. See in this regard his letter to Uhlig of November 12, 1851 (Wagner, *Letters* [Spencer & Millington], 232–34; *Briefe* [Strobel & Wolf], 4: 176), or the letter to Liszt of January 30, 1852, in Wagner, *Briefe* [Strobel & Wolf], 4: 269–74; here 270; in English in *Correspondence of Wagner and Liszt*, trans. Francis Hueffer, revised by W. Ashton Ellis, 1: 188–94; here 188–89.

6. "The Artwork of the Future," in *PW*, 1: 67–213; here 135, emphasis in original, trans. modified. In German: "Das Kunstwerk der Zukunft," in *GS*, 3: 42–177, here 104. Hereafter, references to these works will be abbreviated "Artwork" and "Kunstwerk," respectively.

7. See "Kunstwerk," *GS*, 3: 105–6, and "Artwork," *PW*, 1: 136.

8. For a more detailed discussion of the aesthetic politics of *Die Meistersinger von Nürnberg*, see my "Reading Beckmesser Reading: Antisemitism and Aesthetic Practice in *Die Meistersinger von Nürnberg*," in *New German Critique* 69 (Fall 1996): 127–46. Hereafter, "Reading Beckmesser Reading."

9. See "Kunstwerk," *GS*, 3: 105, and "Artwork," *PW*, 1: 136–37, trans. modified; emphasis in original.

10. *Letters* [Spencer & Millington], 223; emphasis in original, trans. modified; *Briefe* [Strobel & Wolf], 4: 44.

11. My wording is intentionally vague here, since Ernest Newman, among others, has pointed out that Wagner's recollection in *My Life* is mistaken. Wagner claims that he read the completed first draft of the poem to Devrient: "When I read my poem aloud after its completion to Eduard Devrient . . . he expressed utter amazement." But since that first draft contained the revisions that Devrient proposes, it seems clear that Wagner in fact read the first prose *sketch* of the work, concluded in October of 1848, and not the draft of the poem. For Wagner's claim, see *My Life*, 380; for Newman's argument, see *The Wagner Operas*, vol. 2, chap. 1, "The Nibelung's Ring," sec. 7, 401–2. Hereafter, *Wagner Operas*. Devrient (1801–77) was a librettist and singer who, after losing much of his voice in the early 1830s, became a stage director, writer, and administrative director for the court theaters of Dresden (1844–46) and Karlsruhe (1852–70).

12. *My Life*, 381; trans. modified; *Mein Leben*, 394.

13. Wagner contributed to the letter's fame, when he cited it (in a letter to Uhlig of December 3, 1851) as the clearest statement of his latest plans: "Already I very much wanted to let you (especially the R[itter]s) read my last letter to Liszt, because I have most clearly explained in it the motives which led to my latest decision with regard to my future artistic plans." Wagner, *Briefe* [Strobel & Wolf], 4: 206; in English in: *Wagner's Letters to His Dresden Friends*, trans. J. S. Shedlock, 149.

14. Wagner, *Letters* [Spencer & Millington], 237; *Briefe* [Strobel & Wolf], 4: 186.

15. The point recurs in Wagner's letters. On November 12, 1851, Wagner writes to Uhlig and reiterates some of these ideas. Thus, for example, he explains his decision to expand the work in the following terms: "all that remained of the overall context—which alone gives the characters their enormous, striking significance—was *epic narration* [*epische Erzählung*], a communication to the mind. In order, therefore, to render *Siegfried's Death* feasible, I wrote *Young Siegfried*: but the more imposing a structure the whole thing assumed, the more it was bound to dawn on me, as I began the scenico-musical realization of *Young Siegfried*, that all I had done was to increase the need for a clearer presentation **to the senses** of the total context. I now see that, in order to be fully understood from the stage, I must present the entire myth in vivid, plastic terms [*den ganzen Mythos plastisch ausführen*]." (Wagner, *Letters* [Spencer & Millington], 232–33; trans. modified, bold in original, emphasis added; *Briefe* [Strobel & Wolf], 4: 174.)

16. At least in address, the trajectories envisioned by Wagner (from narration to *Darstellung*) and Freud (from *id* to *ego*) appear to be headed in opposite directions. For whereas Freud directs his observation to the salutary effects of medi-

ating and constricting the *id*, Wagner seeks, in a sense, to bypass that constriction in order to address himself fully and without inhibition to "the senses."

17. The example appears in the letter to Liszt. See Wagner, *Letters* [Spencer & Millington], 238; Wagner, *Briefe* [Strobel & Wolf], 4: 188.

18. *Letters* [Spencer & Millington], 238; trans. modified; *Briefe* [Strobel & Wolf], 4: 187–88.

19. In an extremely suggestive essay on the dramaturgy of Wagner's orchestral narration, Rheinhold Brinkmann argues that Wagner remained occupied with the attempt to devise a properly dramatic form of musical narration from *Tannhäuser* onward. See Rheinhold Brinkmann, "Richard Wagner der Erzähler," *Österreichische Musik Zeitschrift* 37, no. 6 (June 1982): 297–306, here 302.

20. Among the myriad works charting the evolution of the theory and practice of the *Gesamtkunstwerk* from the writings of the Zurich period to the later compositions for the stage, see Borchmeyer, *Richard Wagner: Theory and Theatre*, trans. Stewart Spencer, especially chapter 6. See also Barry Millington's *Wagner*, rev. ed., 125, 202–8, 233–35, 247–49, 259–60.

21. See Richard Wagner, *Opera and Drama*, vol. 2 of *Richard Wagner's Prose Works*, trans. William Ashton Ellis. In German: *Oper und Drama* in *GS*, 3 (part one) and 4 (parts two and three). Hereafter, references to this work will be abbreviated *O&D* [Eng.], or *OuD* [Ger.], including the volume and page number. For a thorough yet unpedantic account of the publication history of *Oper und Drama*, see Klaus Kropfinger, "Text und Edition von *Oper und Drama*," in Richard Wagner, *Oper und Drama*, ed. Klaus Kropfinger, 450–78.

22. "Art and Revolution," in *PW*, 1: 30–65, here 44; "Die Kunst und die Revolution," in *GS*, 3: 8–41, here 20–21.

23. *O&D* [Eng.], *PW*, 2: 372, trans. modified; *OuD*, *GS*, 4: 225.

24. See James Treadwell, "The *Ring* and the Conditions of Interpretation: Wagner's Writing, 1848 to 1852," in *Cambridge Opera Journal* 7, no. 3 (November 1995): 207–31. Hereafter, Treadwell, "The *Ring*."

25. Jean-Jacques Nattiez offers a detailed and convincing account of the construction and deployment of this logic in the Zurich period writings in *Wagner Androgyne*, trans. Stewart Spencer, 12–37.

26. Treadwell, "The *Ring*," 228.

27. Carolyn Abbate, *Unsung Voices*, 161.

28. Abbate, *Unsung Voices*, 161.

29. Ibid.

30. Treadwell, "The *Ring*," 219.

31. Treadwell, "The *Ring*," 230–31. The passage from Wagner's prose works cited in the quotation is from Wagner's "A Theatre in Zurich" in *PW*, 3: 43. Brünnhilde's quotation appears in the third act of *Siegfried* (Spencer, 267).

32. Here, I am concurring with Carolyn Abbate's position that "the very genesis of the *Ring* attests to a longing for presentation, for the physical force of

embodiment in performance, over representation and the suspicions attached to the written and silently read word." *Unsung Voices*, 160.

33. This is a point made most forcefully in the "Communication to My Friends." In that essay, Wagner suggests that while the critic is busy dissecting the printed pages of the artwork and resisting its "sensual appearance," his "friends" are necessarily swept away by the sensuality of the work. ("Mitteilung," *GS*, 4: 291; "Communication," *PW*, 1: 273, my trans.)

34. Marc Weiner argues forcefully that the distinction between Wagner's appeal to the mind and the heart has a racial correlative. Thus, according to Weiner, cerebral artworks that appeal to the intellect are understood to be "superficial" and "Judaized" in Wagner's vocabulary, while "deep," "Germanic" artworks would appeal to and spring from the sensibilities of the *Volk*. See Marc A. Weiner, *Richard Wagner and the Anti-Semitic Imagination*, 22. A bit further on, Weiner strengthens the point and, in so doing, weakens his argument, by claiming that the "topos juxtaposing impoverished surface appearance and superior and above all *privileged* depths functions as the fulcrum of Wagner's aesthetics, providing a motif upon which many of the metaphors of his theoretical writings and music dramas are based." See Weiner, *Anti-Semitic Imagination*, 41; emphasis in original. While the topos is undoubtedly a recurring phenomenon (perhaps we could term it a node?), I would argue that it is surely not "the" fulcrum of Wagner's aesthetics. Indeed, I would argue that Weiner himself makes this clear, given the proliferation of fulcrums presented in his study.

35. Treadwell, "The *Ring*," 228.

36. Weiner puts it sharply and well: "The Mime of *Siegfried*, then, is an apelike Francophilic copycat: Metaphorically, he is that which his name reveals him to be, a mime . . ." Weiner, *Anti-Semitic Imagination*, 89.

37. See, in this regard, the extraordinary diatribe presented in "The Artwork of the Future": "It's not you intellectuals who are inventive, but the *Volk*. . . . [A]ll great inventions are deeds of the *Volk*, in contrast to which, the inventions of the intelligentsia are merely exploitations, distortions, indeed splinterings, mutilations of the great inventions of the *Volk*. It was not you who invented *language*, but the *Volk*; you could only ruin its sensuous beauty, only break its strength, only lose its inner comprehension, only laboriously explore again what was lost." See "Artwork," *PW*, 1: 80; my trans.; emphasis in original; in German: "Das Kunstwerk der Zukunft," in *GS*, 3: 53.

38. Like Abbate, Treadwell argues that "the narratives of the *Ring* repeatedly remind us—urge us—to complete them ourselves." Treadwell, "The *Ring*," 231.

39. See *My Life*: "So I wrote the poem of *Das Rheingold* in October and November of that year, whereby I brought the whole cycle of my Nibelung dramas to completion in reverse order" (*My Life*, 489; *Mein Leben*, 501–2). Robert Donington is just one of the critics who has (mis-)read the libretto as an account of the origins of the world: "It might, perhaps, not have occurred to anyone but

Wagner to start an operatic libretto with the beginning of the world and to end with its destruction." In *Wagner's 'Ring' and Its Symbols*, 22.

40. "The Sorrows and Grandeur of Richard Wagner," in Thomas Mann, *Pro and Contra Wagner*, trans. Allan Blunden, 102. In German: Thomas Mann, "Leiden und Größe Richard Wagners," in *Wagner und unsere Zeit*, ed. Erika Mann, 63–121, here 73–74. Hereafter, Mann, "Sorrows" and Mann, "Leiden," respectively. There is some confusion and debate about the sequence of this spiral and whether it truly began at the end and concluded at the beginning. The *Wagner Werk-Verzeichnis* suggests that Wagner may well have prepared the prose sketch of *Das Rheingold* before *Die Walküre*, although he evidently prepared the full texts in reverse order, that is, first *Die Walküre*, then *Das Rheingold*). See John Deathridge, Martin Geck, and Egon Voss, *Wagner Werk-Verzeichnis*, sect. 86, 406. Hereafter, references to this work will be abbreviated *WWV*.

41. Siegmund's "Wes Herd dies auch sei, hier muß ich rasten!" in *Die Walküre*, or Mime's "Zwangvolle Plage! Müh ohne Zweck!" in *Siegfried* articulate an urgent predicament. Part of that predicament and its urgency derives from the fact that these characters have no one to talk to: for the moment, the audience is their sole (and wholly implicit) interlocutor. *Götterdämmerung*, on the other hand, opens with an odd, meta-diegetic conversation in which the Norns talk and weave amongst themselves, reviewing the dramatic events that have preceded the scene that is about to open. Their conversation is followed by—and the Prelude to *Götterdämmerung* concludes with—a second scene, the much less confounding exchange between Siegfried and Brünnhilde: thus, the Prelude presents two successive conversations.

42. Stewart Spencer discusses the range of critical responses to Woglinde's opening lines in the first pages of his essay "The Language and Sources of *Der Ring des Nibelungen*," in Ursula and Ulrich Müller, eds., *Richard Wagner und sein Mittelalter*, 141–55.

43. On the Prelude as an allegory of origins, see Newman, *Wagner Operas*, 451–52; Thomas Mann, "Leiden," 79, 80. The argument presented here does not account for the thorny problem of musical reference, which would call into question music's ability to signify *anything*. In *Oper und Drama* Wagner himself dismisses the notion that music can be dramatic, or that it can become the content of drama: "Bei allen verkehrten Bestrebungen ist die Musik, die irgend wirkungsvolle Musik, wirklich auch nichts anderes geblieben als Ausdruck: jenen Bestrebungen, sie zum Inhalte—und zwar zum Inhalte des Dramas—selbst zu machen, entsprang aber das, was wir als den folgerichtigen Verfall der Oper, und somit als die offenkundige Darlegung der gänzlichen Unnatur dieses Kunstgenres zu erkennen haben." (*OuD*, *GS*, 3: 244)

44. *My Life*, 499; trans. modified; *Mein Leben*, 512.

45. See, for example, Stewart Spencer's "Introductory Essay: 1849–1858," in Wagner, *Letters* [Spencer & Millington], 157–68, as well as John Deathridge, "Life," in *The New Grove Wagner*, 39.

46. See, for example, Nattiez's discussion at the outset of chapter 3: "The Ring as a Mythic Account of the History of Music," in his *Wagner Androgyne*, 53–55.

47. Newman, *Wagner Operas*, 451.

48. For an eclectic and inventive history of theatrical lighting practices, see Wolfgang Schivelbusch, *Lichtblicke*, 193–201, especially 198. In English: *Disenchanted Night*, 203–12, especially 210.

49. Jean-Jacques Nattiez presents a similar argument in *Wagner Androgyne*, arguing that "by electing to sing a folk melody, Woglinde attests to the union of poetry and music at the very dawn of human history" and, a bit later, "Following the birth of harmony, Woglinde allows us to witness the birth of that melody which issues from harmony." See Nattiez, *Wagner Androgyne*, 58, 59.

50. *Das Rheingold*, trans. Stewart Spencer in Stewart Spencer and Barry Millington, eds., *Wagner's Ring of the Nibelung*, 57–118, here 57. The Spencer/Millington edition includes an excellent English translation and a reliable version of the German text with notes and an appendix listing variants. Reference notes will include the corresponding title of each work in the tetralogy (i.e., *Rheingold*, *Walküre*, etc.) followed by page references to the Spencer edition. In adjusting the translations, I have referred to William Mann's excellent, if little-known, English translation of the tetralogy, published by the Friends of Covent Garden in 1964.

51. Seconding Tibor Kneif, Nattiez associates the three Rhine maidens with the three sisters (dance, music, and poetry) introduced in *The Artwork of the Future*. While Nattiez thus attributes the rupture of linguistic unity to Alberich's arrival, I read that rupture earlier, in Wellgunde's query. See Nattiez, *Wagner Androgyne*, 55–60, especially 60. Kneif's argument appears in "Zur Deutung der Rheintöchter in Wagners *Ring*," *Archiv für Musikwissenschaft* 26 (1969): 297–306. In English: "On the Meaning of the Rhinemaidens in Wagner's *Ring*," trans. Stewart Spencer, in *Wagner* 10 (1989): 21–28.

52. For an excellent account of Wagner's use of *Stabreim*, see Stewart Spencer, "The Language and Sources of *Der Ring des Nibelungen*." For a more general account of the cultural and political resonance of linguistic theory in Europe in the nineteenth century, see Maurice Olender, *The Languages of Paradise*, trans. Arthur Goldhammer, esp. 140–41, where Olender briefly considers the allegory of origins in the *Ring*.

53. *O&D* [Eng.], 2: 224; *OuD, GS*, 4: 91.

54. *O&D* [Eng.], 2: 226; *OuD GS*, 4: 93.

55. See *O&D* [Eng.], 2: 229. The neuter form corresponds to the German where the child's gender remains undetermined. See *OuD, GS*, 4: 96.

56. In Wagner's astonishing formulation: "Let us first notice, however, with what instinctive care this language only very gradually distanced itself from its nourishing mother's breast, Melody, and her breast-milk, the open tone." (*O&D* [Eng.], 2: 226; *OuD, GS*, 4: 93)

57. O&D [Eng.], 2: 227. In German: "die urälteste Eigenschaft aller dichterischen Sprache." Wagner's full formulation reads: "Dieses dichtende Moment der Sprache ist die *Alliteration* oder der *Stabreim*, in dem wir die urälteste Eigenschaft aller dichterischen Sprache erkennen." (*OuD, GS,* 4: 94; emphasis in original)

58. O&D [Eng.], 2: 227; *OuD, GS,* 4: 94.

59. O&D [Eng.], 2: 229; *OuD, GS,* 4: 96.

60. It would be fascinating to pursue a more sustained narratological reading of Wagner's polemical writings, for very often his arguments set—as they do here—particularly vivid scenes. To what extent can we read the writings as allegorical tales? These questions arise all the more forcefully in the wake of two recent and extremely suggestive analyses of the dramaturgical implications of Wagner's prose, namely Nattiez's *Wagner Androgyne* and Treadwell's "The Ring."

61. See, for example, O&D [Eng.], 2: 229–30: "When language had thus lost an instinctive understanding of her own roots—only possible through feeling,—she naturally could no longer answer *in these* to the intonations of that nourishing mother-melody. She either contented herself—where dance remained an inseparable portion of the lyric—by clinging as keenly as possible to the *rhythm* of the melody: or she sought—where dance had more and more completely separated itself from the lyric, as in the modern nations—for another tie to bind her to the melodic breathing intervals; and this she procured in *end-rhyme.*" (In German: *OuD, GS,* 4: 96–97.)

In *Richard Wagners Musikdramen,* Carl Dahlhaus notes but hardly explains Wagner's return to end-rhyme in *Parsifal.* See *Richard Wagners Musikdramen,* 149. In English: *Richard Wagner's Music Dramas,* trans. Mary Whittall, 151. Given the allegorical tenor of Wagner's scenario of language as prodigal son, we can read *Parsifal* as staging—through its title character—certain principles of aberration and return that are contradicted, as they are restaged, on the level of language. As Parsifal moves toward the enlightenment that will allow him to return to Monsalvat and save the Grail society, he seems to abandon *Stabreim* and embrace *Endreim.* We can compare his end-rhymed remonstration to Kundry in act II with his initial appearance in the first scene of the opera, as an ambassador from the linguistic wilds of *Stabreim*: "Im Fluge treff' ich was fliegt!" See *Parsifal,* in *GS,* 10: 324–75. Material quoted above appears on 334; for Parsifal's extended foray into end-rhyming, see 361. I will have to bracket this dramaturgical anomaly for now, since further analysis—which it certainly deserves—will lead us too far astray.

62. O&D [Eng.], 2: 265; trans. modified, emphasis in original; *OuD, GS,* 4: 128.

63. See *OuD* [Eng.], 2: 229; *OuD, GS,* 4: 96.

64. One of the most sententious formulations of the incompatibility of art and modern language appears in *Oper und Drama*: "In der modernen Sprache

kann nicht *gedichtet* werden, d.h., eine dichterische Absicht kann in ihr nicht *verwirklicht*, sondern eben nur *als solche* ausgesprochen werden" (*OuD, GS,* 4: 98; emphasis in original). For Wagner's argument in favor of artistic expression situated way above everyday expression, see *OuD, GS,* 4: 100–101.

65. Wagner is not the only one to argue thus. In *The Wagner Operas,* Ernest Newman parrots Wagner's position, albeit with reference to the need for "muscular" rather than aboriginal language. "[Wagner's] young Siegfried, the symbol of a new and ardent life, could not possibly express himself in regularly shaped verse such as that of *Lohengrin;* a mode of speech would have to be found for him as forthright, as muscular, as himself." See Newman, *The Wagner Operas,* 406.

66. "Communication," 376; trans. modified; "Mitteilung," *GS,* 4: 230–344, here 329.

67. As Catherine Clément puts it, "the prelude to the *Ring* . . . is a specific desire. A desire for the 'first time,' roused by primitive cosmology and demiurgic hope." Later in the same chapter, Clément suggests that the experience of origins, which is particular to *Das Rheingold,* is particularly pleasurable. And yet, while Clément describes this pleasure in lyrical detail, she does not explain or analyze it. Thus, some of the questions that arise in the wake of her consideration remain unaddressed—such as, wherein lies the pleasure? How does it operate? Why is it irretrievable? Here is the text of Clément's later claim: "*Rheingold* sets it all in place starting with its first chords, in the river waters. What is played out is also a method and a spectacle unlike any other, interlocking ear and eye, at the same time as the unconscious takes over the weaving of something soon to affect you. But never again are you to have the illusion of an origin, the pleasure of beginnings. You will discover as you go along that the first threads of the story are the most beautiful, the most powerful, and the most true." See "The Tetralogic of the *Ring,* or the Daughter Done for," in *Opera, or the Undoing of Women,* trans. Betsy Wing, 137–72. The two excerpts quoted above appear on pages 137 and 147, respectively.

68. See Mann, "Sorrows," 102. On this point, see also Nattiez, *Wagner Androgyne,* 53–55.

69. *O&D* [Eng.], 2: 265; trans. modified; *OuD, GS,* 4: 127.

70. Sander Gilman considers a very similar structure in the course of an analysis of the linguistics of anti-Semitism in the second half of the nineteenth century. According to Gilman, "The idea of the cultural contribution of the Jews, of the Jews' aesthetic language as the indicator of their Otherness within a new science of race, appealed to those Germans who were still attempting to create a political as well as cultural identity out of the chaos of the German states." See chapter 5, section 1, "The Linguistics of Anti-Semitism," in Gilman, *Jewish Self-Hatred,* 209–19; here 212. Gilman begins the chapter with a brief consideration of Wagner's "Judaism in Music."

71. Every time Woglinde's line is repeated, Wagner violates a cardinal rule of his newly formulated dramaturgy, for insofar as she speaks, she invokes this

history, and as we have seen, Wagner is intent upon recuperating narration for *Darstellung*.

72. *Siegfried*, Spencer, 199; trans. modified.

73. *Siegfried*, Spencer, 197, trans. modified.

74. Ibid.

75. Here as elsewhere, that rapport will find musical expression *within* the diegesis. Thus, Siegfried communicates with nature by means of his horn, and in doing so, he would communicate a specific intention:

> ob sich froh mir gesellte
> ein guter Freund?
> das frug' ich mit dem Getön'.
> Aus dem Busche kam ein Bär.
>
> [would some good-hearted friend
> be glad to join me
> I asked by means of that sound.
> From the bushes came a bear.] (*Siegfried*, Spencer, 197)

Wagner is savvy enough to limit the extent of the exchange; thus it remains unclear whether the bear understood that intention or whether he was simply drawn by the sheer force of Siegfried's natural charisma.

76. *Siegfried*, Spencer, 200, trans. modified. Siegfried's sentiment follows and echoes his response to Mime's "rearing song":

> Vieles lehrtest du, Mime,
> und Manches lernt' ich von dir;
> doch was du am liebsten mich lehrtest,
> zu lernen gelang mir nie:—
> wie ich dich leiden könnt'.—
>
> [Much, Mime, have you taught me, and I've learned plenty from you, but what you most wanted to teach me, I never managed to learn: how to abide you . . .] (*Siegfried*, Spencer, 200, trans. modified)

77. *Siegfried*, Spencer 201, trans. modified.

78. Here are the terms of Siegfried's inquiry to Mime:

> Ei, Mime, bist du so witzig,
> so lass' mich eines noch wissen!
> Es sangen die Vöglein
> so selig im Lenz,
> das eine lockte das and're:
> du sagtest selbst—
> da ich's wissen wollt'—
> das wären Männchen und Weibchen.

Sie kos'ten so lieblich,
und ließen sich nicht;
sie bauten ein Nest
und brüteten drin:
da flatterte junges
Geflügel auf,
und beide pflegten der Brut.—
. . . Da lernt' ich wohl
was Liebe sei:
. . . Wo hast du nun, Mime,
dein minniges Weibchen,
daß ich es Mutter nenne?

[Hey, Mime, if you're so clever, tell me one thing more. In spring the birds would sing so blithely, the one would entice the other: you said so yourself—since I wanted to know—that they were a little husband and a little wife. They cuddled so lovingly and never left one another's side; they built a nest and hatched their eggs in it. Young fledglings then would flutter out and both of them tended their brood.— . . . There I learned what love is. . . . Now, Mime, where is your loving little wife, that I may call her mother?] (*Siegfried*, Spencer 201–2, trans. modified)

79. *Siegfried*, Spencer, 202, trans. modified.

80. The missing mother—a recurring and motivating fantasy in Wagner's works—constitutes the vulnerable spot in Mime's account, and—to borrow a Freudian locution from the introductory chapter—*dort setzt die Mimedeutung an*.

81. *Siegfried*, Spencer, 202. Siegfried rejects this unnatural fusion not with reference to its biological implausibility but to its unnatural appearance: since a son must naturally resemble his parents, and since Siegfried and Mime look so radically different, Mime must be lying.

82. "The mirror stage as formative of the function of the I as revealed in psychoanalytic experience" [lecture first delivered on July 14, 1949], in *Écrits: A Selection*, trans. Alan Sheridan, 1–7.

83. *Siegfried*, Spencer, 202–3.

84. *Siegfried*, Spencer, 203, trans. modified.

85. *Siegfried*, Spencer, 205, trans. modified.

86. See *Siegfried*: in full score, reprint of the first edition, originally published in 1876, 47. This manner of quotation appears throughout Siegfried's exchange with Mime; see also 43, 44, 45, 46.

87. *Siegfried*, Spencer, 205–6, trans. modified.

88. According to Weiner, the regime of vision inspires a particular form of exclusionary identification: "the eye always has racist implications in Wagner's

thought and provides a link between the essays apparently bereft of overt anti-Semitism and the more obviously anti-Semitic tracts. It also provides . . . a direct link between Wagner's theoretical reflections and the texts of his music dramas." (*Anti-Semitic Imagination*, 36). Weiner devotes the second chapter of his book to this question.

89. Wagner, "Was ist Deutsch?" in *GS*, 10: 36–53, here 44; "What Is German?" in *PW*, 4: 149–69, here 159.

90. Later on in the same chapter, Weiner presents a detailed and suggestive reading of the scene of Siegfried's confrontation with Mime. See *Anti-Semitic Imagination*, 84–88.

91. According to Shaw,

> Siegfried inherits from Wotan a mania for autobiography, which leads him to inflict on everyone he meets the story of Mime and the dragon, although the audience have spent a whole evening witnessing the events he is narrating. Hagen tells the story to Gunther; and that same night Alberich's ghost tells it to Hagen, who knows it already as well as the audience. Siegfried tells the Rhine maidens as much of it as they will listen to, and then keeps telling it to his hunting companions until they kill him.

See Shaw, *The Perfect Wagnerite*, 109. Franco Moretti cites this passage at the outset of his discussion of the *Ring*. See Moretti, *Modern Epic*, 101.

92. *Walküre*, Spencer 152, trans. modified.

93. *Walküre*, Spencer, 131.

94. *Walküre*, Spencer, 132, trans. modified.

95. *Walküre*, Spencer, 177–78, trans. modified.

96. Of course, the logic of the leitmotif is such that it renders our recognition of this new musical material (as "the Siegfried motif") necessarily *nachträglich*. Each theme can only be recognized at some later point of its recurrence, and even then, that recurrence is never identical or unchanged. Theodor Adorno, Carl Dahlhaus, and Anthony Newcomb have each argued against a simplistic understanding of the operations of the leitmotif. See, for instance, Anthony Newcomb, "The Birth of Music out of the Spirit of Drama," in *Nineteenth Century Music*, 5, no. 1 (Summer 1981): 38–66. At the conclusion of his essay, Newcomb argues eloquently that "[Wagnerian] forms are constantly becoming something else as we move through them in time, and their ends and beginnings are elided with great care. It is to the appreciation and illumination of this art of blurred edges, this characteristically Wagnerian *Kunst des Übergangs*, that we should dedicate ourselves" (64).

97. For in remaking the sword, Siegfried is evidently making himself anew—determined to leave his lifetime home, which he now recognizes as illegitimate, in order to head off into the world.

98. See in this regard Lutz Köpnick's imaginative and insightful essay " 'Nothung! Nothung! Neidlicher Stahl!': Die Phantasmagorie des Schwertes in

Wagners *Der Ring des Nibelungen*," *German Quarterly* 66, no. 4 (Fall 1993): 490–509.

99. *Siegfried*, Spencer, 195.

100. Ibid., trans. modified.

101. Although I have not quoted the line above, Mime's lament includes the following, more explicit admission:

> Ein Schwert nur taugt zu der That;
> nur Nothung nützt meinem Neid,
> wenn Siegfried sehrend ihn schwingt:—
> und ich kann's nicht schweißen,
> Nothung das Schwert!

> [One sword alone befits the deed and only Nothung serves my grudge, if Siegfried wields it with fell intent:—yet I cannot forge it, Nothung the sword!] (*Siegfried*, Spencer, 196)

102. See Brünnhilde's exhortation to Sieglinde, quoted above:

> den hehrsten Helden der Welt
>   heg'st du, o Weib,
>   im schirmenden Schooß!—
> [*Sie zieht die Stücken von Siegmunds Schwert unter ihrem Panzer hervor und überreicht sie Sieglinde*]
>   Verwahr' ihm die starken
>   Schwertes-Stücken;
>   seines Vaters Walstatt
>   entführt' ich sie glücklich:
>   der neu gefügt
>   das Schwert einst schwingt,
> den Namen nehm' er von mir—
> rSiegfried€ erfreu' sich des Sieg's!

103. The lament with which Mime opens the opera concludes:

> könnt' ich die starken
> Stücken schweißen,
> die meine Kunst
> nicht zu kitten weiß.
> Könnt' ich's dem Kühnen schmieden,
> meiner Schmach erlangt' ich da Lohn!

> [could I but weld the mighty shards which my art cannot piece together. If I could only forge it for that hothead, I'd find a due reward for all my shame!] (*Siegfried*, Spencer, 195; trans. modified)

104. *Wagner Androgyne*, 71.

105. Ernest Newman has noted that the moment when Mime bemoans having stolen the sword—"verfluchter Stahl, daß ich dich gestohlen" (*Siegfried*, Spencer, 214)—is a contradiction carried over from the draft of *Der junge Siegfried*. See *Wagner Operas*, 429. The apparent confusion over whether Mime stole or received the sword makes those origins even less clear than they would otherwise be.

106. *Siegfried*, Spencer, 213, trans. modified.

107. *Siegfried*, Spencer, 214, trans. modified.

108. Ibid.

109. *Siegfried*, Spencer, 220, emphasis added.

110. *Siegfried*, Spencer, 227, trans. modified.

111. *Siegfried*, Spencer, 227–28.

112. *Siegfried*, Spencer, 227, trans. modified.

113. When Siegfried kills Fafner in *Siegfried*, act II, scene ii, he juxtaposes the impossibility of garnering any further advice from a dead dragon—one to whom, however, he has just spoken—with the determination to gain direction from his "living sword." "Zur Kunde taugt kein Todter," Siegfried reasons, "so leite mich denn / mein lebendes Schwert!" [Nothing can be explained by something dead, so you must lead me, my living sword!], *Siegfried*, Spencer, 242, trans. modified.

114. *Siegfried*, Spencer, 223, trans. modified. In German: "[die] eigene Waffe, die er sich gewonnen."

115. *Siegfried*, Spencer, 224. In German: "bald schwing' ich dich als mein Schwert!"

116. *Siegfried*, Spencer, 228.

117. *Siegfried*, Spencer, 224.

118. *Walküre*, Spencer, 178.

119. This transition is thematized in the text. Thus Mime notes

> Zu Schanden kam ein Schmied,
> den Lehrer sein Knabe lehrt;
> mit der Kunst nun ist's beim Alten aus,
> als Koch dient er dem Kind:
> brennt es das Eisen zu Brei,
> aus Eiern brau't
> der Alte ihm Sud. (*Er fährt fort zu kochen*).

> [A smith has been put to shame: his boy is teaching his teacher; the old man's art is over and done with, he serves the child as cook: while he smelts the iron to pulp, the old man cooks him broth from eggs. (*He continues cooking*).] (*Siegfried*, Spencer 224)

120. *Siegfried*, Spencer, 242–43. Siegfried's question here is richer than this translation allows. The question, "Nützte mir das des Blutes Genuß?" relies upon the notion that the blood was tasty and tasting it had some utility. Thus,

the question could also be translated: "Is that what I gained from having tasted [or 'having enjoyed the taste of'] the blood?" Later in my discussion of this passage, I will consider this ambiguity in greater detail.

121. It is unclear why the bird would so instruct Siegfried; after all, in following these directions, Siegfried unwittingly assumes the curse upon the ring. The words of the "voice of the woodbird (in the linden tree)" are as follows:

> Hei! Siegfried gehört
> nun der Niblungen Hort:
> o fänd' in der Höhle
> den Hort er jetzt!
> Wollt' er den Tarnhelm gewinnen,
> der taugt ihm zu wonniger That:
> doch möcht' er den Ring sich errathen,
> der macht' ihn zum Walter der Welt! (*Siegfried*, Spencer, 243)

122. *Siegfried*, Spencer, 247, trans. modified.

123. Ibid.

124. *Siegfried*, Spencer, 248–49, trans. modified.

125. Weiner argues that Mime's *voice* gives him away—in tone and in vocal range. That is, Mime mimics (and mimes) "the lilting sweetness of the sounds of love, sounds with which he himself has no affinity but which he believes will convince and fool the young German hero" *and* "he cannot but sing as a high tenor, cannot change the nature of his voice, which is physiologically different from that of the Germanic *Heldentenor*. His elevated tessitura, contrasted with the lower vocal writing for Siegfried, gives him away . . ." (*Anti-Semitic Imagination*, 169, 170).

126. As such, Siegfried's actions could be read as a grotesque staging of the aggression implicit in Freud's scenario. Of course, Siegfried himself will be caught in the same scenario in *Götterdämmerung*.

127. We learn this in an important exchange between Brünnhilde and Hagen in act II, scene v of *Götterdämmerung* (see chapter 1, note 58, above).

128. *Siegfried*, Spencer, 251.

129. *Siegfried*, Spencer, 252.

130. *Siegfried*, Spencer, 206–7.

131. *Götterdämmerung*, Spencer, 294.

132. Ibid.

133. Although Hagen will die at the end of the work, and will be revealed as the villain earlier still, his narrative manipulations will have taken their toll.

134. See *Götterdämmerung*, Spencer, 288.

135. See *Götterdämmerung*, Spencer, 289:

> Ein Weib weiß ich,
> das herrlichste der Welt:—
> auf Felsen hoch ihr Sitz;

ein Feuer umbrennt ihren Saal:
nur wer durch das Feuer bricht,
darf Brünnhildes Freier sein.

[I know of a woman, the noblest in the world:—high on a fell her home;
a fire burns round her hall: only he who breaks through the fire may
sue for Brünnhilde's love.]

136. *Götterdämmerung*, Spencer, 320.

137. This is an insight staged quite pointedly in Patrice Chéreau's centenary
Bayreuth production of the *Ring* when the Gibichungen society bears explicitly
contemporary, nineteenth-century attributes.

138. *Götterdämmerung*, Spencer, 339.

139. Here, then, is the locus of my disagreement with James Treadwell. For in
my view, it is important to keep in mind Wagner's extremely ambivalent relationship to narration and the resultant distinction in his works between forms of
narration. While some characters in the works narrate in good faith, others use
narration to eminently bad ends. Not coincidentally, they bear the marks of that
which, in Wagner's eyes, undermines social and aesthetic integrity; that is, the
integrity of society and the *Gesamtkunstwerk*.

140. *Götterdämmerung*, Spencer, 341.

141. *Siegfried*, Spencer, 247.

142. Of course, that is not all it accounts for. In Wagner's writings, it is just
such an uncritical receptiveness that accounts for the dominance of Meyerbeer
in Paris and Rossini in Italy.

143. See Slavoj Zizek, *The Sublime Object of Ideology*, 125..

144. Zizek makes this point in *Sublime Object*: "the figure of the Jew condenses opposing features, features associated with lower and upper classes: Jews
are supposed to be dirty *and* intellectual, voluptuous *and* impotent, and so on"
(125).

145. See, in this regard, Jacob Katz's discussion of the rise of the notion of the
Christian State in the 1840s as a state that constitutes itself in a double negative,
that is, as *not not* Christian. See Jacob Katz, "The Christian State," in *From
Prejudice to Destruction*, 195–202. In *Entertaining the Third Reich*, Linda
Schulte-Sasse examines the function of the Jew in the consolidation of commu-
nity in the cinema of the Nazi period. Unfortunately, I was unable to consult
Schulte-Sasse's text in the preparation of my argument.

146. *Judentum und Modernität*, 13; my trans.

147. Gilman argues that, "with the secularization of the stereotype of the Jew
(now the antithesis of the Aryan) . . . the Jew became an exclusionary category.
The Jew defined what the Aryan was not. It was that which the Aryan neither
was nor ever would be. The Jew became the projection of all the anxieties about
control present within the Aryan." *Freud, Race, and Gender*, 9.

148. *Sublime Object*, 126.

149. Ibid.

150. Ibid.

151. I have chosen to cite a recent—and excellent—translation of the original 1850 version of Wagner's essay, published in *Wagner 9* (1988): 20–33. In addition, I will provide page references for the more readily available (but much less precise) translation by William Ashton Ellis, which is based upon Wagner's revised edition of the essay, published in 1869. See "Judaism in Music," in *Prose Works*, 3: 79–100. The most readily available German edition of the essay as it originally appeared in 1850 is in Richard Wagner, *Drei Essays*, 53–77. Hereafter, references to the various versions of the work will be abbreviated "Judaism-WAE" (for the English edition by William Ashton Ellis), "Judaism-*Wag*" (for the English edition that appeared in *Wagner*), and "Judentum" (for the German-language edition). A facsimile of the original articles as they appeared in the *Neue Zeitschrift für Musik* 19 (Sep. 3, 1850) and 20 (Sep. 6, 1850) appears in Manfred Eger, ed., *Wagner und die Juden*, 9–19.

152. The bibliography of works on Wagner and the Jews is extensive, ranging from National Socialist celebrations of Wagner's perspicuity in matters of racial purity to dogged defenders of the irrelevance of Wagner's social or political views. Among the most important recent works on the subject are Marc A. Weiner's, *Anti-Semitic Imagination*; Jacob Katz's *The Darker Side of Genius*; and Paul Lawrence Rose, *Wagner: Race and Revolution*. Hereafter, references to these latter works will be abbreviated *Darker Side* and *Race and Revolution*. While Katz provides a comprehensive historical account of Wagner's anti-Semitism, he refuses to speculate on whether anti-Semitism can be found in the stage works. Rose chastises Katz for his reticence; he and Weiner go to the works and find them suffused with anti-Semitism—although in different ways. Earlier contributions to the debate include Peter Viereck, "Hitler and Richard Wagner," *Common Sense* 8 (Nov/Dec 1939); Thomas Mann's response to Viereck in *Common Sense* 9 (January 1940); Leon Poliakov, *The History of Modern Anti-Semitism* (4 vols.), trans. Miriam Kochan; Otto Dov Kulka, "Richard Wagner und die Anfänge des modernen Antisemitismus," *Bulletin des Leo Baeck Instituts* 4 (1961): 290–96; Leon Stein, *The Racial Thinking of Richard Wagner*, especially 70–91; and, from the National Socialist perspective, Karl Richard Ganzer's *Richard Wagner und das Judentum*.

153. I have presented some of the following argument in the course of an essay on the aesthetics of anti-Semitism in Wagner's *Die Meistersinger von Nürnberg*. See my "Reading Beckmesser Reading."

154. See Adorno, *Search*, 19; Adorno, *Versuch*, 18. For a particularly provocative semifictional (and semiautobiographical) account of Wagner's relationship to Levi, interweaving the author's own, largely unsavory experiences at Bayreuth with an attempt to somehow reconstruct Levi's enigmatic character and his exceedingly precarious position in the Wagner circle, see Rolf Schneider, *Die Reise zu Richard Wagner*.

155. Adorno, *Search*, 23; Adorno, *Versuch*, 21. Nattiez explores this claim in *Wagner Androgyne*. See, for example, 69–70 (on Alberich and Mime).

156. Adorno, *Search*, 23; Adorno, *Versuch*, 21.

157. See, for example, Weiner, *Anti-Semitic Imagination*, 3–5; Deathridge, *New Grove Wagner*, 1–5; Katz, *Darker Side*, 120–23; Ernest Newman, *Life of Wagner*, 4 vols., 1: 3–18 and 2: 608–13; and (on Newman's position) Stein, *Racial Thinking*, 236–37. I discuss some of these positions below.

158. Friedrich Nietzsche, "The Case of Wagner," in *The Birth of Tragedy and The Case of Wagner*, trans. Walter Kaufmann, 153–92. Passage cited here appears in a footnote to the first Postscript, 182. In German: "War Wagner überhaupt ein Deutscher? Man hat einige Gründe, so zu fragen. Es ist schwer, in ihm irgend einen deutschen Zug ausfindig zu machen. . . . Sein Vater war ein Schauspieler Namens Geyer. Ein Geyer ist beinahe schon ein Adler. . . . Das, was bisher als 'Leben Wagner's' in Umlauf gebracht ist, ist fable convenue, wenn nicht Schlimmeres. Ich bekenne mein Mistrauen gegen jeden Punkt, der bloss durch Wagner selbst bezeugt ist. Er hatte nicht Stolz genug zu irgend einer Wahrheit über sich, Niemand war weniger stolz; er blieb, ganz wie Victor Hugo, auch im Biographischen sich treu,—er blieb Schauspieler." See Friedrich Nietzsche, [erste] Nachschrift, "Der Fall Wagner," *Sämtliche Werke: Kritische Studienausgabe*, 13 vols., 6: 1–69, here 41.

159. See Katz, *Darker Side*, 120–23; Peter Burbidge, "The Man and the Artist," in Burbidge and Sutton, *Wagner Companion*, 15–16; Sander Gilman, *Jewish Self-Hatred*, 210.

160. See the "Introductory Essay: 1813–1839" in Wagner, *Letters* [Spencer & Millington], 3–10. Text quoted above appears on 3.

161. *Anti-Semitic Imagination*, 5. As indicated above, Weiner is not the only one to make this claim. In a deft and surprising argument, Paul Lawrence Rose suggests that Wagner's youthful anxieties concerning his own Jewishness derived more from his financial situation than his ancestry. According to Rose, "A recurrent theme in Wagner's letters before 1850 is his self mocking accusation of his own 'Jewishness'. This was not so much a reference to his secret—and groundless—fear of being of Jewish descent through his probable father Ludwig Geyer, but rather alluded to his constant egoistic need for money. Wagner often ironically describes the solution of his own money problems as being his 're-demption' (*Erlösung*, *Auflösung*, and so on), acclaiming Meyerbeer as his 're-deemer' (*Erlöser*). Psychologically, therefore, the attack on Meyerbeer in 1850 neatly solved for Wagner the problem of his 'Jewishness', for it enabled him to blame his desperate desire for money on a type of 'Jewishness' that he had destroyed in himself by his repudiation of Meyerbeer as its true epitome." (Rose, *Wagner*, 86)

162. *Search*, 23–24; trans. modified. For Siegfried's diatribe against Mime, see *Siegfried*, Spencer, 200. Wagner's diatribe against the "Jewish way of speaking" appears in Judaism-*Wag*, 24; Judaism-WAE, 85; and *Judentum*, 59. (I have inter-

polated the text from Stewart Spencer's translations of "Judaism in Music" and *Siegfried* into the Adorno passage.)

163. According to Adorno, "Wagner recoiled with shock from the similarity between Mime and himself" (*Search*, 24; *Versuch*, 22).

164. See, for example, Katz, *Darker Side*, chapter 5, 47–64; Weiner, *Anti-Semitic Imagination*, 52–53; Rose, *Race and Revolution*, chapter 3, 40–48; and chapter 5, 73–88.

165. For a discussion of the volatile political history of the concept of the *Volk* and, in particular, its predictable antagonism to the concept of the Jew, see chapter 1 of George Mosse, *Germans and Jews*, 8–33.

166. It is interesting to note in this regard the occasional moments when Wagner seems to identify with the predicament of the homeless, rootless Jew. In *My Life*, for instance, Wagner recalls how his trip to Genoa in the fall of 1853 sent him into a delicious state of delirium: "For a few days I was as if intoxicated; but it was no doubt my great loneliness amid all these impressions which soon made me feel again the alien quality of this world and realize that I would never feel myself at home in it" (*My Life*, 498; trans. modified; *Mein Leben*, 511).

167. In his "The *Ring* and the Conditions of Interpretation," James Treadwell makes a similar point.

> "The interchangeability of nationalist fantasy and theatrical reform is clear from 'Jewishness in Music,' where Wagner's racist vision of a redeemed community is expressed through an assault on the operatic aesthetic of Mendelssohn and Meyerbeer. The public that sponsors their works and finds its own values (luxury, triviality) reflected in them is the degenerate echo of the idealized Greek audience. In *Opera and Drama*, *A Theatre in Zurich*, and *A Communication to My Friends*, Wagner develops a notion of the public's unconscious resistance to this degeneracy, identical with the 'collective Want' of the *Volk*." (Treadwell, "The *Ring*," 213)

The question, of course, is how and whether this notion, developed in the writings, finds expression in the *Ring*. According to Weiner, it is developed precisely through the motif of vision, a motif reproduced in Treadwell's argument, where Wagner's conception of the redeemed community is characterized as a "racist vision"; or where the degenerate public finds its own values "reflected" in degenerate artworks. (See Weiner, *Anti-Semitic Imagination*, 56.) In my argument, that expression will take the (ambivalent) form of resistance to narrative transmission.

168. Judaism-*Wag*, 23–24, trans. modified, emphasis in original; Judaism-WAE, 84; Judentum, 58.

169. Not surprisingly, the same argument reappears in Wagner's "What Is German?" published more than twenty-five years later. See "Was ist Deutsch?" *GS*, 10: 36–53; *PW*, 4: 149–69.

170. *Siegfried*, Spencer, 197, trans. modified.

171. Judaism-*Wag*, 23, Judaism-WAE, 83; Judentum, 57.

172. Judaism-*Wag*, 23, trans. modified, emphasis in original; Judaism-WAE, 83–84; Judentum, 57–58.

173. In fact, in the later version of the essay, printed in 1869, the phrase is changed to the plural: languages.

174. The same logic applies, in different ways, to Wagner's other works as well. For a reading of its deployment in the *Meistersinger*, see my "Reading Beckmesser Reading." Wagner's comedy has served as a flashpoint for discussions—often heated—concerning the presence or absence of anti-Semitism in his stage-works. See, in this regard, Barry Millington's famous essay "Nuremberg Trial: Is There Anti-Semitism in *Die Meistersinger*?" *Cambridge Opera Journal* 3, no. 3 (1991): 247–60. Hans Rudolf Vaget takes strenuous exception to Millington's claims in his provocative "Sixtus Beckmesser—A 'Jew in the Brambles'?" *Opera Quarterly* 12, no. 1 (1995): 35–45. Marc Weiner devotes a good deal of space to the question: see *Anti-Semitic Imagination*, especially 66–72, 117–35, and 215–21. Paul Lawrence Rose devotes less space to the question, but his position is probably even more controversial: see Rose, *Race and Revolution*, 110–12.

175. Wolf Rosenberg, "Versuch über einen Janusgeist," *Musik Konzepte* 5 (June 1981): 40–49, here 42.

176. Abbate, *Unsung Voices*, 161.

CHAPTER THREE

1. Fritz Lang, "Arbeitsgemeinschaft im Film," *Kinematograph* (887), February 17, 1924. Here and throughout this chapter, translations are mine unless otherwise noted. A substantial number of Lang's essays and interviews from the period between 1922 and 1933, including "Arbeitsgemeinschaft im Film," have been collected and republished in Fred Gehler and Ullrich Kasten's extremely useful compilation, *Fritz Lang: Die Stimme von Metropolis*. "Arbeitsgemeinschaft im Film" appears on 164–68, here 165. Hereafter, references to this collection will be abbreviated "Gehler & Kasten."

2. Lang, "Arbeitsgemeinschaft im Film," in Gehler & Kasten, 165–66.

3. See, for example, Thomas J. Saunders, *Hollywood in Berlin*, and Sabine Hake, *The Cinema's Third Machine*.

4. Fritz Lang, "Worauf es beim Nibelungen-Film ankam," reprinted in Gehler & Kasten, 170. Lang's prose here bears many of the hallmarks of Harbou's [ghost-?]writing, employing a rather complicated syntactical structure in the service of an overblown pathos and reactionary, *völkisch* sentiment. Karin Bruns presents a perceptive genealogical account of the rhetorical constellation and aspirations of Harbou's prose in the twenty years preceding *Die Nibelungen*. See Karin Bruns, *Kinomythen 1920–1945*, 7–41. Although I will not do so here, it

would be interesting to compare the prose styles of Lang and Harbou. I am not at all convinced that their markedly different styles are properly read as expressions of their political differences.

5. See Raymond Belour, "On Fritz Lang," trans. Tom Milne, in Stephen Jenkins, ed., *Fritz Lang*, 26–37, here 28.

6. Among the exceptions are Thomas Elsaesser's "Film History and Visual Pleasure: Weimar Cinema," in *Cinema Histories, Cinema Practices*, ed. Patricia Mellencamp and Philip Rosen, 47–87; hereafter, "Film History." In addition, see Klaus Kanzog, "Der Weg der Nibelungen ins Kino: Fritz Langs Film-Alternative zu Hebbel und Wagner," in Borchmeyer, ed., *Wege des Mythos in der Moderne*, 202–23.

7. Siegfried Kracauer, *From Caligari to Hitler*, hereafter, *Caligari*.

8. Before Kracauer's book was published, criticism of the film was much less thematically focused. Although some critics dismissed the film upon its release in February 1924, they were hardly riled by its architectural aesthetics. An extensive and partially annotated list of early reviews is included in E. Ann Kaplan, *Fritz Lang: A Guide to References and Sources* , 46–48 and 137–43. Hans Helmut Prinzler includes a substantial list of early reviews in the German press in his Appendix to Frieda Grafe, et. al, *Fritz Lang*. A number of books on Lang include reprints of reviews of the film: brief excerpts of glowing notices (including a review of the revival of the work in the "new Germany" of 1933) are included in Frederick Ott, *The Films of Fritz Lang*, 110–20. Martin Dey published an extended and blistering attack upon the film shortly after its release. See his *Nibelungenbuch und Nibelungenfilm*.

9. Kracauer, *Caligari*, 94–95.

10. For an eclectic study of the aestheticization of power in National Socialism see the extensive catalogue of the Neue Gesellschaft für Bildende Kunst exhibit *Inszenierung der Macht*.

11. See Kracauer, *Caligari*, 272.

12. Lotte Eisner, *The Haunted Screen*, 160.

13. Here I am in overall agreement with Sabine Hake's argument in "Architectural Hi/stories: Fritz Lang and the Nibelungs" in *Wide Angle* 12, no. 3 (July 1990): 38–57. As Hake puts it, "the film, as film, must not be reduced to its ideological effects" (39).

14. Elsaesser, "Film History," 58.

15. Elsaesser, "Film History," 74.

16. See Laura Mulvey, "Visual Pleasure and Narrative Cinema," in her *Visual and Other Pleasures*, 19.

17. Karin Bruns discusses the cultural resonances of Siegfried's physique in *Kinomythen*, 39–40.

18. In this sense, it is significant that Kriemhild is repeatedly shown to have her own visions, which take the form of fantastical dreams. In making space for

these dreams on screen, the film marks Kriemhild as bearing an unusual (because individual) power of vision. We can read the revenge that she wreaks and that which is wrought upon her as retribution for the singularity of that vision.

19. The screenplay indicates that Hagen does not reserve that stare for Siegfried. He first employs it when Kriemhild passes him on her way to gaze out the window near the outset of the second canto (shot 166). For a complete index of shots (based on the Munich print) and a complete transcription of intertitles, see the appendix to Angelika Breitmoser-Bock, *Bild, Filmbild, Schlüsselbild*, 191–257. Hereafter, references to this work will be abbreviated *Bild*.

20. This and all subsequent quotations from the film are taken from the intertitles of the Munich print listed in the appendix to Breitmoser-Bock, *Bild*, here 212. In "Fritz Lang's Definitive *Siegfried* and Its Versions," Victoria Stiles includes the text of the first two cantos of the Munich/Patalas print (in German and English translation) and compares it to the sequencing and texts of the other two major prints in circulation (Blackhawk and the 1933/Nazi reissue). See "Fritz Lang's Definitive *Siegfried* and Its Versions," *Literature/Film Quarterly* 13, no. 4 (1985): 258–74; here 265–73. In an earlier essay, Stiles considers the various sources used in preparing the Nibelungen film. See "The Siegfried Legend and the Silent Screen: Fritz Lang's Interpretation of a Hero Saga," *Literature/Film Quarterly* 8, no. 4 (1980): 232–36. Until the mid-1990s, the screenplay of the film was presumed lost. It is now available in the archives of the Stiftung Deutsche Kinemathek in Berlin.

21. Thea von Harbou, *Das Nibelungenbuch*, 32.

22. Thus, in his first appearance in Harbou's novel, Hagen juxtaposes King Gunther's blindness to his own acute vision:

> Do you observe Kriemhild's route every morning, when she and her ladies-in-waiting go to Siegfried? Not you, Sir Gunther, but I do! Do you count the money that Kriemhild's ladies-in-waiting carry in their coats, red gold from the Nibelungen stash, taken each and every morning from the treasure? Not you, Sir Gunther, but I do! Do you count the beggars that Kriemhild invites in to her, whom she has line up to see her in front of Siegfried's tomb? Not you, Sir Gunther, but I do! Do you hear them asking: "Your majesty, Queen, what shall we do for you?" Do you see the look in Kriemhild's eyes, when she bids them: "Nothing!"—for this woman, she knows all too well that eventually, without any of her doing, without her command, out of these thick beggar brains one day there will spring the desire to thank Siegfried, the dead hero, for his gold and to seek justice for his widow. That's what the lady is waiting for. That's what you're all waiting for! You too, King Gunther. But not me! (Harbou, *Nibelungenbuch*, 31–32)

23. Although I will be arguing that Siegfried is tainted by losing control over his appearance, some early reviewers were interested in Siegfried's precarious moral standing in the film. Thus, for example, Roland Schacht argues that the

film does not present Siegfried as an unmitigated hero: "But doesn't Siegfried play a really blameworthy role in the film? Granted: a hero. He kills the dragon, defeats Alberich, enslaves twelve kings. But what's the deal with Brunhild? In perpetrating this scam to win blond Kriemhild, where are the heroic ethics?" *Das Blaue Heft* 5, no. 6 (March 1, 1924).

24. In the screenplay, the scene is described thus: "Siegfried only half hears what Gunther says. He again turns his gaze upon Kriemhild. She stands with her hands crossed beneath her breast like a pretty, immobile picture with her eyes upon the ground." Harbou, *"Die Nibelungen: Ein deutsches Heldenlied."* In place of consecutive page numbers, the screenplay is labeled by a combination of scene and page. The quotation above appears on the third page of scene 48, which is thus designated *48/III*; previous pages in that scene are labeled 48/I, 48/II, etc. Hereafter, *"Siegfried* screenplay" followed by pagination corresponding to the original.

25. Although it would take me too far afield to present the argument in the detail that it deserves, I am convinced that this inflection of Kriemhild's transgressive lack of self-restraint can be read in light of Harbou's polemical sense of a woman's proper place in wartime. See her books *Die deutsche Frau im Weltkrieg,* and *Deutsche Frauen im Kampfe des Lebens,* as well as the collection of novellas *Der Krieg und die Frauen.*

26. Von Harbou, *Nibelungenbuch,* 54.

27. In his *Memoirs,* Kettelhut suggests that in the film Siegfried was supposed to appear *as Gunther*:

> [Gunther] knew that he would never be able to defeat [Brunhild], whose warrior powers were legendary—and Hagen Tronje knew it too. Only Siegfried could match Brunhild and defeat her. Gunther had promised Siegfried the hand of lovely Kriemhild and thus it was up to Siegfried to take the magic cap that he had won from Alberich the Nibelung and tuck it under his belt. The magic cap could render him invisible and allow him to assume any appearance he wished; and by appearing as Gunther here in Isenheim and by vanquishing the strong queen of the northern land he would win his beloved Kriemhild. This great deception— conceived by a cunning Hagen, executed by an unsuspecting and amorous Siegfried, tolerated by Gunther, fully aware of his own incapacities—is of course the impetus for the fatal destiny that was to bring death to almost everyone involved. (Erich Kettelhut, "Erinnerungen," unpublished typescript in the holdings of the Stiftung Deutsche Kinemathek, 501–2)

A brief excerpt from the section of the Memoirs relating to the Nibelungen films appears as "Fritz Lang und die Nibelungen: Erinnerungen an die Dreharbeiten," in Wolfgang Jacobsen, ed., *Babelsberg,* 77–80.

28. The text of Brunhild's threat: "Before evening, King Gunther, your broken weapons will be added to those already adorning my hall." Breitmoser-Bock, *Bild,* 217.

29. In the film, Brunhild's army consists entirely of women. In the *Nibelungenlied*, it is populated by men and women.

30. Here the triangular structure of homosocial bonding takes as its object the disempowerment of this eminently powerful woman. What makes the arrangement unusual, however, is that its third term is rendered invisible: the arrangement "between men" would appear to be an arrangement solely between a man and a woman.

31. Here the familial link between Alberich and Hagen looms large, for Hagen "produces" Siegfried's appearance (as a shadow) in peculiarly cinematic terms and Alberich is presented as a veritable father of cinema. While Wagner presents Hagen as Alberich's son, no such family link is proposed in the Nibelungen film.

32. See adventure 10 of *NL*, 637:

> Di füeze unt ouch die hende   si im zesamne bant,
> si truoc in z'einem nagele   unt hienc in an die want,
> do er si slâfes irte.   die minne si im verbôt.
> jâ het er von ir krefte   vil nâch gewúnnén den tôt.

> [For in return for being baulked of her sleep, she bound him hand and foot, carried him to a nail, and hung him on the wall. She had put a stop to his love-making! As to him, he all but died, such strength had she exerted.] (*NL-Eng*, 88)

33. See adventure 8, *NL*, 75; *NL-Eng*, 527–28. There is mention here that Brünhild is not willing to sleep with Gunther on board but no intimation of serious trouble.

34. Breitmoser-Bock, *Bild*, 224.

35. See *NL-Eng*, 88; *NL*, 633–43.

36. *NL-Eng*, 90, trans. modified; *NL*, 652.4–653.3. In the original:

> "ez muoz diu vrouwe Prünhilt   noch hînaht wérdén dîn wîp."
> Er sprach: "ich kum' noch hînte   ze der kémenâten dîn
> alsô tougenlîchen   in der tárnkáppen mîn,
> daz sich mîner liste   mac niemen wol verstên."

37. Breitmoser-Bock, *Bild*, 228.

38. Breitmoser-Bock *Bild*, 239. Hagen's claim represents a rather clumsy instance of foreshadowing. In Hagen's eyes, Siegfried's big mouth will remain worse than—and thus proper justification for—the murder Hagen will commit to avenge it. Here, then, the intertitle literalizes Hagen's foresight, for his comment suggests that he foresees not just the consequences of Siegfried's actions but the moral justification that will be needed to support his retribution.

39. After all, how much of the rape which the gesture arguably metonymizes could the filmmakers show?

40. See Saunders, *Hollywood in Berlin*, especially chapters 3 and 4. On the prehistory of this "invasion" see Deniz Göktürk, "Moving Images of America in Early German Cinema," in Thomas Elsaesser, ed., *A Second Life*, 93–100.

41. See Saunders, *Hollywood in Berlin*, chapter 4. The appetite of the German public for Hollywood films persisted well into the Third Reich. In this regard, see "German Fantasies, American Dreams," in Eric Rentschler, *Ministry of Illusion*, 103–12.

42. See in this regard, Karl Figdor in *Erste Internationale Film-Zeitung*, January 3, 1920; Robert Bogyansky, "Der deutsche Film," *Film-Kurier*, March 4, 1920.

43. In "Weimar Cinema and National Identity," Thomas Saunders lists these qualities and observes that participants in the *Weltbühne* debate of 1921 "agreed on the qualities assigned the respective national cinemas but disagreed on which corresponded to the inherent character of film." Thomas J. Saunders, "History in the Making: Weimar Cinema and National Identity," in Bruce A. Murray and Christopher J. Wickham, eds., *Framing the Past*, 42–67, here 51 and 50, respectively.

44. Saunders "History in the Making," 52.

45. Here are the exact terms of the screenplay: "In der Höhlung des [verkrüppelten] Baumstumpfes kauert, als wäre er ein Teil des Baumes selbst, Alberich" (*Siegfried* screenplay, 23).

46. Breitmoser-Bock, *Bild*, 204.

47. *Siegfried*—screenplay, 29/I.

48. See Miriam Hansen, *Babel and Babylon*, 25; hereafter, *Babel*.

49. For example, the Wintergarten program of the Skladanowsky brothers in Berlin in November 1895—credited as the first occasion where film is presented to a paying audience—included two films of ethnic dancing, while the Lumière brothers included a short film of a train pulling into a station in their Grand Café show in Paris in December 1895.

50. Hansen, *Babel*, 26. In having the projectionist behind the screen, Porter arguably compensates for the much more pressing fear, namely that there is no one and nothing back there at all.

51. See Lotte Eisner, *Fritz Lang*, 79.

52. See Darrell William Davis, *Picturing Japaneseness*, 15.

53. Davis, *Picturing Japaneseness* 22.

54. During the Third Reich, the fantasy would become doxa. In *The Ministry of Illusion*, Eric Rentschler reviews some of the terms by which Jews are fantasized as having gained control over German cinema. See "Masks of a Monster," in *Ministry of Illusion*, 154–58.

55. Kracauer, *Caligari*, 94.

56. Ibid.

57. *Siegfried*—screenplay, 30/I.

58. See Janet Bergstrom, "Psychological Explanation in the Films of Lang and Pabst," in E. Ann Kaplan, ed., *Psychoanalysis and Cinema*, 163–80, here 169.

59. Harbou, "Vom Epos," 139. I consider this quote in greater detail below. The terms of this notion of exhaustion are not new. In the early years of cinema, the ponderousness of German culture (often associated with Wagner's music dramas) and the exhaustion of the German worker were often juxtaposed to the fast pace and visual stimulation provided by American film. See, in this regard, Deniz Göktürk, "Moving Images," 94.

60. On the distinctions between Lang's prose style and Harbou's, see note 4 above. Fritz Lang, "Stilwille im Film," in *Jugend*, 3 (Feb. 1, 1924), reprinted in Gehler & Kasten, 161–64, here 162.

61. Günther Hess argues that the generalized need for images of heroism became much more tightly connected to the Nibelungen material around 1925. See his "Siegfrieds Wiederkehr."

62. Harbou "Vom Epos," 139. Although Harbou has routinely (and rightly) been associated with a jingoistic celebration of the German *Geist*, a number of writers have argued that Fritz Lang was himself a thoroughgoing nationalist. See, in this regard, Reinhold Keiner, *Thea von Harbou und der deutsche Film bis 1933*, 62, and Gösta Werner, "Fritz Lang and Goebbels: Myth and Facts," in *Film Quarterly* 43, no. 3 (Spring 1990): 24–27.

63. Harbou "Vom Epos," 139.

64. Fritz Lang, "Kitsch—Sensation—Kultur und Film," in *Das Kulturfilm-buch*, 28–31, here 31. The essay also appears in Gehler & Kasten, 202–6.

65. In his essay on visual pleasure in Weimar film, Thomas Elsaesser notes that "Fritz Lang's interviews and essays in the quality monthlies and weekly press throughout his German career were always conscious of what cultural prejudices he had to flatter in order to subvert" (Elsaesser, "Film History," 71). In this case, Lang is clearly positioning film—and by extension, *his* film—as an international rather than a national product: thus, *The Nibelungen* would be seen as a work of interest to the world (read: the export market) despite its dedication to the German people.

66. See Breitmoser-Bock, *Bild*, 201, shot 158.

67. The image is unanchored in the sense that we cannot determine whether it records Siegfried's vision of the tale being told or the storyteller's vision or the shared vision of the on-screen audience.

68. Breitmoser-Bock, *Bild*, 201.

69. The title of the second canto is "How Volker Sang For Kriemhild, and How Siegfried Came to Worms."

70. The term *Nibelungentreue* was first introduced into political discourse in Chancellor Fürst Bülow's speech to the Reichstag on March 29, 1909, in an attempt to ensure the solidarity of the German Reich with Austria-Hungary. For a brief history of the political appropriation of the term in German politics with particular focus on Hermann Göring's notorious Stalingrad speech, see Peter

Krüger, "Etzels Halle und Stalingrad: Die Rede Görings vom 30. 1. 1943," in Heinzle and Waldschmidt, *Die Nibelungen*, 151–69.

71. Harbou, "Vom Epos," 139.

POSTSCRIPT

1. Sigmund Freud, "Fetishism," in *Standard Edition*, 21: 149–57, here 153, trans. modified. In German: "Fetischismus" in *Studienausgabe*, 3: 379–88, here 384. Hereafter, references to the essay will be abbreviated "Fetishism," *SE* and "Fetischismus," *SA*, respectively.

2. "Fetishism," *SE*, 153; "Fetischismus," *SA*, 384.

3. Thus, for example, in the Collier Books edition of *The Collected Papers of Sigmund Freud*, the passage cited above concludes as follows: "If we wish to differentiate between what happens to the *idea* as distinct from the *affect*, we can restrict 'repression' to relate to the affect; the correct word for what happens to the idea is then 'denial'." See "Fetishism," in Sigmund Freud, *Sexuality and the Psychology of Love*, 214–19, here 215.

4. See, in this regard, Michael Franz Basch, "The Perception of Reality and the Disavowal of Meaning," in *Annual of Psychoanalysis* 11 (1983): 25–53. Here is how Basch puts the problem:

> In psychosis the offending percept is decathected; it no longer exists for the ego which is then free to falsify reality. I think there can be little argument but that this is what English-speaking psychiatrists and psychoanalysts term "denial," "denial of reality," or "psychotic denial." . . . In this instance, I believe, conceptual accuracy would have been served if Mr. Strachey [general editor and translator of the *Standard Edition* of Freud's works] had translated Freud's *verleugnen* as "deny," using "disavow" for cases . . . where the percept has not been eliminated but only its significance for the observer has been distorted, rationalized, or misinterpreted in the interest of preventing anxiety. (129)

My argument is indebted to Basch's informative and intelligent paper.

5. See "Some Psychical Consequences of the Anatomical Distinction Between the Sexes," in Freud, *Standard Edition*, 19 (1961): 243–60, here 252; emphasis added, trans. modified. In German: "wenn der kleine Knabe die Genitalgegend des Mädchens zuerst erblickt, benimmt er sich unschlüssig, zunächst wenig interessiert; er sieht nichts, oder er verleugnet seine Wahrnehmung, schwächt sie ab, sucht nach Auskünften, um sie mit seiner Erwartung in Einklang zu bringen." See Freud, "Einige psychische Folgen des anatomischen Geschlechtsunterschieds," in *Studienausgabe*, 5: 253–66, here 260. For a helpful introductory discussion regarding the distinction between disavowal and negation, see the respective entries in Jean Laplanche and J.-B. Pontalis, *The Language of Psychoanalysis*, 118–21 and 261–63.

6. In summarizing the inflection of *Verleugnung* in the 1925 essay, Basch proposes a similar scenario: "It is not the perceptual fact but the deficit that it implies that is rejected by the little boy—*it only looks as if it is not there because it is small, it will grow, etc.*" For Freud as for Basch, the perception generates a practice that would redress that shortcoming through an alternative figuration. See Basch, "Perception," 130; emphasis added.

7. "Fetishism," *SE*, 152; "Fetischismus," *SA*, 383.

8. It is surprising that Freud does not comment further upon the flimsiness of the mediation here. If Freud's analysis is correct, then the formulation of the fetish as a simple homonym would seem to compel its discovery. The recurring crudity of figuration in fetishism seems worthy of further consideration.

9. Surprisingly, Freud does not explore an obvious resonance of the term, namely, as glans. Thus the "glance" vouchsafes the boy's investment of the nose with the value of the missing penis more completely—and more literally—than Freud seems to think.

10. *The Nasty Girl* [*Das schreckliche Mädchen*], a film written and directed by Michael Verhoeven, starring Lena Stolze. Sentana Filmproduktion; distributed in the U.S. by Miramax Films and HBO Video.

11. Although we can only know this in retrospect, since we have not been introduced to the character: these are her first lines.

12. *NL*, 1; *NL-Eng*, 17.

13. Verhoeven invents Pfilzing as his heroine's hometown. As he explains in the opening roll of text, the town is fictional, but stands for any and all German towns.

14. It is a wonderfully ironic turn, for here the ex-Nazis, and not the Jews, control the media and the university.

15. Thus, for example, in an earlier scene, Sonja's family sat in a living room, listening to a series of harangues left on Sonja's new answering machine. But instead of being enclosed within walls, the room is situated upon a moving platform that encircles the town's main square, incongruously placing the family simultaneously at home and very much out in the open, exposed to public view.

16. Here is a translation of Sonja's harangue:

> *Sonja*: I won't let you put me in the town hall as a bust; I'm a living person!
>
> *Mom*: Sonja, what's got into you?
>
> *Sonja*: Nothing's gotten into me; but I'm not falling for that trick! Just because you all are scared shitless? Because you're scared of what else I might dig up?
>
> *Mom*: Sonja, please, be quiet.
>
> *Sonja*: I won't be quiet! That's exactly what they want! Don't you see that? But I'm not falling for that trick! I won't do you people that favor! It's a load of crap! You just want to make a fool of me! [*Ihr wollt mich*

ja umscheißen] You want me to shut up; to keep quiet! [Her mother attempts to smack her, but misses; she smacks her mother back, hard. Her father faints.]

Person 1: And you *should* keep quiet!

Person 2: You ungrateful thing!

Person 3: Go to the DDR!

Sonja: Kiss my ass! This is *my* country. *My* country [swatting at her grandmother, who is trying to restrain her] You're all assholes!

17. In doing so, the film fetishizes its claim to present live events—a problematic but familiar conceit.

18. The scene's overriding concern with turning Sonja to stone echoes as it inverts the film's more general and implicit association of Sonja with the figure of Medusa. In the town's eyes, Sonja is aligned with the Gorgon: she is a dreadful, horrifying figure, who, herself turned to stone, would become much less threatening, much more reassuring.

𝔚𝔬𝔯𝔨𝔰 ℭ𝔦𝔱𝔢𝔡

Bibliographical Note: Unless otherwise noted, all references to Wagner's prose works are taken from the *Gesammelte Schriften und Dichtungen* and the *Prose Works*. I have not listed individual essays and works here. References to Wagner's prose published in other sources are listed here, by title.

Abbate, Carolyn. *Unsung Voices: Opera and Musical Narrative in the Nineteenth Century*. Princeton: Princeton University Press, 1991.

Adorno, Theodor. "Bürgerliche Oper." In *Gesammelte Schriften*, vol. 16, Musikalische Schriften I–III, ed. Rolf Tiedemann. Frankfurt am Main: Suhrkamp, 1978. 24–39. English translation: "Bourgeois Opera." In *Opera Through Other Eyes*, ed. David J. Levin. 25–43.

———. *Versuch über Wagner*. In *Gesammelte Schriften*, vol. 13, ed. Gretel Adorno and Rolf Tiedemann. Frankfurt am Main: Suhrkamp, 1971. 7–148. English translation: *In Search of Wagner*. Trans. Rodney Livingstone. London: NLB, 1981.

Anderson, Benedict. *Imagined Communities: Reflections on the Origin and Spread of Nationalism*. Rev. ed. New York: Verso, 1991.

Andersson, Theodore M. *Preface to the Nibelungenlied*. Stanford: Stanford University Press, 1987.

———. "Why Does Siegfried Die?" In *Germanic Studies in Honor of Otto Springer*, ed. Stephen J. Kaplowitt. Pittsburgh: K & S Enterprises, 1978. 29–39.

Bartetzko, Dieter. *Illusionen in Stein: Stimmungsarchitektur im deutschen Faschismus. Ihre Vorgeschichte in Theater- und Film-Bauten*. Reinbek: Rowohlt, 1985.

Basch, Michael Franz. "The Perception of Reality and the Disavowal of Meaning." In *Annual of Psychoanalysis* 11 (1983): 25–53.

Bekker, Hugo. *The Nibelungenlied: A Literary Analysis*. Toronto: University of Toronto Press, 1971.

Belour, Raymond. "On Fritz Lang." Trans. Tom Milne. In *Fritz Lang: The Image and the Look*, ed. Stephen Jenkins. London: British Film Institute, 1981. 26–37.

Bergstrom, Janet. "Psychological Explanation in the Films of Lang and Pabst." In *Psychoanalysis and Cinema*, ed. E. Ann Kaplan. New York: Routledge, 1990. 163–80.

Bhabha, Homi K., ed. *Nation and Narration*. New York: Routledge, 1990.

Botstein, Leon. *Judentum und Modernität: Essays zur Rolle der Juden in der deutschen und österreichischen Kultur 1848 bis 1938*. Vienna: Böhlau, 1991.

Borchmeyer, Dieter. *Das Theater Richard Wagners*. Stuttgart: Reclam, 1982. In English: *Richard Wagner: Theory and Theatre*. Trans. Stewart Spencer. New York: Oxford University Press, 1991.

———, ed. *Wege des Mythos in der Moderne: Richard Wagner, Der Ring des Nibelungen*. Munich: Deutscher Taschenbuch Verlag, 1987.

Brackert, Helmut. *Das Nibelungenlied*. Mittelhochdeutscher Text und Übertragung. 2 vols. Frankfurt am Main: Fischer, 1971.

———. "Nibelungenlied und Nationalgedanke: Zur Geschichte einer deutschen Ideologie." In *Mediaevalia Litteraria: Festschrift für Helmut de Boor*, ed. Ursula Hennig and Herbert Kolb. Munich: C. H. Beck, 1971. 343–64.

Breitmoser-Bock, Angelika. *Bild, Filmbild, Schlüsselbild: Zu einer kunstwissenschaftlichen Methodik der Filmanalyse am Beispiel von Fritz Langs "Siegfried."* Diskurs Film: vol. 5. Munich: Shaudig, Bauer, Ledig, 1992.

Brinkmann, Rheinhold. "Richard Wagner der Erzähler." *Österreichische Musik Zeitschrift* 37, no. 6 (June 1982): 297–306.

Bruns, Karin. *Kinomythen 1920–1945: Die Filmentwürfe der Thea von Harbou*. Stuttgart: Metzler, 1995.

Burbidge, Peter. "Richard Wagner: The Man and the Artist." In *The Wagner Companion*, ed. Burbidge and Richard Sutton. Boston: Faber and Faber, 1979.

Burger, Harald. "Vorausdeutung und Erzählstruktur in mittelalterlichen Texten." In *Zeitgestaltung in der Erzählkunst*, ed. Alexander Ritter. Darmstadt: Wissenschaftliche Buchgesellschaft, 1978. 247–77.

Clément, Catherine. *Opera, or the Undoing of Women*. Trans. Betsy Wing. Minneapolis: University of Minnesota Press, 1988.

Dahlhaus, Carl. *Richard Wagners Musikdramen*. Velber: Friedrich, 1971. English translation: *Richard Wagner's Music Dramas*. Trans. Mary Whittall. New York: Cambridge University Press, 1992.

Davis, Darrell William. *Picturing Japaneseness: Monumental Style, National Identity, Japanese Film*. New York: Columbia University Press, 1996.

de Boor, Helmut, ed. *Das Nibelungenlied*. Nach der Ausgabe von Karl Bartsch. 17th printing. Wiesbaden: Brockhaus, 1963.

Deathridge, John. "Life." In *The New Grove Wagner*, ed. Carl Dahlhaus and John Deathridge. New York: Norton, 1984. 1–67.

———. Book Review Essay in *Nineteenth Century Music* 5, no. 1 (Summer 1981): 81–89.

———, Martin Geck, and Egon Voss. *Wagner Werk-Verzeichnis: Verzeichnis der musikalischen Werke Richard Wagners und ihrer Quellen*. Mainz: Schott, 1986.

Dey, Martin. *Nibelungenbuch und Nibelungenfilm: Betrachtungen eines Laien*. Dortmund: Ruhfuss, 1924.

Dickerson, Jr., Harold D. "Hagen: A Negative View." *Semasia: Beiträge zur germanisch-romanischen Sprachforschung* 2 (1975): 43–59.

Donington, Robert. *Wagner's 'Ring' and Its Symbols: The Music and the Myth.* New York: St. Martin's, 1969.

Edmundson, Mark. *Towards Reading Freud: Self-Creation in Milton, Wordsworth, Emerson, and Sigmund Freud.* Princeton: Princeton University Press, 1990.

Eger, Manfred, ed. *Wagner und die Juden: Fakten und Hintergründe.* Bayreuth: Druckhaus Bayreuth, 1985.

Eggert, Mara, and Hans-Klaus Jungheinrich. *Die Oper Frankfurt: Durchbrüche. 10 Jahre Musiktheater mit Michael Gielen.* Weinheim, Berlin: Quadriga, 1987.

Ehrismann, Otfrid. *Nibelungenlied: Epoche—Werk—Wirkung.* Munich: C. H. Beck, 1987.

———. *Nibelungenlied in Deutschland: Studien zur Rezeption des Nibelungenlieds von der Mitte des 18. Jahrhunderts bis zum Ersten Weltkrieg.* Munich: Wilhelm Fink, 1975.

———. "*Nibelungenlied* und Nationalgedanke: Zu Geschichte und Psychologie eines nationalen Identifikationsmusters." *Damals: Zeitschrift für geschichtliches Wissen* 12 (1980): 942–60, 1033–46; 13 (1981): 21–35, 115–32.

———. "Strategie und Schicksal—Hagen." In *Literarische Symbolfiguren: Von Prometheus bis Svejk,* ed. Werner Wunderlich. Facetten deutscher Literatur. St. Galler Studien. Vol. 1. Bern: Haupt, 1989. 89–115.

Eisner, Lotte. *Fritz Lang.* London: Secker & Warburg, 1976/repr. New York: Da Capo, n.d.

———. *The Haunted Screen: Expressionism in the German Cinema and the Influence of Max Reinhardt.* Trans. Roger Greaves (from the French). Berkeley: University of California Press, 1973.

Elsaesser, Thomas. "Film History and Visual Pleasure: Weimar Cinema." In *Cinema Histories, Cinema Practices,* ed. Patricia Mellencamp and Philip Rosen. Westport, CT: Greenwood Publishing Group, 1984. 47–87.

Felman, Shoshana. *Jacques Lacan and the Adventure of Insight: Psychoanalysis in Contemporary Culture.* Cambridge, MA: Harvard University Press, 1987.

Frakes, Jerold. *Brides and Doom: Gender, Property, and Power in Medieval German Women's Epic.* Philadelphia: University of Pennsylvania Press, 1994.

Freeman, Mark. *Rewriting the Self: History, Memory, Narrative.* New York: Routledge, 1993.

Freud, Sigmund. "Einige psychische Folgen des anatomischen Geschlechtsunterschieds." In *Studienausgabe.* 10 vols. Frankfurt am Main: Fischer, 1969–79. Vol. 5 (1972). 253–72. English translation: "Some Psychical Consequences of the Anatomical Distinction Between the Sexes." Trans. James Strachey. *Standard Edition of the Complete Psychological Works of Sigmund Freud.* 24 vols. London: Hogarth, 1953–73. Vol. 19 (1961). 243–60.

Freud, Sigmund. "Die endliche und die unendliche Analyse" (1937). In *Studienausgabe*. Vol. 2. Frankfurt am Main: Fischer, 1972. Ergänzungsband. 351–92. English translation: "Analysis: Terminable and Interminable." In *Standard Edition*. Vol. 23 (1958). 209–53.

———. "Fetischismus." In *Studienausgabe*. Vol. 3. Frankfurt am Main: Fischer, 1975. 379–88. English translation: "Fetishism." In *Standard Edition*. Vol. 21 (1961). 149–57.

———. *Sexuality and the Psychology of Love*, ed. Philip Rieff. New York: Collier, 1963.

———. *Die Traumdeutung*. In *Studienausgabe*. Vol. 2. Frankfurt am Main: Fischer, 1972. 10 vols. English translation: *The Interpretation of Dreams*. In *Standard Edition*. Vols. 4 and 5.

Frühwald, Wolfgang. "Wandlungen eines Nationalmythos: Der Weg der Nibelungen ins 19. Jahrhundert." In *Wege des Mythos in der Moderne: Richard Wagner, Der Ring des Nibelungen*, ed. Dieter Borchmeyer. Munich: Deutscher Taschenbuch Verlag, 1987. 17–40.

Ganzer, Karl Richard. *Richard Wagner und das Judentum*. Hamburg: Hanseatische Verlagsanstalt, 1938.

Gehler, Fred, and Ulrich Kasten. *Fritz Lang: Die Stimme von Metropolis*. Berlin: Henschel, 1990.

Genette, Gérard. *Narrative Discourse: An Essay in Method*. Trans. Jane E. Lewin. Ithaca, NY: Cornell University Press, 1980.

Gilman, Sander. *Freud, Race, and Gender*. Princeton: Princeton University Press, 1993.

———. *Jewish Self-Hatred: Anti-Semitism and the Hidden Language of the Jews*. Baltimore: Johns Hopkins University Press, 1986.

Göktürk, Deniz. "Moving Images of America in Early German Cinema." In *A Second Life: German Cinema's First Decades*, ed. Thomas Elsaesser. Amsterdam: Amsterdam University Press, 1996. 93–100.

Grafe, Frieda, et al. *Fritz Lang*. Reihe Film 7, Reihe Hanser 208. Munich: Carl Hanser, 1976.

Graus, Frantisek. "Von der Siegfriedsage zum Nibelungenmythos." In *Lebendige Vergangenheit: Überlieferung im Mittelalter und in den Vorstellungen vom Mittelalter*. Köln: Böhlau, 1975. 275–289.

Hake, Sabine. "Architectural Hi/stories: Fritz Lang and *The Nibelungs*." *Wide Angle* 12, no. 3 (July 1990): 38–57.

———. *The Cinema's Third Machine: Writing on Film in Germany 1907–1933*. Lincoln: University of Nebraska Press, 1993.

Hansen, Miriam. *Babel and Babylon: Spectatorship in American Silent Film*. Cambridge, MA: Harvard University Press, 1991.

Harbou, Thea von. "Aus dem Manuskript des Films *Die Nibelungen*." In *Das Kulturfilmbuch*, ed. E. Beyfuss and A. Kossowsky. Berlin: Carl P. Chryselius, 1924. 246–60.

———. *Die deutsche Frau im Weltkrieg: Einblicke und Ausblicke.* Leipzig: 1916.

———. *Deutsche Frauen im Kampfe des Lebens.* Leipzig: 1924.

———. *Der Krieg und die Frauen: Novellen.* Stuttgart: Cotta, 1913/rpt 1916.

———. "*Die Nibelungen: Ein deutsches Heldenlied. Erster Teil: Siegfried.*" Unpublished screenplay in the holdings of the Stiftung Deutsche Kinemathek, n.d., n.p.

———. *Das Nibelungenbuch.* Munich: Drei Masken Verlag, 1923.

———. "Vom Epos zum Film." *Die Woche* 26, no. 6 (February 9, 1924): 138–40.

Hart Nibbrig, Christiaan L., ed. *Was heisst "Darstellen."* Frankfurt am Main: Suhrkamp, 1994.

Hatto, A. T., trans. *The Nibelungenlied.* London: Penguin, 1969.

Haymes, Edward R. *The Nibelungenlied: History and Interpretation.* Chicago: University of Illinois Press, 1986.

Heinzle, Joachim, and Anneliese Waldschmidt, eds. *Die Nibelungen: Ein deutscher Wahn, ein deutscher Alptraum. Studien und Dokumente zur Rezeption des Nibelungenstoffs im 19. und 20. Jahrhundert.* Frankfurt am Main: Suhrkamp, 1991.

Helfer, Martha B. *The Retreat of Representation: The Concept of Darstellung in German Critical Discourse.* Albany: SUNY Press, 1996.

Hess, Günther. "Siegfrieds Wiederkehr: Zur Geschichte einer deutschen Mythologie in der Weimarer Republik." *Internationales Archiv für Sozialgeschichte der deutschen Literatur* 6 (Tübingen: 1981): 112–44.

Homann, Holgar. "The Hagen Figure in the *Nibelungenlied*: Know Him by His Lies." *Modern Language Notes* 97, no. 3 (1982): 759–69.

Hughes, Michael. *Nationalism and Society: Germany 1800–1945.* London: Edward Arnold, 1988.

Julius, Anthony. *T. S. Eliot, Anti-Semitism, and Literary Form.* Cambridge: Cambridge University Press, 1995.

Kanzog, Klaus. "Der Weg der Nibelungen ins Kino: Fritz Langs Film-Alternative zu Hebbel und Wagner." In *Wege des Mythos in der Moderne,* ed. Borchmeyer. 202–23.

Kaplan, E. Ann. *Fritz Lang: A Guide to References and Sources.* Boston: G. K. Hall, 1981.

———, ed. *Psychoanalysis and Cinema.* New York: Routledge, 1990.

Katz, Jacob. *The Darker Side of Genius: Richard Wagner's Anti-Semitism.* Tauber Institute for the Study of European Jewry, vol. 5. Hanover, NH: University Press of New England, 1986. German original: *Richard Wagner: Vorbote des Antisemitismus.* Königstein/Ts: Jüdischer Verlag, Athenäum, 1985.

———. *From Prejudice to Destruction: Anti-Semitism, 1700–1933.* Cambridge, MA: Harvard University Press, 1980.

Keiner, Reinhold. *Thea von Harbou und der deutsche Film bis 1933.* Hildesheim: Georg Olms, 1984.

Kettelhut, Erich. "Erinnerungen." Unpublished typescript in the holdings of the

Stiftung Deutsche Kinemathek. A brief excerpt appears as "Fritz Lang und die Nibelungen: Erinnerungen an die Dreharbeiten." In *Babelsberg: Ein Filmstudio 1912–1992*, ed. Wolfgang Jacobsen. Berlin: Argon, 1992. 77–80.

Klein, Melanie. "Notes on Some Schizoid Mechanisms." In *International Journal of Psychoanalysis* 27 (1946): 99–110.

———. "On Identification." In Melanie Klein, Paula Heimann, R. E. Money-Kyrle, eds. *New Directions in Psychoanalysis*. New York: Basic Books, 1957. 309–45.

Kneif, Tibor. "Zur Deutung der Rheintöchter in Wagners *Ring*." *Archiv für Musikwissenschaft* 26 (1969): 297–306. English translation: "On the Meaning of the Rhinemaidens in Wagner's *Ring*." Trans. Stewart Spencer. In *Wagner* 10. London: Wagner Society, 1989. 21–28.

Köpnick, Lutz. "'Nothung! Nothung! Neidlicher Stahl!': Die Phantasmagorie des Schwertes in Wagners *Der Ring des Nibelungen*." *German Quarterly* 66, no. 4 (Fall 1993): 490–509.

Kracauer, Siegfried. *From Caligari to Hitler: A Psychological History of the German Film*. Princeton: Princeton University Press, 1947.

Kropfinger, Klaus. "Text und Edition von *Oper und Drama*." In Richard Wagner, *Oper und Drama*. Stuttgart: Reclam, 1984. 450–78.

Krüger, Peter. "Etzels Halle und Stalingrad: Die Rede Görings vom 30. 1. 1943." In Heinzle and Waldschmidt, eds. *Die Nibelungen*. 151–69.

Kulka, Otto Dov. "Richard Wagner und die Anfänge des modernen Antisemitismus." *Bulletin des Leo Baeck Instituts* 4 (1961): 290–96.

Lacan, Jacques. "The Mirror Stage as Formative of the Function of the I as Revealed in Psychoanalytic Experience" (lecture of July 14, 1949). In *Écrits: A Selection*. Trans. Alan Sheridan. New York: Norton, 1977. 1–7.

Lacoue-Labarthe, Philippe. *Musica Ficta: Figures of Wagner*. Stanford: Stanford University Press, 1994.

Lang, Fritz. "Arbeitsgemeinschaft im Film." *Kinematograph* (887), February 17, 1924. Reprinted in Gehler and Kasten. *Fritz Lang: Die Stimme von Metropolis*. 164–68.

———. "Kitsch—Sensation—Kultur und Film." In *Das Kulturfilmbuch*, ed. E. Beyfuss and A. Kossowsky. Berlin: Carl P. Chryselius, 1924. 28–31. Reprinted in Gehler and Kasten. *Fritz Lang*. 202–6.

———. "Stilwille im Film." In *Jugend*, 3 (Feb. 1, 1924). Reprinted in Gehler and Kasten. *Fritz Lang*. 161–64.

———. "Worauf es beim Nibelungen-Film ankam." Reprinted in Gehler and Kasten. *Fritz Lang*. 170–74.

Laplanche, Jean, and J.-B. Pontalis. *The Language of Psychoanalysis*. Trans. Donald Nicholson-Smith. New York: Norton, 1973.

Levin, David J., ed. *Opera Through Other Eyes*. Stanford: Stanford University Press, 1994.

————. "Reading Beckmesser Reading: Antisemitism and Aesthetic Practice in *Die Meistersinger von Nürnberg.*" *New German Critique* 69 (Fall 1996): 127–46.

Magee, Elizabeth. *Richard Wagner and the Nibelungs.* Oxford: Oxford University Press, 1990.

Mahlendorf, Ursula R., and Frank J. Tobin. "Hagen: A Reappraisal." In *Monatshefte* 63, no. 2 (1971): 125–40.

Mann, Thomas. "Leiden und Größe Richard Wagners." In *Wagner und unsere Zeit*, ed. Erika Mann. Frankfurt am Main: Fischer, 1983. 63–121. English trans.: "The Sorrows and Grandeur of Richard Wagner." In Thomas Mann, *Pro and Contra Wagner.* Trans. Allan Blunden. Chicago: University of Chicago Press, 1985. 91–148.

————. "To the Editor of *Common Sense*" in *Common Sense* 9 (January 1940).

Mann, William. *The Ring of the Nibelung: Das Rheingold, Die Walküre, Siegfried, Götterdämmerung.* Libretto in German by Richard Wagner. English trans. William Mann. London: Friends of Covent Garden, 1964.

McCarthy, Sister Mary Frances. "The Use of Rhetoric in the *Nibelungenlied*: A Stylistic and Structural Study of *Aventiure 5.*" *Modern Language Notes* 87 (1972): 683–700.

Millington, Barry. *Wagner.* Rev. ed. Princeton: Princeton University Press, 1984.

————. "Nuremberg Trial: Is There Anti-Semitism in *Die Meistersinger?*" *Cambridge Opera Journal* 3, no. 3 (1991): 247–60.

Moretti, Franco. *Modern Epic: The World-System from Goethe to García Márquez.* Trans. Quintin Hoare. New York: Verso, 1996.

Mosse, George. *Germans and Jews.* New York: Howard Fertig, 1970.

Mulvey, Laura. "Visual Pleasure and Narrative Cinema." In her *Visual and Other Pleasures.* Bloomington: Indiana University Press, 1989. 14–26.

Münkler, Herfried, and Wolfgang Storch. *Siegfrieden: Politik mit einem deutschen Mythos.* Berlin: Rotbuch, 1988.

Nattiez, Jean-Jacques. *Wagner Androgyne: A Study in Interpretation.* Trans. Stewart Spencer. Princeton: Princeton University Press, 1993.

Newcomb, Anthony. "The Birth of Music out of the Spirit of Drama." *Nineteenth Century Music* 5, no. 1 (Summer 1981): 38–66.

Newman, Ernest. *Life of Wagner.* 4 vols. New York: Knopf, 1933–46.

————. *The Wagner Operas.* 2 vols. New York: Knopf, 1949.

Neue Gesellschaft für Bildende Kunst. *Inszenierung der Macht: Aesthetische Faszination im Faschismus.* Berlin: Dirk Nishen, 1987.

Nietzsche, Friedrich. "Der Fall Wagner." [erste] Nachschrift, [1888]. *Sämtliche Werke: Kritische Studienausgabe*, 13 vols. Munich: Deutscher Taschenbuch Verlag, 1980. 6: 1–69. English translation: "The Case of Wagner." In *The Birth of Tragedy and The Case of Wagner.* Trans. Walter Kaufmann. New York: Random House, 1967. 153–92.

Olender, Maurice. *The Languages of Paradise: Race, Religion, and Philology in the Nineteenth Century*. Trans. Arthur Goldhammer. Cambridge, MA: Harvard University Press, 1992.

Ott, Frederick W. *The Films of Fritz Lang*. Secaucus, NJ: Citadel Press, 1979.

Poliakov, Leon. *The History of Modern Anti-Semitism*. 4 vols. Trans. Miriam Kochan. New York: Vanguard Press, 1965.

Rentschler, Eric. *The Ministry of Illusion: Nazi Cinema and Its Afterlife*. Cambridge, MA: Harvard University Press, 1996.

Rose, Paul Lawrence. *Wagner: Race and Revolution*. New Haven: Yale University Press, 1992.

Rosenberg, Wolf. "Versuch über einen Janusgeist." *Musik Konzepte* 5 (June 1981): 40–49.

Saunders, Thomas J. "History in the Making: Weimar Cinema and National Identity." In Bruce A. Murray and Christopher J. Wickham, eds. *Framing the Past: The Historiography of German Cinema and Television*. Carbondale: Southern Illinois University Press, 1992. 42–67.

———. *Hollywood in Berlin: American Cinema and Weimar Germany*. Berkeley: University of California Press, 1994.

Schafer, Roy. "Narration in the Psychoanalytic Dialogue" In *On Narrative*, ed. W.J.T. Mitchell. Chicago: University of Chicago Press, 1981. 25–49.

———."Narratives of the Self." In *Retelling a Life: Narration and Dialogue in Psychoanalysis*. New York: Basic Books, 1992. 21–35.

Schivelbusch, Wolfgang. *Lichtblicke: zur Geschichte der künstlichen Helligkeit im 19. Jahrhundert*. Frankfurt am Main: Fischer, 1986. English translation: *Disenchanted Night: The Industrialization of Light in the Nineteenth Century*. Trans. Angela Davies. Berkeley: University of California Press, 1988.

Schneider, Rolf. *Die Reise zu Richard Wagner*. Vienna: Paul Zsolnay, 1989.

Schulte-Sasse, Linda. *Entertaining the Third Reich: Illusions of Wholeness in Nazi Cinema*. Durham: Duke University Press, 1996.

Schweitzer, Edward. "Tradition and Originality in the Narrative of Siegfried's Death in the *Nibelungenlied*." *Euphorion* 66, no. 4 (1972): 355–64.

Segal, Hanna. *Introduction to the Work of Melanie Klein*. London: Hogarth Press, 1982.

Shaw, George Bernard. *The Perfect Wagnerite*. New York: Dover, 1967/rept 1888.

Spencer, Stewart. "The Language and Sources of *Der Ring des Nibelungen*." In *Richard Wagner und sein Mittelalter*. Ursula and Ulrich Müller, eds. Anif/Salzburg: Ursula Müller-Speiser, 1989. 141–55.

Stein, Leon. *The Racial Thinking of Richard Wagner*. New York: Philosophical Library, 1950.

Stiles, Victoria. "Fritz Lang's Definitive *Siegfried* and Its Versions." *Literature/Film Quarterly* 13, no. 4 (1985): 258–74.

———. "The Siegfried Legend and the Silent Screen: Fritz Lang's Interpretation of a Hero Saga." *Literature/Film Quarterly* 8, no. 4 (1980): 232–36.

Storch, Wolfgang. *Die Nibelungen: Bilder von Liebe, Verrat und Untergang*. Munich: Prestel, 1987.

Tisdell, Marie-Elisabeth. *Studien zur Erzählweise einiger mittelhochdeutscher Dichtungen*. Bern: P. Lang, 1978.

Treadwell, James. "The *Ring* and the Conditions of Interpretation: Wagner's Writing, 1848 to 1852." In *Cambridge Opera Journal* 7, no. 3 (November 1995): 207–31.

Vaget, Hans Rudolf. "Sixtus Beckmesser—A 'Jew in the Brambles'?" *Opera Quarterly* 12, no. 1 (1995): 35–45.

Viereck, Peter. "Hitler and Richard Wagner." *Common Sense* 8 (Nov/Dec 1939).

von der Hagen, Friedrich Heinrich. *Der Niebelungen Lied*. 2nd ed. Breslau: Max und Komp., 1816.

Wagner, Richard. *Correspondence of Wagner and Liszt*. 2 vols. Trans. Francis Hueffer, revised by W. Ashton Ellis. New York: Scribner's, 1897.

———. *Gesammelte Schriften und Dichtungen*, 10 vols. Leipzig: E. W. Fritzsch, 1887–88.

———. "Das Judentum in der Musik." In *Drei Essays*, ed. Tibor Kneif. Munich: Rogner und Bernhard, 1975. 53–77. English translation in *Wagner 9*. London: Wagner Society, 1988. 20–33.

———. *Wagner's Letters to His Dresden Friends*. Trans. J. S. Shedlock. New York: Scribner & Welford, 1890.

———. *Mein Leben*, ed. Martin Gregor-Dellin. Mainz: B. Schott, 1983. English translation: *My Life*, ed. Mary Whittall, trans. Andrew Gray. Cambridge: Cambridge University Press, 1983/rpt 1988.

———. *Oper und Drama*, ed. Klaus Kropfinger. Stuttgart: Reclam, 1984.

———. *Parsifal* in *Die Musikdramen*. Munich: Deutscher Taschenbuch Verlag, 1981. 821–65.

———. *Richard Wagner's Prose Works*. 8 vols. Trans. William Ashton Ellis. New York: Broude Bros., 1966/rpt of London: 1893.

———. *Wagner's Ring of the Nibelung: A Companion*, ed. Stewart Spencer and Barry Millington. Full German text with a new translation by Stewart Spencer. New York: Thames & Hudson, 1993.

———. *Sämtliche Briefe*, ed. Gertrud Strobel and Werner Wolf. Leipzig: VEB Deutscher Verlag für Musik, 1979.

———. *Selected Letters of Richard Wagner*, ed. and trans. Stewart Spencer and Barry Millington. New York: Norton, 1987.

———. *Siegfried: In full score*. Reprint of the first edition, 1876. New York: Dover, 1983.

Weiner, Marc A. *Richard Wagner and the Anti-Semitic Imagination*. Lincoln: University of Nebraska Press, 1995.

Werner, Gösta. "Fritz Lang and Goebbels: Myth and Facts." *Film Quarterly* 43, no. 3 (Spring 1990): 24–27.

Wunderlich, Werner. *Der Schatz des Drachentödters: Materialien zur Wirkungsgeschichte des Nibelungenliedes.* Stuttgart: Klett, 1977.

Zelinsky, Hartmut. "Die deutsche Losung Siegfried: oder die 'innere Notwendigkeit' des Juden-Fluches im Werk Richard Wagners." In *In den Trümmern der Eignen Welt: Richard Wagners "Der Ring des Nibelungen,"* ed. Udo Bermbach. Hamburg and Berlin: Dietrich Reimer, 1989. 201–49.

———. "Die 'feuerkur' des Richard Wagner oder die 'neue religion' der 'Erlösung' durch 'Vernichtung.'" *Musik Konzepte* 5 (June 1981): 79–112.

———. *Richard Wagner: Ein deutsches Thema.* Frankfurt am Main: Zweitausendeins, 1976.

Zizek, Slavoj. *The Sublime Object of Ideology.* New York: Verso, 1989.

Index

Abbate, Carolyn, 14, 39–41, 95, 153n.23, 162n.32, 163n.38

Adorno, Theodor W., 9, 14, 88–90, 158n.57, 170n.96, 176–77n.162, 177n.163

Alberich:
—in the *Ring*, 9, 10, 11, 89, 176n.155, and bad language 51, 165n.51; compared to Alberich in Nibelungen film, 126
—in the Nibelungen film, as bad object, 10, 98, 105, 137; compared to Alberich in *Ring*, 126, 182n.31; compared to Siegfried, 134; compared to Volker's cinema, 134–36; confrontation with Siegfried, 116–28, 140, 180–81n.23, 181n.27, 183n.45; and disavowal, 137, 139; as foreign film man, 125; as Jew, 123–27, 144, 152n.13; mesmerizing Siegfried, 119–23; relationship to film and viewing, 122

allegory: of language in Wagner, 166n.61; of narrative control, 7, 21; of national film culture in the Nibelungen film, 116–17; of origins in the *Ring*, 42–44, 50, 165n.52; of visual power in the Nibelungen film, 98–99, 132–40

Anderson, Benedict, 151n.3

Andersson, Theodore, 154n.31, 157n.51

anti-Semitism: as aesthetic problem in the Nibelungen film, 99–101, 123–29, 143–44; as aesthetic problem in Wagner, 88–95, 152n.12, 169–70n.88, 178n.174; aesthetics of, 10; and Alberich in the Nibelungen film, 124–27, 152n.13; and social cohesion, 86–7, 167n.70. *See also* Jews

bad object, 11; in the *Nasty Girl*, 148–50; in the Nibelungen film, 102, 105, 137; in the *Nibelungenlied*, 23–24; in Wagner, 88–94, 143–44. *See also* Melanie Klein

Bakhtin, Mikhail, 39

Basch, Michael Franz, 142, 185n.4, 186n.6

Beckmesser, 9, 89

Bekker, Hugo, 154n.29

Bellour, Raymond, 98

Benjamin, Walter, 90

Berghaus, Ruth, x

Bergstrom, Janet, 128

Bhabha, Homi K., 151n.3

Bogyansky, Robert, 183n.42

Borchmeyer, Dieter, 162n.20

Botstein, Leon, 86–87

Brackert, Helmut, 21, 151nn. 2 and 6, 154n.32, 155n.39

Breitmoser-Bock, Angelika, 180nn. 19 and 20

Brinkmann, Rheinhold, 162n.19

Brunhild (Nibelungen film), 104, 109–14, 180–81n.23; contest with Gunther, 109, 110; as threat to male power, 109–10, 181n.28, 182n.29

Brünhild (*Nibelungenlied*), 182n.29; conjugal night, 112–13, 182n.33; desire to speak, 22, 155n.40

Brünnhilde (*Ring*), 80, 94, 162n.31, 164n.41; and rhetoric of predetermination, 66–67, 72, 171n.102; and Siegfried's invulnerability, 28, 77, 159n.58, 173n.127

Bruns, Karin, 178n.4, 179n.17

Bülow, Chancellor Prince Bernhard von, 184n.71